Second Edition

Bureau of Land Management Camping

Directory of 1,273 Camping Areas in 14 States

Published by:

Roundabout Publications
PO Box 569
LaCygne, KS 66040

Phone: 800-455-2207
Internet: www.RoundaboutPublications.com

Library of Congress Control Number: 2021943923

ISBN-10: 1-885464-81-9
ISBN-13: 978-1-885464-81-1

Table of Contents

Introduction

Bureau of Land Management Camping

The Bureau of Land Management (or BLM) was established in 1946 by President Harry S. Truman. The agency manages more surface land (245 million acres) and more subsurface mineral estate (700 million acres) than any other government agency in the United States. Management responsibilities include renewable energy development, conventional energy development, livestock grazing, hardrock mining, timber harvesting, and outdoor recreation. This book focuses on the outdoor recreation aspect and features 1,273 camping areas managed by the agency. To learn more about the Bureau of Land Management, visit their website:

www.blm.gov

State Maps

A state map is provided to aid you in locating camping areas. A grid overlay on each map is used when cross-referencing with each camping area.

Alphabetical List

Following the state map is an alphabetical list of each location within the state. The list provides each location's number, map grid ID, and whether the camping area is suitable for RVs or tents. It also identifies camping areas that are free of charge.

Camping Area Details

Camping area details include information about each public camping area within the state. Preceding each location's name is a number and map grid ID, which is used when referencing the state map.

Details for each camping area generally include the following information:

- Total number of sites or dispersed camping
- Number of RV sites
- Sites with electric hookups
- Full hookup sites, if available
- Water (central location or spigots at site)
- Showers
- RV dump station
- Toilets (flush, pit/vault, or none)
- Laundry facilities
- Camp store
- Maximum RV size limits (if any)
- Reservation information (accepted, not accepted, recommended or required)
- Generator use and hours (if limited)
- Operating season
- Camping fees charged
- Miscellaneous notes
- Length of stay limit
- Elevation in feet and meters
- Telephone number
- Nearby city or town
- Managing agency
- GPS coordinates

About The Ultimate Public Campground Project

The Ultimate Public Campground Project was conceived in 2008 to provide a consolidated and comprehensive source for public campgrounds of all types. It all began with a simple POI (Point of Interest) list of GPS coordinates and names, nothing more, totaling perhaps 5,000 locations. As the list grew in size and information provided, a website was designed to display the data on a map. Next came mobile apps; first iOS and Mac apps and more recently Android versions.

Ultimate Campgrounds is NOT the product of some large company with deep pockets. We are a team of three, all working on this as a part-time avocation: Ted is the founder of Ultimate Campgrounds and its Data Meister, Bill is our iOS and Mac developer and Geoff is our Android guy. Both Ted and Bill have been camping for many years and Ultimate Campgrounds reflects their interest in accurate and useful campground information.

Please note that despite our best efforts, there will always be errors to be found in the data. With over 45,000 records in our database, it is impossible to ensure that each one is always up-to-date. Ted tries to work his way through the data at least once a year to pick up things like increased fees and URL's that always seem to be changing. On an annual basis, it requires reviewing over 123 locations each and every day of the year – that's a pretty tall order.

Thus we always appreciate input from users who have found errors…or would like to submit a new location. Our goal is accuracy and we will gratefully accept any and all input.

We decided some years ago to focus on just one thing, publicly-owned camping locations, and try to be the best at it.

You can find much more information about the Ultimate Public Campground Project on our website:

www.ultimatecampgrounds.com.

Feel free to address any questions or comments by sending an email to the following:

info@ultimatecampgounds.com.

Happy Camping!

Abbreviations

ATV	All-Terrain Vehicle
BLM	Bureau of Land Management
CG	Campground
CR	County Road
FSR	Forest Service Road
LTVA	Long Term Visitors Area
NCA	National Conservation Area
NHS	National Historic Site
NM	National Monument
NNL	National Natural Location
OHV	Off-Highway Vehicle
OHVA	Off-Highway Vehicle Area
ORV	Off-Road Vehicle
RA	Recreation Area
RMA	Recreation Management Area
RNA	Research Natural Area
SRMA	Special Recreation Management Area
TH	Trail Head
TMA	Travel Management Area
WA	Wildlife Area
WSA	Wilderness Study Area

Alaska

Alaska

Alaska State Office
222 W 7th Avenue #13
Anchorage AK 99513

Phone: 907-271-5960

Name	ID	Map	RVs	Tents	Free
Arctic Circle Wayside	3	B3	✓	✓	✓
Brushkana	13	C3	✓	✓	
Clearwater Creek Wayside	14	C3	✓	✓	✓
Cripple Creek	4	B3	✓	✓	
Eagle	10	B4	✓	✓	
Galbraith Lake	1	A3	✓	✓	✓
Marion Creek	5	B3	✓	✓	
Mount Prindle	6	B3	✓	✓	
Ophir Creek	7	B3	✓	✓	
Otto Lake Road	8	B3	✓	✓	✓
Paxson Lake	15	C3	✓	✓	
Salmon Lake	2	B2	✓	✓	✓
Sixty-Mile	9	B3	✓	✓	✓
Sourdough Creek	16	C3	✓	✓	
Tangle Lakes	17	C3	✓	✓	
Walker Fork	11	B4	✓	✓	
West Fork	12	B4	✓	✓	

1 • A3 | Galbraith Lake

Total sites: 30, RV sites: 30, No water, Vault/pit toilet, Tent & RV camping: Free, Open Jun-Sep, Reservations not accepted, Stay limit: 14 days, Elevation: 2798ft/853m, Telephone: 907-474-2200. Nearest town: Prudhoe Bay. GPS: 68.453436, -149.483227

2 • B2 | Salmon Lake

Total sites: 6, RV sites: 6, No water, Vault/pit toilet, Tent & RV camping: Free, Open Jun-Oct, Reservations not accepted, Elevation: 457ft/139m. Nearest town: Nome. GPS: 64.916681, -164.960638

3 • B3 | Arctic Circle Wayside

Total sites: 7, RV sites: 7, No water, Vault/pit toilet, Tent & RV camping: Free, Reservations not accepted, Elevation: 1308ft/399m. Nearest town: Coldfoot. GPS: 66.558352, -150.794434

4 • B3 | Cripple Creek

Total sites: 19, RV sites: 12, Central water, Vault/pit toilet, No showers, No RV dump, Tent & RV camping: $6, Open Jun-Nov, Reservations not accepted, Stay limit: 10 days, Elevation: 1223ft/373m, Telephone: 907-474-2200. Nearest town: Fox. GPS: 65.275394, -146.647167

5 • B3 | Marion Creek

Total sites: 27, RV sites: 27, Central water, Vault/pit toilet, No showers, No RV dump, Tent & RV camping: $8, Open Jun-Sep, Reservations not accepted, Stay limit: 14 days, Elevation: 1105ft/337m, Telephone: 907-474-2200. Nearest town: Coldfoot. GPS: 67.317386, -150.162546

6 • B3 | Mount Prindle

Total sites: 13, RV sites: 13, Central water, Vault/pit toilet, No showers, No RV dump, Tent & RV camping: $6, Open May-Sep, Reservations not accepted, Stay limit: 10 days, Elevation: 2506ft/764m. GPS: 65.368231, -146.593062

7 • B3 | Ophir Creek

Total sites: 19, RV sites: 19, Central water, Vault/pit toilet, No showers, No RV dump, Tent & RV camping: $6, Open May-Sep, Reservations not accepted, Stay limit: 10 days, Elevation: 1655ft/504m, Telephone: 907-474-2200. Nearest town: Fox. GPS: 65.368537, -147.085537

8 • B3 | Otto Lake Road

Dispersed sites, No water, No toilets, Tent & RV camping: Free, Reservations not accepted, Elevation: 1765ft/538m. Nearest town: Healy. GPS: 63.845503, -149.016103

9 • B3 | Sixty-Mile

Total sites: 30, RV sites: 30, Central water, Vault/pit toilet, No showers, RV dump, Tent & RV camping: Free, Open May-Sep, Reservations not accepted, Stay limit: 14 days, Elevation: 507ft/155m, Telephone: 907-474-2200. GPS: 65.925711, -149.838698

10 • B4 | Eagle

Total sites: 18, RV sites: 18, Central water, Vault/pit toilet, No showers, No RV dump, Tent & RV camping: $10, Open May-Sep, Reservations not accepted, Stay limit: 10 days, Elevation: 1010ft/308m, Telephone: 907-474-2200. Nearest town: Eagle. GPS: 64.791386, -141.233616

11 • B4 | Walker Fork

Total sites: 18, RV sites: 18, Central water, Vault/pit toilet, No showers, No RV dump, Tent & RV camping: $10, Open May-Sep, Reservations not accepted, Stay limit: 10 days,

Elevation: 1907ft/581m, Telephone: 907-474-2200. Nearest town: Boundary. GPS: 64.078934, -141.642733

12 • B4 | West Fork

Total sites: 25, RV sites: 25, No water, Vault/pit toilet, Tent & RV camping: $10, Open May-Sep, Reservations not accepted, Stay limit: 10 days, Elevation: 1902ft/580m, Telephone: 907-474-2200. Nearest town: Tok. GPS: 63.887335, -142.237043

13 • C3 | Brushkana

Total sites: 22, RV sites: 22, Central water, Vault/pit toilet, No showers, No RV dump, Tents: $6-12/RVs: $12, Open Jun-Oct, Reservations not accepted, Stay limit: 14 days, Elevation: 2551ft/778m, Telephone: 907-822-3217. Nearest town: Cantwell. GPS: 63.289329, -148.066052

14 • C3 | Clearwater Creek Wayside

Dispersed sites, No water, Vault/pit toilet, Tent & RV camping: Free, Reservations not accepted, Elevation: 2921ft/890m, Telephone: 907-822-3217. Nearest town: Paxson. GPS: 63.041587, -146.881685

15 • C3 | Paxson Lake

Total sites: 50, RV sites: 50, Central water, Vault/pit toilet, No showers, RV dump, Tents: $6-12/RVs: $12, Also walk-to sites, Open Jun-Oct, Reservations not accepted, Stay limit: 14 days, Elevation: 2598ft/792m, Telephone: 907-822-3217. Nearest town: Paxson. GPS: 62.884426, -145.524164

16 • C3 | Sourdough Creek

Total sites: 42, RV sites: 42, Central water, Vault/pit toilet, No showers, No RV dump, Tents: $6/RVs: $12, Also walk-to sites, 2 walk-in sites, Open May-Oct, Reservations not accepted, Stay limit: 14 days, Elevation: 1916ft/584m, Telephone: 907-822-3217. Nearest town: Gakona. GPS: 62.527061, -145.518931

17 • C3 | Tangle Lakes

Total sites: 45, RV sites: 45, Central water, Vault/pit toilet, No showers, No RV dump, Tents: $6/RVs: $12, Also walk-to sites, Open Jun-Oct, Reservations not accepted, Stay limit: 14 days, Elevation: 2850ft/869m. Nearest town: Paxson. GPS: 63.049836, -146.007497

Arizona

NEVADA

UTAH

CO

NM

ARIZONA

CALIFORNIA

MEXICO

Gulf of California

Page
Kayenta
Flagstaff
Winslow
Springerville
Kingman
Camp Verde
Payson
Globe
Willcox
Phoenix
Tucson
Benson
Gila Bend
Dateland
Yuma

15
93
89
160
89
40
40
40
191
93
17
260
77
60
87
79
77
70
10
8
8
19

1 2 3 4 5 6 7
9 20 23 11
8 10 22 21
12-19 33
43 34
26 40,42
53 52
64 57
50 31 54 51
24
35 46 32 47 56
29,30 55 44,45 41 48 49 36-39
25,27,28 86
74 69 79 78
65-67,70-73 58,59 60 80,81 76,77 93 62
61 63,82 68 75
94-96 98 92 89
91 93
97
88 89 99 90
102 103 106
100 105 101 104
113 114 112 108 107 109 115 110 111
120 118 116 117 119
121

A B C D E
1 2 3 4

Arizona

Arizona State Office
One North Central Ave Suite 800
Phoenix AZ 85004

Phone: 602-417-9200

Name	ID	Map	RVs	Tents	Free
17 Mile Road	57	C2	✓	✓	✓
Agua Caliente Road	87	D2	✓	✓	✓
Agua Fria NM	58	C2	✓	✓	✓
Agua Fria NM – Badger Spring Dispersed	59	C2	✓	✓	✓
Agua Fria NM – Bloody Basin Rd	60	C2	✓	✓	✓
Alley Road Dispersed	88	D2	✓	✓	✓
Baker Canyon WSA	121	E4		✓	✓
Black Mountain Rock Art	5	A2	✓	✓	✓
BLM Road 9331 Dispersed	61	C2	✓	✓	✓
Boulders OHV	62	C2	✓	✓	✓
Bouse	24	C1	✓	✓	✓
Box Wash	63	C2	✓	✓	✓
Burro Creek	64	C2	✓	✓	
Cedar Pocket Road Dispersed	1	A1	✓	✓	✓
Cedar Pocket Road Dispersed	2	A1		✓	✓
Cerbat Foothills Rec Area	8	B1	✓	✓	✓
Chloride	9	B1	✓	✓	✓
Cholla Road Dispersed	25	C1	✓	✓	✓
Christmas	100	D3		✓	✓
County Road 193	10	B1	✓	✓	✓
Craggy Wash Dispersed	26	C1	✓	✓	✓
Crown King Road Dispersed 1	65	C2	✓	✓	✓
Crown King Road Dispersed 2	66	C2	✓	✓	✓
Crown King Road Dispersed 3	67	C2	✓	✓	✓
Crozier Ranch Dispersed	11	B1	✓	✓	✓
Darby Wells Road Dispersed	89	D2	✓	✓	✓
Dome Rock Dispersed	27	C1	✓	✓	✓
Dome Rock Mountain	28	C1	✓	✓	✓
Eagle Eye Road Dispersed	68	C2	✓	✓	✓
East Stanton Road	69	C2	✓	✓	✓
Ehrenberg Sandbowl	29	C1	✓	✓	✓
Ehrenburg-Cibola Road	30	C1	✓	✓	✓
Fortuna Pond	83	D1	✓	✓	✓

Name	ID	Map	RVs	Tents	Free
Fourmile Canyon	101	D3	✓	✓	
FSR 259 Dispersed 1	70	C2	✓	✓	✓
FSR 259 Dispersed 2	71	C2	✓	✓	✓
FSR 259 Dispersed 3	72	C2	✓	✓	✓
FSR 259 Dispersed 4	73	C2	✓	✓	✓
FSR 62 Dispersed 1	116	E3	✓	✓	✓
Ghost Town Rd	74	C2	✓	✓	✓
Gibraltar Mountain	31	C1	✓	✓	✓
Gold Nugget Road Dispersed	32	C1	✓	✓	✓
Golden Shores	33	C1	✓		✓
Gunsight Wash Dispersed	90	D2	✓	✓	✓
Hackel Road Dispersed	107	D4	✓	✓	✓
Hackle Road	108	D4	✓	✓	✓
Harquahala Mountains – Eagle Eye Road	75	C2	✓	✓	✓
Havasu Heights	34	C1	✓	✓	✓
Hi Jolly	35	C1	✓		✓
Hidden Shores Concession	84	D1	✓		
Hot Well Dunes	109	D4	✓	✓	
Indian Bread Rocks	110	D4	✓	✓	✓
Ironwood Forest NM Dispersed	102	D3	✓	✓	✓
La Posa North LTVA	36	C1	✓		
La Posa South LTVA	37	C1	✓		
La Posa Tyson Wash LTVA	38	C1	✓		
La Posa West LTVA	39	C1	✓		
Lake Havasu Dispersed	40	C1	✓	✓	✓
Las Cienegas NCA – Cieneguita Dispersed	117	E3	✓	✓	✓
Las Cienegas NCA – Oak Canyon Dispersed	118	E3	✓	✓	✓
Las Cienegas NCA – Road Canyon	119	E3	✓	✓	✓
Levee Road	41	C1	✓	✓	✓
Lone tree Dispersed	42	C1	✓	✓	✓
Margies Cove West	91	D2	✓	✓	✓
Mittry Lake WA	85	D1	✓	✓	✓
Muleshoe Ranch	111	D4		✓	✓
Natural Gas Road Dispersed	92	D2	✓	✓	✓
Needle Mountain Road Dispersed	43	C1	✓	✓	✓
North Little Grand Canyon Rd Site 1	76	C2	✓	✓	✓
North Little Grand Canyon Rd Site 2	77	C2	✓	✓	✓
North Pump Station Road	103	D3	✓	✓	✓
Oatman-Topock Road Site 1	12	B1	✓	✓	✓

Name	ID	Map	RVs	Tents	Free
Oatman-Topock Road Site 2	13	B1	✓	✓	✓
Oatman-Topock Road Site 3	14	B1	✓	✓	✓
Oatman-Topock Road Site 4	15	B1	✓	✓	✓
Oatman-Topock Road Site 5	16	B1	✓	✓	✓
Oatman-Topock Road Site 6	17	B1	✓	✓	✓
Oatman-Topock Road Site 7	18	B1	✓	✓	✓
Oatman-Topock Road Site 8	19	B1	✓	✓	✓
Owl Creek	112	D4	✓	✓	
Ox Bow Road	44	C1	✓	✓	✓
Ox Bow Road Dispersed	45	C1	✓	✓	✓
Packsaddle	20	B1	✓	✓	✓
Painted Rock Petroglyph Site	93	D2	✓	✓	
Plomosa	46	C1	✓		✓
Ramsey Mine Road Dispersed	47	C1	✓	✓	✓
Red Knolls Amphitheater	113	D4	✓	✓	✓
Redfield Canyon	104	D3	✓	✓	✓
Riverview	114	D4	✓	✓	
Road 129 Dispersed	21	B1	✓	✓	✓
Road Runner	48	C1	✓	✓	✓
Round Mountain Rockhound Area	115	D4	✓	✓	✓
Round Top Mesa Dispersed	7	A4	✓	✓	✓
S Cibola Lake Road Dispersed	86	D1	✓	✓	✓
Saddle Mountain Dispersed 1	94	D2	✓	✓	✓
Saddle Mountain Dispersed 2	95	D2	✓	✓	✓
Saddle Mountain Dispersed 3	96	D2	✓	✓	✓
Scaddan Wash	49	C1	✓		✓
Shea Road Dispersed 1	50	C1	✓	✓	✓
Shea Road Dispersed 2	51	C1	✓	✓	✓
Shores	105	D3	✓	✓	✓
Snyder Hill Dispersed	106	D3	✓	✓	✓
Sophie Flats Dispersed	78	C2	✓	✓	✓
South of North Ranch	79	C2	✓	✓	✓
Standard Wash Dispersed 1	52	C1	✓	✓	✓
Standard Wash Dispersed 2	53	C1	✓	✓	✓
Swansea Ghost Town	54	C1	✓	✓	✓
Table Mesa OHV Little Pan	80	C2	✓	✓	✓
Table Mesa OHV Remote	81	C2	✓	✓	✓
Tom Wells Road Dispersed	55	C1	✓	✓	✓
Vekol Valley	97	D2	✓	✓	✓
Vicksburg	56	C1	✓	✓	✓
Virgin Mountains	3	A1	✓	✓	✓

Name	ID	Map	RVs	Tents	Free
Virgin River Gorge RA – Cedar Pockets	4	A1	✓	✓	
Vulture Mine Road	82	C2	✓	✓	✓
West Dobbs Road Dispersed	98	D2	✓	✓	✓
White House Canyon Road Dispersed	120	E3	✓	✓	✓
White Pocket TH	6	A3	✓	✓	✓
Wild Cow Springs	22	B1	✓	✓	
Wild Woman	99	D2	✓	✓	✓
Windy Point	23	B1	✓	✓	

1 • A1 | Cedar Pocket Road Dispersed

Dispersed sites, No water, No toilets, Tent & RV camping: Free, Reservations not accepted, Elevation: 2302ft/702m. Nearest town: Littlefield. GPS: 36.956902, -113.801984

2 • A1 | Cedar Pocket Road Dispersed

Dispersed sites, No water, No toilets, Tents only: Free, 4x4 recommended, Reservations not accepted, Elevation: 2769ft/844m. Nearest town: Littlefield. GPS: 36.972549, -113.797039

3 • A1 | Virgin Mountains

Dispersed sites, No water, No toilets, Tent & RV camping: Free, Elevation: 3566ft/1087m, Telephone: 702-515-5000. Nearest town: Mesquite. GPS: 36.676183, -114.012013

4 • A1 | Virgin River Gorge RA – Cedar Pockets

Total sites: 77, RV sites: 77, Central water, Flush toilet, No showers, No RV dump, Tent & RV camping: $8, Elevation: 2257ft/688m, Telephone: 435-688-3200. Nearest town: Littlefield. GPS: 36.951095, -113.793449

5 • A2 | Black Mountain Rock Art

Dispersed sites, No water, Vault/pit toilet, Tent & RV camping: Free, Elevation: 2897ft/883m, Telephone: 435-688-3200. Nearest town: St George, UT. GPS: 36.982706, -113.502915

6 • A3 | White Pocket TH

Dispersed sites, No water, No toilets, Tent & RV camping: Free, 4x4 high-clearance vehicles required, Reservations not accepted, Elevation: 5678ft/1731m, Telephone: 453-688-3200. GPS: 36.955133, -111.893558

7 • A4 | Round Top Mesa Dispersed

Dispersed sites, No water, No toilets, Tent & RV camping: Free, Elevation: 5128ft/1563m. Nearest town: Dennehotso. GPS: 36.917778, -109.762615

8 • B1 | Cerbat Foothills Rec Area

Dispersed sites, No water, Vault/pit toilet, Tent & RV camping: Free, Parking lot at trailhead, Reservations not accepted, Elevation: 3682ft/1122m, Telephone: 928-718-3700. Nearest town: Kingman. GPS: 35.205394, -114.095641

9 • B1 | Chloride

Dispersed sites, No water, No toilets, Tent & RV camping: Free, Rough road, Elevation: 3917ft/1194m. Nearest town: Kingman. GPS: 35.417562, -114.226842

10 • B1 | County Road 193

Dispersed sites, No water, No toilets, Tent & RV camping: Free, Elevation: 4659ft/1420m. Nearest town: Kingman. GPS: 35.148288, -113.810092

11 • B1 | Crozier Ranch Dispersed

Dispersed sites, No water, No toilets, Tent & RV camping: Free, Elevation: 4218ft/1286m. Nearest town: Crozier. GPS: 35.452145, -113.623744

12 • B1 | Oatman-Topock Road Site 1

Dispersed sites, No water, No toilets, Tent & RV camping: Free, Elevation: 722ft/220m. Nearest town: Topock. GPS: 34.816031, -114.467838

13 • B1 | Oatman-Topock Road Site 2

Dispersed sites, No water, No toilets, Tent & RV camping: Free, Elevation: 756ft/230m. Nearest town: Topock. GPS: 34.824316, -114.466454

14 • B1 | Oatman-Topock Road Site 3

Dispersed sites, No water, No toilets, Tent & RV camping: Free, Elevation: 817ft/249m. Nearest town: Topock. GPS: 34.834032, -114.462687

15 • B1 | Oatman-Topock Road Site 4

Dispersed sites, No water, No toilets, Tent & RV camping: Free, Elevation: 977ft/298m. Nearest town: Topock. GPS: 34.855483, -114.449305

16 • B1 | Oatman-Topock Road Site 5

Dispersed sites, No water, No toilets, Tent & RV camping: Free, Elevation: 1300ft/396m. Nearest town: Oatman. GPS: 34.900895, -114.427191

17 • B1 | Oatman-Topock Road Site 6

Dispersed sites, No water, No toilets, Tent & RV camping: Free, Elevation: 1426ft/435m. Nearest town: Oatman. GPS: 34.927636, -114.424609

18 • B1 | Oatman-Topock Road Site 7

Dispersed sites, No water, No toilets, Tent & RV camping: Free, Elevation: 1498ft/457m. Nearest town: Oatman. GPS: 34.936917, -114.419908

19 • B1 | Oatman-Topock Road Site 8

Dispersed sites, No water, No toilets, Tent & RV camping: Free, Elevation: 1799ft/548m. Nearest town: Oatman. GPS: 34.953697, -114.409448

20 • B1 | Packsaddle

Dispersed sites, No water, Vault/pit toilet, Tent & RV camping: Free, Trailers not recommended, Reservations not accepted, Elevation: 5935ft/1809m, Telephone: 928-718-3700. Nearest town: Kingman. GPS: 35.457477, -114.170008

21 • B1 | Road 129 Dispersed

Dispersed sites, No water, No toilets, Tent & RV camping: Free, Elevation: 3865ft/1178m. Nearest town: Flagstaff. GPS: 34.973693, -113.732861

22 • B1 | Wild Cow Springs

Total sites: 24, RV sites: 24, No water, Vault/pit toilet, Tent & RV camping: $8, Group fee: $20, Open May-Oct, Reservations not accepted, Stay limit: 14 days, Elevation: 6174ft/1882m, Telephone: 928-718-3700. Nearest town: Kingman. GPS: 35.064511, -113.869793

23 • B1 | Windy Point

Total sites: 7, RV sites: 7, No water, Vault/pit toilet, Tent & RV camping: $8, High-clearance vehicles recommended, Open May-Oct, Reservations not accepted, Stay limit: 14 days, Elevation: 6132ft/1869m, Telephone: 928-718-3700. Nearest town: Kingman. GPS: 35.435799, -114.160594

24 • C1 | Bouse

Dispersed sites, No water, No toilets, Tent & RV camping: Free, Elevation: 1224ft/373m. Nearest town: Bouse. GPS: 33.843641, -114.047655

25 • C1 | Cholla Road Dispersed

Dispersed sites, No water, No toilets, Tent & RV camping: Free, Elevation: 1003ft/306m. Nearest town: Quartzite. GPS: 33.643726, -114.269429

26 • C1 | Craggy Wash Dispersed

Dispersed sites, No water, No toilets, Tent & RV camping: Free, Reservations not accepted, Elevation: 1017ft/310m. Nearest town: Lake Havasu City. GPS: 34.593024, -114.352601

27 • C1 | Dome Rock Dispersed

Dispersed sites, No toilets, Tent & RV camping: Free, Elevation: 1161ft/354m. Nearest town: Quartzite. GPS: 33.642022, -114.313832

28 • C1 | Dome Rock Mountain

Dispersed sites, No water, No toilets, Tent & RV camping: Free, Stay limit: 14 days, Elevation: 1025ft/312m, Telephone: 928-317-3250. Nearest town: Quartzite. GPS: 33.648725, -114.279206

29 • C1 | Ehrenberg Sandbowl

Dispersed sites, No water, Vault/pit toilet, Tent & RV camping: Free, Reservations not accepted, Elevation: 288ft/88m, Telephone: 928-317-3200. Nearest town: Ehrenberg. GPS: 33.590908, -114.522312

30 • C1 | Ehrenburg-Cibola Road

Dispersed sites, No water, No toilets, Tent & RV camping: Free, Elevation: 485ft/148m. Nearest town: Ehrenburg. GPS: 33.590454, -114.483597

31 • C1 | Gibraltar Mountain

Dispersed sites, No water, No toilets, Tent & RV camping: Free, Elevation: 1043ft/318m. Nearest town: Parker. GPS: 34.121305, -114.061893

32 • C1 | Gold Nugget Road Dispersed

Dispersed sites, No toilets, Tent & RV camping: Free, Elevation: 1503ft/458m. Nearest town: Quartzite. GPS: 33.675482, -114.078084

33 • C1 | Golden Shores

Dispersed sites, No water, No toilets, No tents/RVs: Free, Elevation: 766ft/233m. Nearest town: Golden Shores. GPS: 34.798863, -114.469013

34 • C1 | Havasu Heights

Dispersed sites, No water, No toilets, Tent & RV camping: Free, Elevation: 1402ft/427m. Nearest town: Lake Havasu City. GPS: 34.664812, -114.308965

35 • C1 | Hi Jolly

Dispersed sites, No water, No toilets, No tents/RVs: Free, Open all year, Reservations not accepted, Stay limit: 14 days, Elevation: 840ft/256m, Telephone: 928-317-3200. Nearest town: Quartzite. GPS: 33.708611, -114.216111

36 • C1 | La Posa North LTVA

Dispersed sites, No water, Vault/pit toilet, No tents/RVs: Fee unk, Elevation: 912ft/278m. Nearest town: Quartzsite. GPS: 33.651944, -114.215556

37 • C1 | La Posa South LTVA

Dispersed sites, Central water, Vault/pit toilet, No showers, RV dump, No tents/RVs: $15, Long ($180) or short ($40) term permit required Sep 15-Apr 15, Open all year, Reservations not accepted, Elevation: 1039ft/317m. Nearest town: Quartzsite. GPS: 33.615325, -114.202197

38 • C1 | La Posa Tyson Wash LTVA

Dispersed sites, No water, Vault/pit toilet, No tents/RVs: Fee unk, Elevation: 968ft/295m. Nearest town: Quartzsite. GPS: 33.626667, -114.218889

39 • C1 | La Posa West LTVA

Dispersed sites, No water, Vault/pit toilet, No tents/RVs: Fee unk, Elevation: 902ft/275m. Nearest town: Quartzsite. GPS: 33.651944, -114.218611

40 • C1 | Lake Havasu Dispersed

Dispersed sites, No toilets, Tent & RV camping: Free, Reservations not accepted, Elevation: 1518ft/463m. Nearest town: Lake Havasu City. GPS: 34.644835, -114.316253

41 • C1 | Levee Road

Dispersed sites, No water, No toilets, Tent & RV camping: Free, Reservations not accepted, Elevation: 305ft/93m. Nearest town: Ehrenburg. GPS: 33.512176, -114.564545

42 • C1 | Lone tree Dispersed

Dispersed sites, No water, No toilets, Tent & RV camping: Free, Open all year, Reservations not accepted, Elevation: 1379ft/420m. Nearest town: Lake Havasu City. GPS: 34.626704, -114.327325

43 • C1 | Needle Mountain Road Dispersed

Dispersed sites, No water, No toilets, Tent & RV camping: Free, Elevation: 830ft/253m. Nearest town: Topock. GPS: 34.714164, -114.435406

44 • C1 | Ox Bow Road

Dispersed sites, No water, No toilets, Tent & RV camping: Free, Reservations not accepted, Stay limit: 14 days, Elevation: 266ft/81m. Nearest town: Ehrenberg. GPS: 33.570475, -114.532319

45 • C1 | Ox Bow Road Dispersed

Dispersed sites, No water, No toilets, Tent & RV camping: Free, Numerous spots along Colorado River, Elevation: 259ft/79m. Nearest town: Ehrenberg. GPS: 33.548048, -114.530443

46 • C1 | Plomosa

Dispersed sites, No water, No toilets, No tents/RVs: Free, Stay limit: 14 days, Elevation: 833ft/254m, Telephone: 928-317-3200. Nearest town: Quartzite. GPS: 33.7475, -114.216111

47 • C1 | Ramsey Mine Road Dispersed

Dispersed sites, No water, No toilets, Tent & RV camping: Free, Elevation: 1365ft/416m. Nearest town: Brenda. GPS: 33.674656, -113.961122

48 • C1 | Road Runner

Dispersed sites, No water, No toilets, Tent & RV camping: Free, Stay limit: 14 days, Elevation: 1058ft/322m, Telephone: 928-317-3200. Nearest town: Quartzite. GPS: 33.581503, -114.227473

49 • C1 | Scaddan Wash

Dispersed sites, No water, No toilets, No tents/RVs: Free, Stay limit: 14 days, Elevation: 965ft/294m, Telephone: 928-317-3200. Nearest town: Quartzite. GPS: 33.665833, -114.1875

50 • C1 | Shea Road Dispersed 1

Dispersed sites, No water, No toilets, Tent & RV camping: Free, Elevation: 587ft/179m. Nearest town: Parker. GPS: 34.146957, -114.194157

51 • C1 | Shea Road Dispersed 2

Dispersed sites, No water, No toilets, Tent & RV camping: Free, Elevation: 768ft/234m. Nearest town: Parker. GPS: 34.123806, -114.153406

52 • C1 | Standard Wash Dispersed 1

Dispersed sites, No water, No toilets, Tent & RV camping: Free, Reservations not accepted, Elevation: 1063ft/324m. Nearest town: Lake Havasu City. GPS: 34.419622, -114.198854

53 • C1 | Standard Wash Dispersed 2

Dispersed sites, No water, No toilets, Tent & RV camping: Free, Reservations not accepted, Elevation: 1212ft/369m. Nearest town: Lake Havasu City. GPS: 34.437556, -114.215621

54 • C1 | Swansea Ghost Town

Dispersed sites, No water, No toilets, Tent & RV camping: Free, High-clearance vehicles recommended, Stay limit: 3 days, Elevation: 1263ft/385m, Telephone: 928-505-1200. Nearest town: Parker. GPS: 34.171288, -113.842615

55 • C1 | Tom Wells Road Dispersed

Dispersed sites, No water, No toilets, Tent & RV camping: Free, Numerous locations along road, Open all year, Reservations not accepted, Elevation: 648ft/198m. Nearest town: Ehrenburg. GPS: 33.616538, -114.432455

56 • C1 | Vicksburg

Dispersed sites, No water, No toilets, Tent & RV camping: Free, Open all year, Elevation: 1447ft/441m. Nearest town: Vicksburg. GPS: 33.749361, -113.739943

57 • C2 | 17 Mile Road

Dispersed sites, No water, No toilets, Tent & RV camping: Free, Elevation: 2240ft/683m. Nearest town: Wickenburg. GPS: 34.505972, -113.414432

58 • C2 | Agua Fria NM

Dispersed sites, No water, No toilets, Tent & RV camping: Free, 4x4 recommended, Stay limit: 14 days, Elevation: 3202ft/976m, Telephone: 623-580-5500. Nearest town: Black Canyon City. GPS: 34.237268, -112.109516

59 • C2 | Agua Fria NM – Badger Spring Dispersed

Dispersed sites, No water, No toilets, Tent & RV camping: Free, Elevation: 3135ft/956m. Nearest town: Black Canyon City. GPS: 34.232655, -112.099418

60 • C2 | Agua Fria NM – Bloody Basin Rd

Dispersed sites, No water, No toilets, Tent & RV camping: Free, Reservations not accepted, Elevation: 3766ft/1148m. Nearest town: Cordes Lakes. GPS: 34.232757, -112.021312

61 • C2 | BLM Road 9331 Dispersed

Dispersed sites, No water, No toilets, Tent & RV camping: Free, Reservations not accepted, Elevation: 2120ft/646m. Nearest town: Wenden. GPS: 33.875629, -113.371749

62 • C2 | Boulders OHV

Dispersed sites, No water, Vault/pit toilet, Tent & RV camping: Free, Open all year, Reservations not accepted, Elevation: 2022ft/616m. Nearest town: Morristown. GPS: 33.843795, -112.441924

63 • C2 | Box Wash

Dispersed sites, No water, Vault/pit toilet, Tent & RV camping: Free, Reservations not accepted, Stay limit: 14 days, Elevation: 2528ft/771m, Telephone: 602-417-9200. Nearest town: Wickenburg. GPS: 33.879202, -112.822046

64 • C2 | Burro Creek

Total sites: 21, RV sites: 21, Central water, Flush toilet, No showers, RV dump, Tent & RV camping: $14, Reservable group site $50, Reservations not accepted, Stay limit: 14 days, Elevation: 1923ft/586m, Telephone: 928-718-3700. Nearest town: Wickenburg. GPS: 34.538073, -113.449928

65 • C2 | Crown King Road Dispersed 1

Dispersed sites, No water, No toilets, Tent & RV camping: Free, Reservations not accepted, Elevation: 3805ft/1160m. Nearest town: Spring Valley. GPS: 34.296345, -112.142466

66 • C2 | Crown King Road Dispersed 2

Dispersed sites, No water, No toilets, Tent & RV camping: Free, Reservations not accepted, Elevation: 3692ft/1125m. Nearest town: Spring Valley. GPS: 34.290172, -112.141084

67 • C2 | Crown King Road Dispersed 3

Dispersed sites, No water, No toilets, Tent & RV camping: Free, Reservations not accepted, Elevation: 3657ft/1115m. Nearest town: Spring Valley. GPS: 34.287353, -112.141197

68 • C2 | Eagle Eye Road Dispersed

Dispersed sites, No water, No toilets, Tent & RV camping: Free, Reservations not accepted, Elevation: 1743ft/531m. Nearest town: Tonopah. GPS: 33.710029, -113.307544

69 • C2 | East Stanton Road

Dispersed sites, No water, No toilets, Tent & RV camping: Free, Reservations not accepted, Elevation: 3192ft/973m, Telephone: 623-580-5500. Nearest town: Congress. GPS: 34.162428, -112.758372

70 • C2 | FSR 259 Dispersed 1

Dispersed sites, No water, No toilets, Tent & RV camping: Free, Reservations not accepted, Elevation: 3926ft/1197m. Nearest town: Spring Valley. GPS: 34.294961, -112.139699

71 • C2 | FSR 259 Dispersed 2

Dispersed sites, No water, No toilets, Tent & RV camping: Free, Reservations not accepted, Elevation: 3863ft/1177m. Nearest town: Spring Valley. GPS: 34.298993, -112.140034

72 • C2 | FSR 259 Dispersed 3

Dispersed sites, No water, No toilets, Tent & RV camping: Free, Reservations not accepted, Elevation: 3870ft/1180m. Nearest town: Spring Valley. GPS: 34.300554, -112.146756

73 • C2 | FSR 259 Dispersed 4

Dispersed sites, No water, No toilets, Tent & RV camping: Free, Reservations not accepted, Elevation: 3947ft/1203m. Nearest town: Spring Valley. GPS: 34.290138, -112.175556

74 • C2 | Ghost Town Rd

Dispersed sites, No water, No toilets, Tent & RV camping: Free, Elevation: 3196ft/974m, Telephone: 623-580-5500. Nearest town: Congress. GPS: 34.18882, -112.85422

75 • C2 | Harquahala Mountains – Eagle Eye Road

Total sites: 2, RV sites: 2, No water, Vault/pit toilet, Tent & RV camping: Free, Elevation: 1843ft/562m. Nearest town: Tonopah. GPS: 33.729497, -113.296919

76 • C2 | North Little Grand Canyon Rd Site 1

Dispersed sites, No water, No toilets, Tent & RV camping: Free, Reservations not accepted, Elevation: 1886ft/575m. Nearest town: Phoenix. GPS: 33.989558, -112.174003

77 • C2 | North Little Grand Canyon Rd Site 2

Dispersed sites, No water, No toilets, Tent & RV camping: Free, Reservations not accepted, Elevation: 1916ft/584m. Nearest town: Phoenix. GPS: 33.988202, -112.170237

78 • C2 | Sophie Flats Dispersed

Dispersed sites, No water, No toilets, Tent & RV camping: Free, Mostly equestrian use, Reservations not accepted, Stay limit: 14 days, Elevation: 2509ft/765m. Nearest town: Wickenburg. GPS: 34.006409, -112.694912

79 • C2 | South of North Ranch

Dispersed sites, No water, No toilets, Tent & RV camping: Free, Elevation: 2707ft/825m. Nearest town: Congress. GPS: 34.089406, -112.819489

80 • C2 | Table Mesa OHV Little Pan

Dispersed sites, No water, Vault/pit toilet, Tent & RV camping: Free, Open all year, Stay limit: 14 days, Elevation: 1932ft/589m, Telephone: 623-580-5500. Nearest town: Black Canyon City. GPS: 34.004123, -112.161272

81 • C2 | Table Mesa OHV Remote

Dispersed sites, No water, Vault/pit toilet, Tent & RV camping: Free, Open all year, Reservations not accepted,

Elevation: 2055ft/626m, Telephone: 623-580-5500. Nearest town: Black Canyon City. GPS: 34.014698, -112.156062

82 • C2 | Vulture Mine Road

Dispersed sites, No water, No toilets, Tent & RV camping: Free, Elevation: 2543ft/775m, Telephone: 623-580-5500. Nearest town: Wickenburg. GPS: 33.88118, -112.821226

83 • D1 | Fortuna Pond

Dispersed sites, No water, Vault/pit toilet, Tent & RV camping: Free, Open all year, Stay limit: 14 days, Elevation: 138ft/42m, Telephone: 928-317-3200. Nearest town: Yuma. GPS: 32.724183, -114.453452

84 • D1 | Hidden Shores Concession

Total sites: 575, RV sites: 575, Electric sites: 575, Water at site, Flush toilet, Free showers, RV dump, No tents/RVs: $58-80, Elevation: 197ft/60m, Telephone: 928-783-1448. Nearest town: Yuma. GPS: 32.88273, -114.458874

85 • D1 | Mittry Lake WA

Dispersed sites, No water, Vault/pit toilet, Tent & RV camping: Free, Elevation: 158ft/48m, Telephone: 928-317-3200. Nearest town: Yuma. GPS: 32.817314, -114.472315

86 • D1 | S Cibola Lake Road Dispersed

Dispersed sites, No water, No toilets, Tent & RV camping: Free, The first 1000' is state trust land requiring a permit so go in a little way to hit BLM property, Open all year, Reservations not accepted, Elevation: 279ft/85m. Nearest town: Cibola. GPS: 33.362718, -114.661085

87 • D2 | Agua Caliente Road

Dispersed sites, No water, No toilets, Tent & RV camping: Free, Elevation: 986ft/301m. Nearest town: Gila Bend. GPS: 33.253995, -112.889773

88 • D2 | Alley Road Dispersed

Dispersed sites, No water, No toilets, Tent & RV camping: Free, Reservations not accepted, Elevation: 2095ft/639m. Nearest town: Ajo. GPS: 32.353639, -112.887503

89 • D2 | Darby Wells Road Dispersed

Dispersed sites, No water, No toilets, Tent & RV camping: Free, Elevation: 1788ft/545m. Nearest town: Ajo. GPS: 32.341354, -112.843637

90 • D2 | Gunsight Wash Dispersed

Dispersed sites, No water, No toilets, Tent & RV camping: Free, Elevation: 1801ft/549m, Telephone: 623-580-5500. Nearest town: Why. GPS: 32.238056, -112.751393

91 • D2 | Margies Cove West

Total sites: 3, RV sites: 3, No water, Vault/pit toilet, Tent & RV camping: Free, High clearance vehicle recommended, Reservations not accepted, Stay limit: 14 days, Elevation: 1109ft/338m, Telephone: 623-580-5500. Nearest town: Gila Bend. GPS: 33.125829, -112.581985

92 • D2 | Natural Gas Road Dispersed

Dispersed sites, No water, No toilets, Tents: Fee unk/RVs: Free, Elevation: 945ft/288m. Nearest town: Tonopah. GPS: 33.343076, -112.982421

93 • D2 | Painted Rock Petroglyph Site

Total sites: 50, RV sites: 50, No water, Vault/pit toilet, Tent & RV camping: $8, Open all year, Reservations not accepted, Stay limit: 14 days, Elevation: 577ft/176m, Telephone: 623-580-5500. Nearest town: Gila Bend. GPS: 33.022259, -113.049385

94 • D2 | Saddle Mountain Dispersed 1

Dispersed sites, No water, No toilets, Tent & RV camping: Free, Reservations not accepted, Stay limit: 14 days, Elevation: 1343ft/409m. Nearest town: Tonopah. GPS: 33.453221, -113.023253

95 • D2 | Saddle Mountain Dispersed 2

Dispersed sites, No water, No toilets, Tent & RV camping: Free, Elevation: 1433ft/437m. Nearest town: Tonopah. GPS: 33.451081, -113.036827

96 • D2 | Saddle Mountain Dispersed 3

Dispersed sites, No water, No toilets, Tent & RV camping: Free, Elevation: 1387ft/423m, Telephone: 623-580-5500. Nearest town: Tonopah. GPS: 33.447899, -113.046571

97 • D2 | Vekol Valley

Dispersed sites, No water, No toilets, Tent & RV camping: Free, Reservations not accepted, Elevation: 1814ft/553m. Nearest town: Casa Grande. GPS: 32.806601, -112.253108

98 • D2 | West Dobbs Road Dispersed

Dispersed sites, No water, No toilets, Tent & RV camping: Free, Rough road, Reservations not accepted, Elevation: 1038ft/316m. Nearest town: Tonopah. GPS: 33.369389, -112.993356

99 • D2 | Wild Woman

Dispersed sites, No water, No toilets, Tent & RV camping: Free, Elevation: 1764ft/538m. Nearest town: Ajo. GPS: 32.241228, -112.765296

100 • D3 | Christmas

Dispersed sites, No water, Vault/pit toilet, Tents only: Free, Nothing larger than truck camper, Elevation: 2059ft/628m, Telephone: 520-258-7200. Nearest town: Winkelman. GPS: 33.021768, -110.738938

101 • D3 | Fourmile Canyon

Total sites: 19, RV sites: 19, No water, Vault/pit toilet, No showers, No RV dump, Tent & RV camping: $5, Open all year, Reservations not accepted, Elevation: 3505ft/1068m, Telephone: 928-348-4400. Nearest town: Klondyke. GPS: 32.829632, -110.345451

102 • D3 | Ironwood Forest NM Dispersed

Dispersed sites, No water, No toilets, Tent & RV camping: Free, Elevation: 2194ft/669m. Nearest town: Red Rock. GPS: 32.473635, -111.497934

103 • D3 | North Pump Station Road

Dispersed sites, No water, No toilets, Tent & RV camping: Free, Elevation: 2004ft/611m. Nearest town: Tucson. GPS: 32.436919, -111.371525

104 • D3 | Redfield Canyon

Dispersed sites, No toilets, Tent & RV camping: Free, Open all year, Elevation: 3320ft/1012m, Telephone: 928-348-4400. Nearest town: Safford. GPS: 32.431614, -110.388668

105 • D3 | Shores

Dispersed sites, No water, Vault/pit toilet, Tent & RV camping: Free, Nothing larger than truck camper, Elevation: 2084ft/635m, Telephone: 520-258-7200. Nearest town: Winkelman. GPS: 33.059923, -110.721659

106 • D3 | Snyder Hill Dispersed

Dispersed sites, No water, No toilets, Tent & RV camping: Free, Open all year, Stay limit: 14 days, Elevation: 2493ft/760m. Nearest town: Tucson. GPS: 32.158031, -111.115385

107 • D4 | Hackel Road Dispersed

Dispersed sites, No water, No toilets, Tent & RV camping: Free, Reservations not accepted, Elevation: 3178ft/969m. Nearest town: Safford. GPS: 32.778655, -109.572236

108 • D4 | Hackle Road

Dispersed sites, No water, No toilets, Tent & RV camping: Free, Elevation: 3054ft/931m, Telephone: 928-348-4400. Nearest town: Safford. GPS: 32.782233, -109.605522

109 • D4 | Hot Well Dunes

Total sites: 10, RV sites: 10, No water, Vault/pit toilet, Tent & RV camping: $3, Open all year, Reservations not accepted, Stay limit: 14 days, Elevation: 3380ft/1030m, Telephone: 928-348-4400. Nearest town: Safford. GPS: 32.521154, -109.438562

110 • D4 | Indian Bread Rocks

Total sites: 5, RV sites: 5, No water, Vault/pit toilet, Tent & RV camping: Free, Camp in undeveloped areas, Reservations not accepted, Elevation: 4167ft/1270m, Telephone: 928-348-4400. Nearest town: Bowie. GPS: 32.238443, -109.499676

111 • D4 | Muleshoe Ranch

Dispersed sites, No water, No toilets, Tents only: Free, 4x4, Elevation: 4101ft/1250m, Telephone: 928-348-4400. Nearest town: Willcox. GPS: 32.337855, -110.238692

112 • D4 | Owl Creek

Total sites: 7, RV sites: 7, No water, Vault/pit toilet, Tent & RV camping: $5, Open all year, Reservations not accepted, Stay limit: 14 days, Elevation: 3450ft/1052m, Telephone: 928-348-4400. Nearest town: Clifton. GPS: 32.965887, -109.306595

113 • D4 | Red Knolls Amphitheater

Dispersed sites, No water, No toilets, Tent & RV camping: Free, Elevation: 2797ft/853m. Nearest town: Eden. GPS: 32.961665, -109.939325

114 • D4 | Riverview

Total sites: 13, RV sites: 13, Central water, Vault/pit toilet, No showers, No RV dump, Tent & RV camping: $5, Open all year, Reservations not accepted, Stay limit: 14 days, Elevation: 3198ft/975m, Telephone: 928-348-4400. Nearest town: Safford. GPS: 32.887671, -109.479652

115 • D4 | Round Mountain Rockhound Area

Dispersed sites, No water, No toilets, Tent & RV camping: Free, Reservations not accepted, Elevation: 4291ft/1308m. Nearest town: Duncan. GPS: 32.484493, -109.059244

116 • E3 | FSR 62 Dispersed 1

Dispersed sites, No water, No toilets, Tent & RV camping: Free, Elevation: 4038ft/1231m. Nearest town: Green Valley. GPS: 31.777026, -110.848312

117 • E3 | Las Cienegas NCA – Cieneguita Dispersed

Dispersed sites, No water, No toilets, Tent & RV camping: Free, Several spots along road, Reservations not accepted,

Elevation: 4607ft/1404m. Nearest town: Sonoita. GPS: 31.766666, -110.627132

118 • E3 | Las Cienegas NCA – Oak Canyon Dispersed

Dispersed sites, No water, No toilets, Tent & RV camping: Free, Reservations not accepted, Elevation: 4706ft/1434m. Nearest town: Sonoita. GPS: 31.800516, -110.655485

119 • E3 | Las Cienegas NCA – Road Canyon

Total sites: 6, RV sites: 6, No water, No toilets, Tent & RV camping: Free, Open Jul-Mar, Reservations not accepted, Elevation: 4578ft/1395m, Telephone: 520-439-6400. Nearest town: Sonoita. GPS: 31.739234, -110.585718

120 • E3 | White House Canyon Road Dispersed

Dispersed sites, No water, No toilets, Tent & RV camping: Free, Elevation: 3774ft/1150m. Nearest town: Green Valley. GPS: 31.787596, -110.871729

121 • E4 | Baker Canyon WSA

Dispersed sites, Tents only: Free, Elevation: 4380ft/1335m, Telephone: 928-348-4400. Nearest town: Stafford. GPS: 31.347292, -109.063497

California

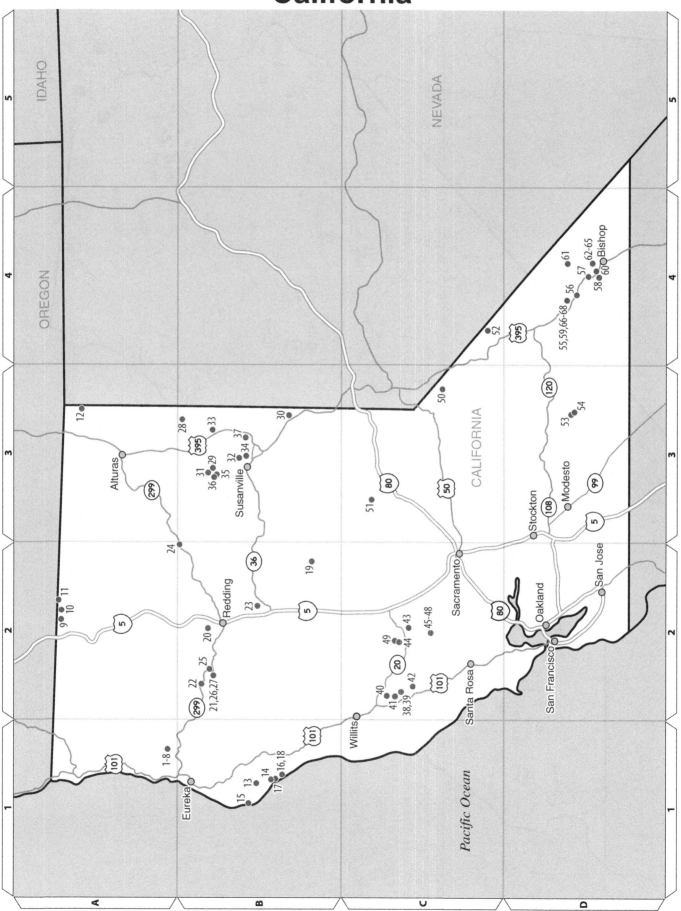

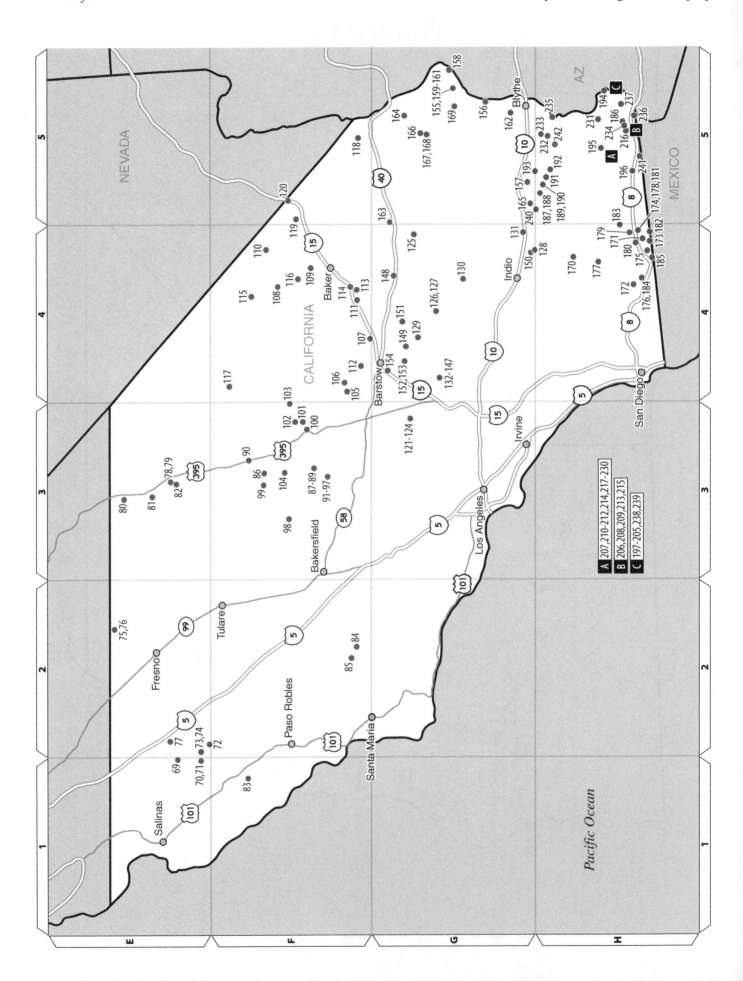

California

California State Office
2800 Cottage Way Suite W1623
Sacramento CA 95825

Phone: 916-978-4400

Name	ID	Map	RVs	Tents	Free
Alabama Hills – Movie Road	78	E3	✓	✓	✓
Alabama Hills RA	79	E3	✓	✓	✓
Amboy Crater	125	G4	✓	✓	✓
American Girl Mine	186	H5	✓	✓	✓
Anza Borego Desert	170	H4	✓	✓	✓
Anza Dispersed	171	H4	✓	✓	✓
Benton Crossing Road Dispersed	55	D4	✓	✓	✓
Bighorn Mountain Wilderness – Barnes Rd	126	G4	✓	✓	✓
Black Mountain Wilderness – Black Canyon	105	F4	✓	✓	✓
Black Mountain Wilderness – Opal	106	F4	✓	✓	✓
Blue Cloud Dispersed	155	G5	✓	✓	✓
Blythe-Vidal	156	G5	✓	✓	✓
Boone Road Dispersed	127	G4	✓	✓	✓
Box Canyon	128	G4	✓	✓	✓
Bradshaw Trail Dispersed 1	187	H5	✓	✓	✓
Bradshaw Trail Dispersed 2	188	H5	✓	✓	✓
Bradshaw Trail Dispersed 3	189	H5	✓	✓	✓
Bradshaw Trail Dispersed 4	190	H5	✓	✓	✓
Bradshaw Trail Dispersed 5	191	H5	✓	✓	✓
Bradshaw Trail Dispersed 6	192	H5	✓	✓	✓
Butte Creek Recreation Area	19	B2	✓	✓	✓
Calico Early Man	107	F4	✓	✓	✓
Camp Ibis	118	F5	✓	✓	✓
Carrizo Plains NM – KCL CG	84	F2	✓	✓	✓
Carrizo Plains NM – Selby CG	85	F2	✓	✓	✓
Chappie – Shasta OHV Area	20	B2	✓	✓	
Chemung Mine	52	C4	✓	✓	✓
Chimney Peak	86	F3	✓	✓	✓
Clark Mountain Camp	119	F5		✓	✓
Condon Peak	72	E2	✓	✓	
Copco Cove	9	A2	✓	✓	✓
Corn Springs	157	G5	✓	✓	
Cottonwood	172	H4	✓	✓	

Name	ID	Map	RVs	Tents	Free
Cow Mountain RA – Buckhorn	38	C2	✓	✓	✓
Cow Mountain RA – Bushy	39	C2	✓	✓	✓
Cow Mountain RA – Mayacamas	40	C2		✓	✓
Cow Mountain RA – Red Mountain	41	C2		✓	✓
Cow Mountain RA – Sheldon Creek	42	C2		✓	✓
Cowboy Camp Horse CG	43	C2	✓	✓	✓
Coyote Dispersed	173	H4	✓	✓	✓
Crossroads	158	G5	✓	✓	
Crowley Lake	56	D4	✓	✓	
Dodge Reservoir	28	B3	✓	✓	
Douglas City	21	B2	✓	✓	
Dove Springs	87	F3	✓	✓	✓
Dove Springs OHV	88	F3	✓	✓	✓
Dove Springs Strip	89	F3	✓	✓	✓
Dumont Dunes OHV	108	F4	✓	✓	
Dunaway Dispersed	174	H4	✓	✓	✓
Dupont Road Dispersed	193	H5		✓	✓
Earp 2 Dispersed	159	G5	✓	✓	✓
Earp 3 Dispersed	160	G5	✓	✓	✓
East Eagle Lake	29	B3	✓		✓
El Mirage Dry Lakebed OHV – Staging Area 1	121	G3	✓	✓	
El Mirage Dry Lakebed OHV – Staging Area 2	122	G3	✓	✓	
El Mirage Dry Lakebed OHV – Staging Area 3	123	G3	✓	✓	
El Mirage Dry Lakebed OHV – Staging Areas 4/5	124	G3	✓	✓	
Fee Reservoir	12	A3	✓	✓	✓
Fergusen Lake	194	H5	✓	✓	✓
Fort Sage OHVA	30	B3	✓	✓	✓
Fossil Falls	90	F3	✓	✓	
Glamis Dispersed	195	H5	✓		✓
Goodale Creek	80	E3	✓	✓	
Gorge Road Dispersed	57	D4	✓		✓
Griswold Hills	69	E1			✓
Hollow Hills Dispersed	109	F4	✓	✓	✓
Holtville Hot Springs LTVA	196	H5	✓	✓	✓
Honeydew	13	B1	✓	✓	✓
Horton Creek	58	D4	✓	✓	
Hot Creek Hatchery Road Dispersed	59	D4	✓	✓	✓
Hwy 62 Dispersed	161	G5	✓		✓

Name	ID	Map	RVs	Tents	Free
Imperial Dam LTVA	197	H5	✓		
Imperial Dam LTVA – Beehive Mesa	198	H5	✓		
Imperial Dam LTVA – Coyote Ridge	199	H5	✓		
Imperial Dam LTVA – Hurricane Ridge	200	H5	✓		
Imperial Dam LTVA – Kripple Creek	201	H5	✓		
Imperial Dam LTVA – Northwest Territory	202	H5	✓	✓	
Imperial Dam LTVA – Quail Hill	203	H5	✓		
Imperial Dam LTVA – Skunk Hollow	204	H5	✓		
Imperial Dam LTVA – South Mesa	205	H5	✓		
Imperial Sand Dunes RA – Buttercup	206	H5	✓		
Imperial Sand Dunes RA – Cement Flats	207	H5	✓		
Imperial Sand Dunes RA – Dunebuggy Flats	208	H5	✓		
Imperial Sand Dunes RA – Dunes Vista	209	H5	✓		
Imperial Sand Dunes RA – Gecko	210	H5	✓		
Imperial Sand Dunes RA – Gecko Loop	211	H5	✓		
Imperial Sand Dunes RA – Glamis Flats	212	H5	✓		
Imperial Sand Dunes RA – Grays Well	213	H5	✓		
Imperial Sand Dunes RA – Keyhole	214	H5	✓		
Imperial Sand Dunes RA – Midway	215	H5	✓		
Imperial Sand Dunes RA – Ogilby	216	H5	✓		
Imperial Sand Dunes RA – Osborne Overlook	217	H5	✓		
Imperial Sand Dunes RA – Pad 1	218	H5	✓		
Imperial Sand Dunes RA – Pad 1.5	219	H5	✓		
Imperial Sand Dunes RA – Pad 2	220	H5	✓		
Imperial Sand Dunes RA – Pad 2.5	221	H5	✓		
Imperial Sand Dunes RA – Pad 3	222	H5	✓		
Imperial Sand Dunes RA – Pad 4	223	H5	✓		
Imperial Sand Dunes RA – Pad 5	224	H5	✓		
Imperial Sand Dunes RA – Palo Verde Flats	225	H5	✓		
Imperial Sand Dunes RA – Roadrunner	226	H5	✓		
Imperial Sand Dunes RA – Wash 10	227	H5	✓		
Imperial Sand Dunes RA – Wash 20	228	H5	✓		
Imperial Sand Dunes RA – Wash 4	229	H5	✓		

Name	ID	Map	RVs	Tents	Free
Imperial Sand Dunes RA – Wash 6	230	H5	✓		
Indian Creek	50	C3	✓	✓	
Indian Pass Wilderness	231	H5	✓	✓	✓
Indian Valley Reservoir – Blue Oaks	44	C2	✓	✓	✓
Ivanpah Dispersed	120	F5	✓		
Jacumba Mountains Wilderness	175	H4	✓	✓	✓
Jade Mill	73	E2	✓	✓	✓
Jawbone Canyon OHV Primitive Area 1	91	F3	✓	✓	✓
Jawbone Canyon OHV Primitive Area 2	92	F3	✓	✓	✓
Jawbone Canyon OHV Staging Area 1	93	F3	✓	✓	✓
Jawbone Canyon OHV Staging Area 2	94	F3	✓	✓	✓
Jawbone Canyon OHV Staging Area 3	95	F3	✓	✓	✓
Jawbone Canyon OHV Staging Area 4	96	F3	✓	✓	✓
Jawbone Canyon OHV Staging Area 5	97	F3	✓	✓	✓
Johnson Valley OHV	129	G4	✓	✓	✓
Joshua Tree Overflow	130	G4	✓	✓	✓
Joshua Tree South	131	G4	✓		✓
Junction City	22	B2	✓	✓	
Juniper Flats Dispersed 01	132	G4	✓	✓	✓
Juniper Flats Dispersed 02	133	G4	✓	✓	✓
Juniper Flats Dispersed 03	134	G4	✓	✓	✓
Juniper Flats Dispersed 04	135	G4	✓	✓	✓
Juniper Flats Dispersed 05	136	G4	✓	✓	✓
Juniper Flats Dispersed 06	137	G4	✓	✓	✓
Juniper Flats Dispersed 07	138	G4	✓	✓	✓
Juniper Flats Dispersed 08	139	G4	✓	✓	✓
Juniper Flats Dispersed 09	140	G4	✓	✓	✓
Juniper Flats Dispersed 10	141	G4	✓	✓	✓
Juniper Flats Dispersed 11	142	G4	✓	✓	✓
Juniper Flats Dispersed 12	143	G4	✓	✓	✓
Juniper Flats Dispersed 13	144	G4	✓	✓	✓
Juniper Flats Dispersed 14	145	G4	✓	✓	✓
Juniper Flats Dispersed 15	146	G4		✓	✓
Juniper Flats Dispersed 16	147	G4	✓	✓	✓
Keysville Rec Site	98	F3	✓	✓	✓
King Range NCA – Horse Mountain	14	B1	✓	✓	
King Range NCA – Mattole	15	B1	✓	✓	
King Range NCA – Nadelos	16	B1		✓	
King Range NCA – Tolkan	17	B1	✓	✓	

Name	ID	Map	RVs	Tents	Free
King Range NCA – Wailaki	18	B1	✓	✓	
Kingston Mountains – Horsethief Camp	110	F4	✓	✓	✓
Knoxville RA – Cedar Creek	45	C2	✓	✓	✓
Knoxville RA – Cement Creek	46	C2	✓	✓	✓
Knoxville RA – Lower Hunting Creek	47	C2	✓	✓	✓
Knoxville RA – Pocock Creek	48	C2	✓	✓	✓
Lacks Creek Mgmt Area – Site 1	1	A1		✓	✓
Lacks Creek Mgmt Area – Site 2	2	A1		✓	✓
Lacks Creek Mgmt Area – Site 3	3	A1		✓	✓
Lacks Creek Mgmt Area – Site 4	4	A1		✓	✓
Lacks Creek Mgmt Area – Site 5	5	A1		✓	✓
Lacks Creek Mgmt Area – Site 6	6	A1		✓	✓
Lacks Creek Mgmt Area – Site 7	7	A1		✓	✓
Lacks Creek Mgmt Area – Site 8	8	A1		✓	✓
Laguna Mountain	70	E1	✓	✓	✓
Long Valley	99	F3	✓	✓	
Lower Lark Canyon	176	H4	✓	✓	
Ludlow	148	G4	✓	✓	✓
Mallard Cove	10	A2	✓	✓	✓
McCabe Flat	53	D3	✓	✓	
Midland LTVA	162	G5	✓		
Mojave Preserve – Kelbaker Rd	163	G5		✓	✓
Mojave Trails NM – Afton Canyon	111	F4	✓	✓	
Mule Mountain – Coon Hollow LTVA	232	H5	✓	✓	
Mule Mountain – Wiley's Well LTVA	233	H5	✓	✓	
North Eagle Lake	31	B3	✓	✓	
Oak Flat	74	E2	✓	✓	✓
Ocotillo Dispersed	177	H4	✓	✓	
Ogilby Road	234	H5	✓	✓	✓
Ord Mountain ORV Route	149	G4	✓	✓	✓
Overlook Dispersed	178	H4	✓	✓	✓
Owl Canyon	112	F4	✓	✓	
Oxbow Lake	235	H5	✓	✓	
Pace Canyon Road Dispersed 1	32	B3	✓	✓	✓
Painted Canyon Dispersed	150	G4	✓	✓	✓
Perry Rifle	23	B2	✓		✓
Pilot Knob	236	H5	✓		
Pit River	24	B2	✓	✓	
Plaster City East OHV	179	H4	✓	✓	✓
Plaster City West OHV	180	H4	✓	✓	✓

Name	ID	Map	RVs	Tents	Free
Powerline	237	H5	✓	✓	✓
PV Pit RA	60	D4	✓	✓	
Railroad Flat	54	D3	✓	✓	
Ramhorn Springs	33	B3	✓	✓	
Rasor OHV Alternate Staging	113	F4	✓	✓	✓
Rasor OHV Main Staging	114	F4	✓	✓	✓
Red Canyon Petroglyphs	61	D4	✓	✓	✓
Rice Canyon OHVA	34	B3	✓	✓	
Rocky Point East	35	B3	✓	✓	
Rocky Point West	36	B3	✓	✓	
Rodman Mountains Wilderness Dispersed	151	G4	✓	✓	✓
San Joaquin River Gorge – Yeh-Gub-Weh-Tuh	75	E2	✓	✓	
Sawtooth Canyon	152	G4	✓	✓	✓
Sawtooth Canyon Dispersed	153	G4	✓	✓	✓
Senator Wash North Shore	238	H5	✓	✓	
Shaffer Mountain	37	B3		✓	✓
Shellbeds Dispersed	181	H4	✓	✓	✓
Shoshone Dispersed	115	F4	✓	✓	✓
Silurian Lake	116	F4	✓	✓	✓
Snaggletooth Dispersed	164	G5	✓		✓
South Yuba	51	C3	✓	✓	
Spangler Hills OHVA – Searles Station	100	F3	✓	✓	✓
Spangler Hills OHVA – Teagle Wash	101	F3	✓	✓	✓
Spangler Hills OHVA – Wagon Wheel	102	F3	✓	✓	✓
Squaw Lake	239	H5	✓	✓	
Squaw Leap Horse Camp	76	E2	✓	✓	
Stateline on the Klamath River	11	A2	✓	✓	✓
Steel Bridge	25	B2	✓	✓	
Steiner Flat	26	B2	✓	✓	✓
Steiner Flat Dispersed	27	B2	✓	✓	✓
Stoddard Valley OHV	154	G4	✓	✓	✓
Summit Dispersed	165	G5	✓	✓	✓
Summit Road Dispersed 1	240	H5		✓	✓
Sunrise Butte Dispersed	182	H4	✓	✓	✓
Superstition Mountain OHV	183	H4	✓	✓	✓
Surprise Canyon Dispersed	117	F4		✓	✓
Symmes Creek	81	E3	✓	✓	
Tamarisk LTVA	241	H5	✓		
Trona Pinnacles NNL	103	F3	✓	✓	✓

Name	ID	Map	RVs	Tents	Free
Tumey Hills	77	E2	✓	✓	✓
Turtle Mountain Road Dispersed	166	G5	✓	✓	✓
Turtle Mountains Wilderness – Brown's Camp	167	G5	✓	✓	✓
Turtle Mountains Wilderness – Lisa Dawn Camp	168	G5	✓	✓	✓
Tuttle Creek	82	E3	✓	✓	
Upper Lark Canyon	184	H4	✓	✓	
Upper Sweetwater	71	E1	✓	✓	✓
Valley of the Moon – Elliot Mine Area	185	H4	✓	✓	✓
Vidal Junction Dispersed	169	G5	✓		
Volcanic Tablelands 1	62	D4	✓	✓	✓
Volcanic Tablelands 2	63	D4	✓	✓	✓
Volcanic Tablelands 3	64	D4	✓	✓	✓
Volcanic Tablelands 4	65	D4	✓	✓	✓
Walker Pass	104	F3	✓	✓	
Whitmore Tubs Road Dispersed	66	D4	✓	✓	✓
Whitmore Tubs Road Dispersed	67	D4	✓	✓	✓
Whitmore Tubs Road Dispersed	68	D4	✓	✓	✓
Wiley Well District Geode Beds	242	H5		✓	✓
Williams Hill Rec Area	83	F1	✓	✓	✓
Wintun	49	C2		✓	✓

1 • A1 | Lacks Creek Mgmt Area – Site 1

Dispersed sites, No water, No toilets, Tents only: Free, Reservations not accepted, Elevation: 3213ft/979m, Telephone: 707-825-2300. Nearest town: Willow Creek. GPS: 40.990462, -123.791504

2 • A1 | Lacks Creek Mgmt Area – Site 2

Dispersed sites, No water, No toilets, Tents only: Free, Nothing larger than TC, Reservations not accepted, Elevation: 3438ft/1048m, Telephone: 707-825-2300. Nearest town: Willow Creek. GPS: 40.996752, -123.789474

3 • A1 | Lacks Creek Mgmt Area – Site 3

Dispersed sites, No water, No toilets, Tents only: Free, Reservations not accepted, Elevation: 3498ft/1066m, Telephone: 707-825-2300. Nearest town: Willow Creek. GPS: 41.002483, -123.779892

4 • A1 | Lacks Creek Mgmt Area – Site 4

Dispersed sites, No water, No toilets, Tents only: Free, Reservations not accepted, Elevation: 3525ft/1074m,

Telephone: 707-825-2300. Nearest town: Willow Creek. GPS: 41.022713, -123.786727

5 • A1 | Lacks Creek Mgmt Area – Site 5

Dispersed sites, No water, No toilets, Tents only: Free, Reservations not accepted, Elevation: 3892ft/1186m, Telephone: 707-825-2300. Nearest town: Willow Creek. GPS: 41.024514, -123.781715

6 • A1 | Lacks Creek Mgmt Area – Site 6

Dispersed sites, No water, No toilets, Tents only: Free, Reservations not accepted, Elevation: 2704ft/824m, Telephone: 707-825-2300. Nearest town: Willow Creek. GPS: 40.999759, -123.797165

7 • A1 | Lacks Creek Mgmt Area – Site 7

Dispersed sites, No water, No toilets, Tents only: Free, Reservations not accepted, Elevation: 2670ft/814m, Telephone: 707-825-2300. Nearest town: Willow Creek. GPS: 41.008084, -123.796523

8 • A1 | Lacks Creek Mgmt Area – Site 8

Dispersed sites, No water, No toilets, Tents only: Free, Reservations not accepted, Elevation: 2467ft/752m, Telephone: 707-825-2300. Nearest town: Willow Creek. GPS: 41.019623, -123.799283

9 • A2 | Copco Cove

Dispersed sites, No water, Vault/pit toilet, Tent & RV camping: Free, Elevation: 2338ft/713m, Telephone: 530-224-2100. Nearest town: Yreka. GPS: 41.976546, -122.398874

10 • A2 | Mallard Cove

Total sites: 4, RV sites: 4, No water, Vault/pit toilet, Tents: Fee unk/RVs: Free, Elevation: 2616ft/797m, Telephone: 530-224-2100. Nearest town: Yreka. GPS: 41.973548, -122.29894

11 • A2 | Stateline on the Klamath River

Dispersed sites, No water, Vault/pit toilet, Tent & RV camping: Free, Reservations not accepted, Stay limit: 14 days, Elevation: 2785ft/849m, Telephone: 530-224-2100. Nearest town: Dorris. GPS: 42.006602, -122.188023

12 • A3 | Fee Reservoir

Total sites: 7, RV sites: 7, No water, Vault/pit toilet, Tent & RV camping: Free, Open all year, Elevation: 5269ft/1606m, Telephone: 530-233-4666. Nearest town: Fort Bidwell. GPS: 41.835107, -120.028776

13 • B1 | Honeydew

Total sites: 5, RV sites: 5, No water, Vault/pit toilet, Tent & RV camping: Free, Reservations not accepted, Stay limit: 14 days, Elevation: 364ft/111m. Nearest town: Garberville. GPS: 40.231601, -124.114586

14 • B1 | King Range NCA – Horse Mountain

Total sites: 9, RV sites: 9, No water, Vault/pit toilet, Tent & RV camping: $5, Reservations not accepted, Stay limit: 14 days, Elevation: 1604ft/489m, Telephone: 707-825-2300. Nearest town: Redway. GPS: 40.105698, -124.066423

15 • B1 | King Range NCA – Mattole

Total sites: 14, RV sites: 14, No water, Vault/pit toilet, No showers, No RV dump, Tent & RV camping: $8, Elevation: 16ft/5m, Telephone: 707-825-2300. Nearest town: Petrolia. GPS: 40.288985, -124.355664

16 • B1 | King Range NCA – Nadelos

Total sites: 8, RV sites: 0, Central water, Vault/pit toilet, No showers, No RV dump, Tents only: $8, Entire CG may be reserved as group site: $85, Reservations not accepted, Elevation: 1936ft/590m, Telephone: 707-825-2300. Nearest town: Redway. GPS: 40.021, -124.006

17 • B1 | King Range NCA – Tolkan

Total sites: 9, RV sites: 5, Central water, Vault/pit toilet, No showers, No RV dump, Tent & RV camping: $8, Reservations not accepted, Stay limit: 14 days, Elevation: 1798ft/548m, Telephone: 707-825-2300. Nearest town: Redway. GPS: 40.082978, -124.056746

18 • B1 | King Range NCA – Wailaki

Total sites: 13, RV sites: 13, Central water, Vault/pit toilet, No showers, No RV dump, Tent & RV camping: $8, Reservations not accepted, Stay limit: 14 days, Elevation: 1923ft/586m, Telephone: 707-825-2300. Nearest town: Redway. GPS: 40.018, -124.003

19 • B2 | Butte Creek Recreation Area

Dispersed sites, No toilets, Tent & RV camping: Free, Stay limit: 14 days, Elevation: 2231ft/680m. Nearest town: Forest Ranch. GPS: 39.836022, -121.666665

20 • B2 | Chappie – Shasta OHV Area

Total sites: 22, RV sites: 22, Central water, Vault/pit toilet, No showers, No RV dump, Tent & RV camping: $10, Open all year, Stay limit: 14 days, Elevation: 689ft/210m, Telephone: 530-224-2100. Nearest town: Redding. GPS: 40.712791, -122.436822

21 • B2 | Douglas City

Total sites: 20, RV sites: 20, Central water, No toilets, No showers, No RV dump, Tent & RV camping: $10, Open May-Oct, Reservations not accepted, Stay limit: 14 days, Elevation: 1654ft/504m, Telephone: 530-224-2100. Nearest town: Douglas City. GPS: 40.648201, -122.953637

22 • B2 | Junction City

Total sites: 22, RV sites: 22, Central water, Vault/pit toilet, No showers, No RV dump, Tent & RV camping: $10, Open May-Nov, Reservations not accepted, Stay limit: 14 days, Elevation: 1519ft/463m, Telephone: 530-224-2100. Nearest town: Junction City. GPS: 40.746102, -123.063515

23 • B2 | Perry Rifle

Dispersed sites, No water, No toilets, No tents/RVs: Free, Must be self-contained, No open fires in summer, Elevation: 342ft/104m. Nearest town: Bend. GPS: 40.294332, -122.178517

24 • B2 | Pit River

Total sites: 8, RV sites: 8, No toilets, Tent & RV camping: $8, Open May-Nov, Elevation: 2910ft/887m, Telephone: 530-233-4666. Nearest town: Burney. GPS: 40.99143, -121.50845

25 • B2 | Steel Bridge

Total sites: 12, RV sites: 12, No water, Vault/pit toilet, Tent & RV camping: $5, Elevation: 1709ft/521m, Telephone: 530-224-2100. Nearest town: Douglas City. GPS: 40.676481, -122.914674

26 • B2 | Steiner Flat

Total sites: 8, RV sites: 8, No water, No toilets, Tent & RV camping: Free, Open all year, Reservations not accepted, Stay limit: 14 days, Elevation: 1618ft/493m, Telephone: 530-224-2100. Nearest town: Douglas City. GPS: 40.654555, -122.953746

27 • B2 | Steiner Flat Dispersed

Dispersed sites, No water, No toilets, Tent & RV camping: Free, Reservations not accepted, Elevation: 1586ft/483m. Nearest town: Douglas City. GPS: 40.658503, -122.967172

28 • B3 | Dodge Reservoir

Total sites: 11, RV sites: 11, No water, Vault/pit toilet, Tent & RV camping: Donation, Open all year, Reservations not accepted, Elevation: 5758ft/1755m, Telephone: 530-257-0456. Nearest town: Susanville. GPS: 40.974156, -120.13295

29 • B3 | East Eagle Lake

Dispersed sites, No water, No toilets, No tents/RVs: Free, Must be self-contained, Reservations not accepted, Elevation: 5131ft/1564m, Telephone: 530-257-0456. GPS: 40.706665, -120.672476

30 • B3 | Fort Sage OHVA

Dispersed sites, No toilets, Tent & RV camping: Free, 3 ton weight limit on a bridge on the access road, Reservations not accepted, Stay limit: 14 days, Elevation: 4738ft/1444m, Telephone: 530-257-0456. Nearest town: Doyle. GPS: 40.060392, -120.072667

31 • B3 | North Eagle Lake

Total sites: 20, RV sites: 20, Central water, Vault/pit toilet, No showers, No RV dump, Tent & RV camping: $8, Open May-Nov, Reservations not accepted, Stay limit: 14 days, Elevation: 5164ft/1574m, Telephone: 530-257-0456. Nearest town: Susanville. GPS: 40.734541, -120.719211

32 • B3 | Pace Canyon Road Dispersed 1

Dispersed sites, No water, No toilets, Tent & RV camping: Free, Reservations not accepted, Elevation: 5245ft/1599m. Nearest town: Susanville. GPS: 40.476188, -120.543261

33 • B3 | Ramhorn Springs

Total sites: 10, RV sites: 10, No water, Vault/pit toilet, Tent & RV camping: Donation, Limited access during wet weather, Open all year, Stay limit: 14 days, Elevation: 5745ft/1751m, Telephone: 530-257-0456. Nearest town: Susanville. GPS: 40.707154, -120.25231

34 • B3 | Rice Canyon OHVA

Dispersed sites, No water, Vault/pit toilet, Tent & RV camping: Free, Reservations not accepted, Stay limit: 14 days, Elevation: 4335ft/1321m, Telephone: 530-257-0456. Nearest town: Susanville. GPS: 40.422112, -120.526392

35 • B3 | Rocky Point East

Dispersed sites, No water, No toilets, Tent & RV camping: Donation, Elevation: 5112ft/1558m, Telephone: 530-257-0456. Nearest town: Susanville. GPS: 40.673572, -120.745552

36 • B3 | Rocky Point West

Dispersed sites, No water, No toilets, Tent & RV camping: Donation, Elevation: 5249ft/1600m, Telephone: 530-257-0456. Nearest town: Susanville. GPS: 40.682601, -120.757589

37 • B3 | Shaffer Mountain

Dispersed sites, No water, No toilets, Tents only: Free, Open Apr-Oct, Elevation: 5639ft/1719m, Telephone: 530-257-0456. GPS: 40.435873, -120.329193

38 • C2 | Cow Mountain RA – Buckhorn

Total sites: 4, RV sites: 4, No water, Vault/pit toilet, Tent & RV camping: Free, No large RVs, Elevation: 2868ft/874m, Telephone: 707-468-4000. Nearest town: Ukiah. GPS: 39.038426, -123.039234

39 • C2 | Cow Mountain RA – Bushy

Dispersed sites, No water, No toilets, Tent & RV camping: Free, Elevation: 2933ft/894m, Telephone: 707-468-4000. Nearest town: Ukiah. GPS: 39.056075, -123.050179

40 • C2 | Cow Mountain RA – Mayacamas

Total sites: 6, RV sites: 0, No water, Vault/pit toilet, Tents only: Free, No large RVs, Open all year, Elevation: 2835ft/864m, Telephone: 707-468-4000. Nearest town: Ukiah. GPS: 39.157134, -123.092257

41 • C2 | Cow Mountain RA – Red Mountain

Total sites: 10, RV sites: 0, No water, Vault/pit toilet, Tents only: Free, No large RVs, Open all year, Elevation: 3041ft/927m, Telephone: 707-468-4000. Nearest town: Ukiah. GPS: 39.078642, -123.090554

42 • C2 | Cow Mountain RA – Sheldon Creek

Total sites: 6, RV sites: 0, No water, Vault/pit toilet, Tents only: Free, No large RVs, Open all year, Elevation: 2310ft/704m, Telephone: 707-468-4000. Nearest town: Cloverdale. GPS: 38.935895, -122.983968

43 • C2 | Cowboy Camp Horse CG

Total sites: 6, RV sites: 6, Vault/pit toilet, Tent & RV camping: Free, Open Apr-Nov, Reservations not accepted, Elevation: 1086ft/331m, Telephone: 707-468-4000. Nearest town: Ukiah. GPS: 38.998453, -122.354526

44 • C2 | Indian Valley Reservoir – Blue Oaks

Total sites: 6, RV sites: 6, No water, Vault/pit toilet, Tent & RV camping: Free, Open all year, Reservations not accepted, Elevation: 1818ft/554m, Telephone: 707-468-4000. Nearest town: Williams. GPS: 39.069533, -122.508668

45 • C2 | Knoxville RA – Cedar Creek

Dispersed sites, No water, No toilets, Tent & RV camping: Free, Reservations not accepted, Elevation: 1299ft/396m, Telephone: 707-468-4000. Nearest town: Napa. GPS: 38.812203, -122.382374

46 • C2 | Knoxville RA – Cement Creek

Dispersed sites, No water, No toilets, Tent & RV camping: Free, Reservations not accepted, Elevation: 892ft/272m, Telephone: 707-468-4000. Nearest town: Napa. GPS: 38.772034, -122.411952

47 • C2 | Knoxville RA – Lower Hunting Creek

Total sites: 8, RV sites: 8, No water, Vault/pit toilet, Tent & RV camping: Free, Reservations not accepted, Elevation: 1119ft/341m, Telephone: 707-468-4000. Nearest town: Clearlake. GPS: 38.808812, -122.374913

48 • C2 | Knoxville RA – Pocock Creek

Dispersed sites, No water, No toilets, Tent & RV camping: Free, Reservations not accepted, Elevation: 935ft/285m, Telephone: 707-468-4000. Nearest town: Napa. GPS: 38.794892, -122.407797

49 • C2 | Wintun

Total sites: 1, RV sites: 0, No water, No toilets, Tents only: Free, Reservations not accepted, Elevation: 3146ft/959m, Telephone: 707-468-4000. Nearest town: Clearlake Oaks. GPS: 39.099718, -122.497791

50 • C3 | Indian Creek

Total sites: 29, RV sites: 19, Central water, Flush toilet, Free showers, RV dump, Tents: $14/RVs: $20, Also walk-to/group sites, Dump fee $10, Group site $50, Open May-Oct, Reservations accepted, Stay limit: 14 days, Elevation: 5640ft/1719m, Telephone: 775-885-6000. Nearest town: Markleeville. GPS: 38.745778, -119.783989

51 • C3 | South Yuba

Total sites: 16, RV sites: 16, Central water, Vault/pit toilet, No showers, No RV dump, Tent & RV camping: $5, 4 ton limit on Edward Crossing Bridge, Open Apr-Oct, Stay limit: 14 days, Elevation: 2674ft/815m, Telephone: 916-941-3101. Nearest town: Nevada City. GPS: 39.341219, -120.971921

52 • C4 | Chemung Mine

Dispersed sites, No water, No toilets, Tent & RV camping: Free, Open all year, Elevation: 8156ft/2486m. Nearest town: Bridgeport. GPS: 38.349707, -119.150441

53 • D3 | McCabe Flat

Total sites: 11, RV sites: 3, No water, Vault/pit toilet, Tent & RV camping: $10, Open all year, Reservations not accepted, Stay limit: 14 days, Elevation: 1132ft/345m, Telephone: 209-379-9414. Nearest town: Briceville. GPS: 37.596949, -120.003529

54 • D3 | Railroad Flat

Total sites: 9, RV sites: 6, No water, Vault/pit toilet, Tent & RV camping: $10, Open all year, Reservations not accepted, Stay limit: 14 days, Elevation: 1138ft/347m, Telephone: 209-379-9414. Nearest town: Briceville. GPS: 37.617811, -120.019841

55 • D4 | Benton Crossing Road Dispersed

Dispersed sites, No water, No toilets, Tent & RV camping: Free, Elevation: 6886ft/2099m. Nearest town: Mammoth Lakes. GPS: 37.660389, -118.788874

56 • D4 | Crowley Lake

Total sites: 47, RV sites: 47, Central water, Vault/pit toilet, No showers, RV dump, Tent & RV camping: $8, $5 dump fee, $300 for season, Open May-Oct, Reservations not accepted, Stay limit: 30 days, Elevation: 6959ft/2121m, Telephone: 760-872-5000. Nearest town: Mammoth Lakes. GPS: 37.573486, -118.769287

57 • D4 | Gorge Road Dispersed

Dispersed sites, No water, No toilets, No tents/RVs: Free, Small pull-off, great view, Reservations not accepted, Elevation: 5181ft/1579m. GPS: 37.467742, -118.565914

58 • D4 | Horton Creek

Total sites: 49, RV sites: 49, Central water, Vault/pit toilet, No showers, RV dump, Tent & RV camping: $5, Dump fee $5, Open May-Oct, Reservations not accepted, Stay limit: 30 days, Elevation: 4967ft/1514m, Telephone: 760-872-5000. Nearest town: Bishop. GPS: 37.383381, -118.578436

59 • D4 | Hot Creek Hatchery Road Dispersed

Dispersed sites, No water, No toilets, Tent & RV camping: Free, Tight turn-around for larger rigs, Elevation: 7074ft/2156m. Nearest town: Mammoth Lakes. GPS: 37.645889, -118.839474

60 • D4 | PV Pit RA

Total sites: 75, RV sites: 75, No water, Vault/pit toilet, Tent & RV camping: $5, Rough access road, Long-term stays available, Open all year, Reservations not accepted, Stay limit: 30 days, Elevation: 4520ft/1378m, Telephone: 760-872-5000. Nearest town: Bishop. GPS: 37.400813, -118.509989

61 • D4 | Red Canyon Petroglyphs

Dispersed sites, No water, No toilets, Tent & RV camping: Free, Reservations not accepted, Elevation: 4903ft/1494m, Telephone: 760-872-5000. Nearest town: Bishop. GPS: 37.650026, -118.435349

62 • D4 | Volcanic Tablelands 1

Dispersed sites, No water, No toilets, Tent & RV camping: Free, Elevation: 4363ft/1330m. Nearest town: Bishop. GPS: 37.423267, -118.416778

63 • D4 | Volcanic Tablelands 2

Dispersed sites, No water, No toilets, Tent & RV camping: Free, Elevation: 4406ft/1343m. Nearest town: Bishop. GPS: 37.426543, -118.421493

64 • D4 | Volcanic Tablelands 3

Dispersed sites, No water, No toilets, Tent & RV camping: Free, Elevation: 4465ft/1361m. Nearest town: Bishop. GPS: 37.430723, -118.423212

65 • D4 | Volcanic Tablelands 4

Dispersed sites, No water, No toilets, Tent & RV camping: Free, Elevation: 4468ft/1362m. Nearest town: Bishop. GPS: 37.437751, -118.430211

66 • D4 | Whitmore Tubs Road Dispersed

Dispersed sites, No water, No toilets, Tent & RV camping: Free, Hot springs, Elevation: 6984ft/2129m. Nearest town: Mammoth Lakes. GPS: 37.660678, -118.811618

67 • D4 | Whitmore Tubs Road Dispersed

Dispersed sites, No water, No toilets, Tent & RV camping: Free, Hot springs, Elevation: 6986ft/2129m. Nearest town: Mammoth Lakes. GPS: 37.648029, -118.804884

68 • D4 | Whitmore Tubs Road Dispersed

Dispersed sites, No water, No toilets, Tent & RV camping: Free, Elevation: 7020ft/2140m. Nearest town: Mammoth Lakes. GPS: 37.648279, -118.812336

69 • E1 | Griswold Hills

Dispersed sites, No water, Vault/pit toilet, Tents only: Free, Elevation: 1282ft/391m, Telephone: 831-630-5000. Nearest town: Paicines. GPS: 36.562052, -120.834979

70 • E1 | Laguna Mountain

Dispersed sites, No water, Vault/pit toilet, Tent & RV camping: Free, Elevation: 2858ft/871m, Telephone: 831-582-2200. Nearest town: Hollister. GPS: 36.367411, -120.830327

71 • E1 | Upper Sweetwater

Total sites: 6, RV sites: 6, No water, Vault/pit toilet, No showers, No RV dump, Tent & RV camping: Free, Elevation: 2841ft/866m, Telephone: 831-630-5000. Nearest town: Hollister. GPS: 36.360436, -120.849341

72 • E2 | Condon Peak

Dispersed sites, No water, Vault/pit toilet, Tent & RV camping: $5, $5/week permit required, Reservations not accepted, Elevation: 2979ft/908m, Telephone: 831-582-2200. GPS: 36.293268, -120.682223

73 • E2 | Jade Mill

Total sites: 5, RV sites: 5, No water, Vault/pit toilet, Tent & RV camping: Free, $5/week, Reservations not accepted, Elevation: 2815ft/858m, Telephone: 831-582-2200. Nearest town: Coalinga. GPS: 36.368068, -120.754211

74 • E2 | Oak Flat

Total sites: 100, RV sites: 100, No water, Vault/pit toilet, Tent & RV camping: Free, $5/week, Open all year, Reservations not accepted, Elevation: 2593ft/790m, Telephone: 831-630-5000. Nearest town: Blythe. GPS: 36.361524, -120.760717

75 • E2 | San Joaquin River Gorge – Yeh-Gub-Weh-Tuh

Total sites: 6, RV sites: 4, Central water, Vault/pit toilet, No showers, No RV dump, Tent & RV camping: $10, Reservations not accepted, Stay limit: 14 days, Elevation: 968ft/295m, Telephone: 661-391-6000. Nearest town: Fresno. GPS: 37.083017, -119.554273

76 • E2 | Squaw Leap Horse Camp

Dispersed sites, Central water, Vault/pit toilet, No showers, No RV dump, Tent & RV camping: Fee unk, Reservations not accepted, Elevation: 843ft/257m, Telephone: 916-985-4474. Nearest town: Oakhurst. GPS: 37.068277, -119.558078

77 • E2 | Tumey Hills

Dispersed sites, Vault/pit toilet, Tent & RV camping: Free, Closed to vehicle access during fire season, Open Oct-Apr, Elevation: 554ft/169m, Telephone: 831-630-5000. Nearest town: Mendota. GPS: 36.624894, -120.659271

78 • E3 | Alabama Hills – Movie Road

Dispersed sites, No water, No toilets, Tent & RV camping: Free, Elevation: 4613ft/1406m, Telephone: 760-872-5000. Nearest town: Lone Pine. GPS: 36.604938, -118.122129

79 • E3 | Alabama Hills RA

Dispersed sites, Tent & RV camping: Free, Elevation: 4429ft/1350m, Telephone: 760-872-5000. Nearest town: Lone Pine. GPS: 36.606285, -118.094571

80 • E3 | Goodale Creek

Total sites: 43, RV sites: 43, Central water, Vault/pit toilet, No showers, No RV dump, Tent & RV camping: $5, $300 for season, Open all year, Reservations not accepted, Stay limit: 14 days, Elevation: 4068ft/1240m, Telephone: 760-872-5008. Nearest town: Independence. GPS: 36.985198, -118.273603

81 • E3 | Symmes Creek

Dispersed sites, No toilets, Tent & RV camping: Fee unk, Elevation: 5128ft/1563m. Nearest town: Independence. GPS: 36.754308, -118.253516

82 • E3 | Tuttle Creek

Total sites: 83, RV sites: 83, Central water, Vault/pit toilet, No showers, RV dump, Tent & RV camping: $8, No water in winter, Dump fee: $5, $300 for season, Open all year, Reservations not accepted, Stay limit: 14 days, Elevation: 5003ft/1525m, Telephone: 760-872-5000. Nearest town: Lone Pine. GPS: 36.565256, -118.124814

83 • F1 | Williams Hill Rec Area

Total sites: 7, RV sites: 7, No water, Vault/pit toilet, Tent & RV camping: Free, Open all year, Reservations not accepted, Stay limit: 14 days, Elevation: 2289ft/698m, Telephone: 831-630-5000. Nearest town: San Miguel. GPS: 35.978291, -121.009757

84 • F2 | Carrizo Plains NM – KCL CG

Total sites: 12, RV sites: 12, No water, Vault/pit toilet, Tent & RV camping: Free, Open all year, Elevation: 2280ft/695m. Nearest town: Taft. GPS: 35.090583, -119.734886

85 • F2 | Carrizo Plains NM – Selby CG

Total sites: 13, RV sites: 13, No water, Vault/pit toilet, Tent & RV camping: Free, Open all year, Stay limit: 14 days, Elevation: 2510ft/765m, Telephone: 661-391-6000. Nearest town: Santa Margarita. GPS: 35.127851, -119.841862

86 • F3 | Chimney Peak

Total sites: 36, RV sites: 36, No water, No toilets, Tent & RV camping: Free, Open all year, Reservations not accepted, Stay limit: 14 days, Elevation: 5626ft/1715m, Telephone: 661-391-6000. Nearest town: Pearsonville. GPS: 35.839094, -118.041035

87 • F3 | Dove Springs

Dispersed sites, No water, Vault/pit toilet, Tent & RV camping: Free, Stay limit: 14 days, Elevation: 3287ft/1002m, Telephone: 760-384-5400. Nearest town: Mohave. GPS: 35.423855, -118.011453

88 • F3 | Dove Springs OHV

Dispersed sites, No water, Vault/pit toilet, Tent & RV camping: Free, 2nd area few hundreds yard to NW, Reservations not accepted, Elevation: 3200ft/975m, Telephone: 760-384-5400. Nearest town: Mohave. GPS: 35.417969, -117.988592

89 • F3 | Dove Springs Strip

Dispersed sites, No water, No toilets, Tent & RV camping: Free, Reservations not accepted, Elevation: 3377ft/1029m, Telephone: 760-384-5400. Nearest town: Mohave. GPS: 35.433484, -117.996312

90 • F3 | Fossil Falls

Total sites: 11, RV sites: 4, Central water, Vault/pit toilet, No showers, No RV dump, Tent & RV camping: $6, Open all year, Elevation: 3317ft/1011m, Telephone: 760-384-5400. Nearest town: Little Lake. GPS: 35.971947, -117.910894

91 • F3 | Jawbone Canyon OHV Primitive Area 1

Dispersed sites, No water, Vault/pit toilet, Tent & RV camping: Free, Open all year, Stay limit: 14 days, Elevation: 2591ft/790m, Telephone: 760-384-5400. Nearest town: Mohave. GPS: 35.317444, -118.078091

92 • F3 | Jawbone Canyon OHV Primitive Area 2

Dispersed sites, No water, Vault/pit toilet, Tent & RV camping: Free, Open all year, Elevation: 2774ft/846m, Telephone: 760-384-5400. Nearest town: Mohave. GPS: 35.305318, -118.106217

93 • F3 | Jawbone Canyon OHV Staging Area 1

Dispersed sites, No water, Vault/pit toilet, Tent & RV camping: Free, Open all year, Elevation: 2482ft/757m, Telephone: 760-384-5400. Nearest town: Mohave. GPS: 35.315949, -118.055112

94 • F3 | Jawbone Canyon OHV Staging Area 2

Dispersed sites, No water, Vault/pit toilet, Tent & RV camping: Free, Open all year, Elevation: 2478ft/755m, Telephone: 760-384-5400. Nearest town: Mohave. GPS: 35.313539, -118.057995

95 • F3 | Jawbone Canyon OHV Staging Area 3

Dispersed sites, No water, Vault/pit toilet, Tent & RV camping: Free, Open all year, Elevation: 2597ft/792m, Telephone: 760-384-5400. Nearest town: Mohave. GPS: 35.320362, -118.077988

96 • F3 | Jawbone Canyon OHV Staging Area 4

Dispersed sites, No water, Vault/pit toilet, Tent & RV camping: Free, Open all year, Elevation: 2630ft/802m, Telephone: 760-384-5400. Nearest town: Mohave. GPS: 35.324217, -118.077715

97 • F3 | Jawbone Canyon OHV Staging Area 5

Dispersed sites, No water, Vault/pit toilet, Tent & RV camping: Free, Open all year, Elevation: 2648ft/807m, Telephone: 760-384-5400. Nearest town: Mohave. GPS: 35.317836, -118.092616

98 • F3 | Keysville Rec Site

Dispersed sites, No water, Vault/pit toilet, Tent & RV camping: Free, Stay limit: 14 days, Elevation: 2506ft/764m, Telephone: 661-391-6112. Nearest town: Lake Isabella. GPS: 35.634392, -118.491874

99 • F3 | Long Valley

Total sites: 13, RV sites: 13, No water, Vault/pit toilet, Tent & RV camping: Donation, Open all year, Reservations not accepted, Stay limit: 14 days, Elevation: 5397ft/1645m, Telephone: 661-391-6000. Nearest town: Bakersfield. GPS: 35.844727, -118.151611

100 • F3 | Spangler Hills OHVA – Searles Station

Dispersed sites, No toilets, Tents: Fee unk/RVs: Free, Elevation: 3202ft/976m, Telephone: 760-384-5400. Nearest town: Red Mountain. GPS: 35.484871, -117.626757

101 • F3 | Spangler Hills OHVA – Teagle Wash

Dispersed sites, No water, No toilets, Tent & RV camping: Free, Elevation: 2628ft/801m, Telephone: 760-384-5400. Nearest town: Ridgecrest. GPS: 35.514407, -117.555961

102 • F3 | Spangler Hills OHVA – Wagon Wheel

Dispersed sites, No water, Vault/pit toilet, Tent & RV camping: Free, Elevation: 3235ft/986m, Telephone: 760-384-5400. Nearest town: Ridgecrest. GPS: 35.572665, -117.548393

103 • F3 | Trona Pinnacles NNL

Dispersed sites, No water, Vault/pit toilet, Tent & RV camping: Free, Road may be closed after heavy rains, Elevation: 1772ft/540m, Telephone: 760-384-5400. Nearest town: Trona. GPS: 35.619093, -117.370247

104 • F3 | Walker Pass

Total sites: 13, RV sites: 2, No water, Vault/pit toilet, Tent & RV camping: Donation, Open all year, Stay limit: 14 days, Elevation: 5039ft/1536m, Telephone: 661-391-6000. Nearest town: Walker Pass. GPS: 35.664025, -118.037851

105 • F4 | Black Mountain Wilderness – Black Canyon

Dispersed sites, No water, No toilets, Tent & RV camping: Free, Elevation: 2609ft/795m, Telephone: 760-252-6000. Nearest town: Barstow. GPS: 35.141115, -117.261162

106 • F4 | Black Mountain Wilderness – Opal

Dispersed sites, No water, No toilets, Tent & RV camping: Free, Elevation: 3339ft/1018m, Telephone: 760-252-6000. Nearest town: Barstow. GPS: 35.156385, -117.182037

107 • F4 | Calico Early Man

Dispersed sites, No water, No toilets, Tent & RV camping: Free, CG closed UFN - vandalism, Elevation: 2110ft/643m. Nearest town: Yermo. GPS: 34.943033, -116.76115

108 • F4 | Dumont Dunes OHV

Dispersed sites, No water, Vault/pit toilet, Tent & RV camping: $30, Fee is for 7 days, $90 for season, Open all year, Reservations not accepted, Stay limit: 14 days, Elevation: 755ft/230m, Telephone: 760-252-6000. Nearest town: Barstow. GPS: 35.686185, -116.230737

109 • F4 | Hollow Hills Dispersed

Dispersed sites, No water, No toilets, Tent & RV camping: Free, Elevation: 1825ft/556m, Telephone: 760-252-6000. Nearest town: Baker. GPS: 35.410324, -116.061485

110 • F4 | Kingston Mountains – Horsethief Camp

Total sites: 4, RV sites: 4, No water, Vault/pit toilet, Tent & RV camping: Free, Elevation: 4057ft/1237m, Telephone: 760-326-7000. Nearest town: Pahrump (NV). GPS: 35.776693, -115.863248

111 • F4 | Mojave Trails NM – Afton Canyon

Total sites: 22, RV sites: 22, Central water, Vault/pit toilet, No showers, No RV dump, Tent & RV camping: $6, Near RR, Open all year, Elevation: 1411ft/430m, Telephone: 760-252-6000. Nearest town: Barstow. GPS: 35.038494, -116.383651

112 • F4 | Owl Canyon

Total sites: 22, RV sites: 22, Central water, Vault/pit toilet, Tent & RV camping: $6, 2 horse corrals, Open all year, Reservations not accepted, Elevation: 3091ft/942m, Telephone: 909-697-5200. Nearest town: Barstow. GPS: 35.022228, -117.021525

113 • F4 | Rasor OHV Alternate Staging

Dispersed sites, No water, No toilets, Tent & RV camping: Free, Elevation: 1202ft/366m, Telephone: 760-252-6000. Nearest town: Baker. GPS: 35.051883, -116.286698

114 • F4 | Rasor OHV Main Staging

Dispersed sites, No water, No toilets, Tent & RV camping: Free, Elevation: 1114ft/340m, Telephone: 760-252-6000. Nearest town: Baker. GPS: 35.088598, -116.265194

115 • F4 | Shoshone Dispersed

Dispersed sites, No toilets, Tent & RV camping: Free, Elevation: 1703ft/519m. Nearest town: Shoshone. GPS: 35.911975, -116.312979

116 • F4 | Silurian Lake

Dispersed sites, No water, No toilets, Tent & RV camping: Free, Elevation: 682ft/208m. Nearest town: Renoville. GPS: 35.51711, -116.16833

117 • F4 | Surprise Canyon Dispersed

Dispersed sites, No water, No toilets, Tents only: Free, Elevation: 2308ft/703m, Telephone: 760-384-5400. Nearest town: Trona. GPS: 36.109785, -117.184186

118 • F5 | Camp Ibis

Dispersed sites, No water, No toilets, Tent & RV camping: Free, Reservations not accepted, Stay limit: 14 days, Elevation: 1775ft/541m. Nearest town: Needles. GPS: 34.972174, -114.831658

119 • F5 | Clark Mountain Camp

Dispersed sites, No water, No toilets, Tents only: Free, 4x4 high clearance vehicle required, Reservations not accepted, Elevation: 6160ft/1878m, Telephone: 760-326-7000. Nearest town: Primm (NV). GPS: 35.515731, -115.578256

120 • F5 | Ivanpah Dispersed

Dispersed sites, No water, No toilets, No tents/RVs: Fee unk, Elevation: 2608ft/795m. GPS: 35.572667, -115.392433

121 • G3 | El Mirage Dry Lakebed OHV – Staging Area 1

Dispersed sites, No water, Vault/pit toilet, Tent & RV camping: $15, $30/week, $90/season, Open all year, Elevation: 2851ft/869m, Telephone: 760-252-6000. Nearest town: Victorville. GPS: 34.625192, -117.547537

122 • G3 | El Mirage Dry Lakebed OHV – Staging Area 2

Dispersed sites, No water, Vault/pit toilet, Tent & RV camping: $15, $90 for season, Open all year, Elevation: 2943ft/897m, Telephone: 760-252-6000. Nearest town: Victorville. GPS: 34.637343, -117.543884

123 • G3 | El Mirage Dry Lakebed OHV – Staging Area 3

Dispersed sites, No water, Vault/pit toilet, Tent & RV camping: $15, $90 for season, Open all year, Elevation: 2984ft/910m, Telephone: 760-252-6000. Nearest town: Victorville. GPS: 34.642467, -117.543757

124 • G3 | El Mirage Dry Lakebed OHV – Staging Areas 4/5

Dispersed sites, No water, Vault/pit toilet, Tent & RV camping: $15, $90 for season, Open all year, Elevation: 3022ft/921m, Telephone: 760-252-6000. Nearest town: Victorville. GPS: 34.647629, -117.543311

125 • G4 | Amboy Crater

Dispersed sites, No water, Vault/pit toilet, Tent & RV camping: Free, Near RR, Camp only in already disturbed areas, Open all year, Stay limit: 14 days, Elevation: 655ft/200m, Telephone: 760-326-7000. Nearest town: Amboy. GPS: 34.557643, -115.776861

126 • G4 | Bighorn Mountain Wilderness – Barnes Rd

Dispersed sites, No water, No toilets, Tent & RV camping: Free, Reservations not accepted, Elevation: 2684ft/818m, Telephone: 760-252-6000. Nearest town: Landers. GPS: 34.39371, -116.5262

127 • G4 | Boone Road Dispersed

Dispersed sites, No water, No toilets, Tent & RV camping: Free, Reservations not accepted, Elevation: 2579ft/786m. Nearest town: Landers. GPS: 34.410761, -116.516435

128 • G4 | Box Canyon

Dispersed sites, No water, No toilets, Tent & RV camping: Free, Rough access road, Beware of flash floods, Open all year, Reservations not accepted, Elevation: 285ft/87m, Telephone: 760-833-7100. Nearest town: Mecca. GPS: 33.587329, -115.977324

129 • G4 | Johnson Valley OHV

Dispersed sites, No water, No toilets, Tent & RV camping: Free, Stay limit: 14 days, Elevation: 3278ft/999m, Telephone: 760-252-6000. Nearest town: Barstow. GPS: 34.561415, -116.769615

130 • G4 | Joshua Tree Overflow

Dispersed sites, No water, No toilets, Tent & RV camping: Free, 4x4 recommended, Must be 300' from roadways, Elevation: 2362ft/720m. Nearest town: 29 Palms. GPS: 34.172966, -116.219087

131 • G4 | Joshua Tree South

Dispersed sites, No water, No toilets, No tents/RVs: Free, Open all year, Elevation: 1775ft/541m. GPS: 33.673505, -115.801266

132 • G4 | Juniper Flats Dispersed 01

Dispersed sites, No water, No toilets, Tent & RV camping: Free, 2nd spot 200' NNE, Reservations not accepted, Stay limit: 14 days, Elevation: 4292ft/1308m, Telephone: 760-252-6000. Nearest town: Hesperia. GPS: 34.382566, -117.164458

133 • G4 | Juniper Flats Dispersed 02

Dispersed sites, No water, No toilets, Tent & RV camping: Free, Reservations not accepted, Stay limit: 14 days, Elevation: 4470ft/1362m, Telephone: 760-252-6000. Nearest town: Hesperia. GPS: 34.373916, -117.173436

134 • G4 | Juniper Flats Dispersed 03

Dispersed sites, No water, No toilets, Tent & RV camping: Free, Reservations not accepted, Stay limit: 14 days, Elevation: 4543ft/1385m, Telephone: 760-252-6000. Nearest town: Hesperia. GPS: 34.370884, -117.176178

135 • G4 | Juniper Flats Dispersed 04

Dispersed sites, No water, No toilets, Tent & RV camping: Free, Reservations not accepted, Stay limit: 14 days, Elevation: 4889ft/1490m, Telephone: 760-252-6000. Nearest town: Hesperia. GPS: 34.401235, -117.184067

136 • G4 | Juniper Flats Dispersed 05

Dispersed sites, No water, No toilets, Tent & RV camping: Free, Reservations not accepted, Stay limit: 14 days, Elevation: 4650ft/1417m, Telephone: 760-252-6000. Nearest town: Hesperia. GPS: 34.368309, -117.198109

137 • G4 | Juniper Flats Dispersed 06

Dispersed sites, No water, No toilets, Tent & RV camping: Free, Reservations not accepted, Stay limit: 14 days, Elevation: 4445ft/1355m, Telephone: 760-252-6000. Nearest town: Hesperia. GPS: 34.407637, -117.165249

138 • G4 | Juniper Flats Dispersed 07

Dispersed sites, No water, No toilets, Tent & RV camping: Free, Reservations not accepted, Stay limit: 14 days, Elevation: 4907ft/1496m, Telephone: 760-252-6000. Nearest town: Hesperia. GPS: 34.373376, -117.108725

139 • G4 | Juniper Flats Dispersed 08

Dispersed sites, No water, No toilets, Tent & RV camping: Free, Reservations not accepted, Stay limit: 14 days, Elevation: 4521ft/1378m, Telephone: 760-252-6000. Nearest town: Hesperia. GPS: 34.378441, -117.113033

140 • G4 | Juniper Flats Dispersed 09

Dispersed sites, No water, No toilets, Tent & RV camping: Free, Reservations not accepted, Stay limit: 14 days, Elevation: 4378ft/1334m, Telephone: 760-252-6000. Nearest town: Hesperia. GPS: 34.384453, -117.115449

141 • G4 | Juniper Flats Dispersed 10

Dispersed sites, No water, No toilets, Tent & RV camping: Free, Reservations not accepted, Stay limit: 14 days, Elevation: 4422ft/1348m, Telephone: 760-252-6000. Nearest town: Hesperia. GPS: 34.386671, -117.120597

142 • G4 | Juniper Flats Dispersed 11

Dispersed sites, No water, No toilets, Tent & RV camping: Free, Reservations not accepted, Stay limit: 14 days, Elevation: 3964ft/1208m, Telephone: 760-252-6000. Nearest town: Hesperia. GPS: 34.394545, -117.123767

143 • G4 | Juniper Flats Dispersed 12

Dispersed sites, No water, No toilets, Tent & RV camping: Free, Reservations not accepted, Stay limit: 14 days, Elevation: 4518ft/1377m, Telephone: 760-252-6000. Nearest town: Hesperia. GPS: 34.374998, -117.116837

144 • G4 | Juniper Flats Dispersed 13

Dispersed sites, No water, No toilets, Tent & RV camping: Free, Reservations not accepted, Stay limit: 14 days, Elevation: 4282ft/1305m, Telephone: 760-252-6000. Nearest town: Hesperia. GPS: 34.375384, -117.144729

145 • G4 | Juniper Flats Dispersed 14

Dispersed sites, No water, No toilets, Tent & RV camping: Free, Reservations not accepted, Stay limit: 14 days, Elevation: 4487ft/1368m, Telephone: 760-252-6000. Nearest town: Hesperia. GPS: 34.359215, -117.188516

146 • G4 | Juniper Flats Dispersed 15

Dispersed sites, No water, No toilets, Tents only: Free, Reservations not accepted, Stay limit: 14 days, Elevation: 5756ft/1754m, Telephone: 760-252-6000. Nearest town: Hesperia. GPS: 34.375625, -117.060252

147 • G4 | Juniper Flats Dispersed 16

Dispersed sites, No water, No toilets, Tent & RV camping: Free, Reservations not accepted, Stay limit: 14 days, Elevation: 5668ft/1728m, Telephone: 760-252-6000. Nearest town: Hesperia. GPS: 34.383018, -117.055119

148 • G4 | Ludlow

Dispersed sites, No water, No toilets, Tent & RV camping: Free, High-clearance vehicle recommended, Open all year, Elevation: 1660ft/506m. Nearest town: Barstow. GPS: 34.732007, -116.163108

149 • G4 | Ord Mountain ORV Route

Dispersed sites, No water, No toilets, Tent & RV camping: Free, Reservations not accepted, Elevation: 4126ft/1258m, Telephone: 760-252-6000. Nearest town: Barstow. GPS: 34.653292, -116.854542

150 • G4 | Painted Canyon Dispersed

Dispersed sites, No water, No toilets, Tent & RV camping: Free, Elevation: 627ft/191m, Telephone: 760-833-7100. Nearest town: Mecca. GPS: 33.619198, -115.999448

151 • G4 | Rodman Mountains Wilderness Dispersed

Dispersed sites, No water, No toilets, Tent & RV camping: Free, Elevation: 4484ft/1367m, Telephone: 760-252-6000. Nearest town: Daggett. GPS: 34.675803, -116.608612

152 • G4 | Sawtooth Canyon

Total sites: 13, RV sites: 13, No water, Vault/pit toilet, Tent & RV camping: Free, Open all year, Elevation: 3607ft/1099m, Telephone: 760-252-6000. Nearest town: Barstow. GPS: 34.670249, -116.983713

153 • G4 | Sawtooth Canyon Dispersed

Dispersed sites, No water, No toilets, Tent & RV camping: Free, Reservations not accepted, Elevation: 3635ft/1108m, Telephone: 760-252-6000. Nearest town: Barstow. GPS: 34.671541, -116.990266

154 • G4 | Stoddard Valley OHV

Dispersed sites, No water, No toilets, Tent & RV camping: Free, Stay limit: 14 days, Elevation: 2615ft/797m, Telephone: 760-252-6000. Nearest town: Barstow. GPS: 34.812727, -117.083377

155 • G5 | Blue Cloud Dispersed

Dispersed sites, No water, No toilets, Tent & RV camping: Free, Reservations not accepted, Stay limit: 14 days, Elevation: 643ft/196m, Telephone: 760-326-7000. Nearest town: Earp. GPS: 34.166516, -114.371843

156 • G5 | Blythe-Vidal

Dispersed sites, No water, No toilets, Tent & RV camping: Free, Reservations not accepted, Elevation: 409ft/125m, Telephone: 760-326-7000. Nearest town: Blythe. GPS: 33.929058, -114.541758

157 • G5 | Corn Springs

Total sites: 9, RV sites: 9, Central water, Vault/pit toilet, No showers, No RV dump, Tent & RV camping: $6, Generator hours: 0800-2100, Open all year, Reservations not accepted, Stay limit: 14 days, Elevation: 1608ft/490m, Telephone: 760-833-7100. Nearest town: Corn Springs. GPS: 33.625732, -115.326172

158 • G5 | Crossroads

Total sites: 26, RV sites: 26, No water, Vault/pit toilet, Tent & RV camping: $5, Reservations accepted, Stay limit: 14 days, Elevation: 374ft/114m, Telephone: 928-505-1200. Nearest town: Lake Havasu City, AZ. GPS: 34.210882, -114.215301

159 • G5 | Earp 2 Dispersed

Dispersed sites, No water, No toilets, Tent & RV camping: Free, Elevation: 751ft/229m. Nearest town: Earp. GPS: 34.177372, -114.391191

160 • G5 | Earp 3 Dispersed

Dispersed sites, No water, No toilets, Tent & RV camping: Free, Elevation: 820ft/250m. Nearest town: Earp. GPS: 34.187875, -114.40348

161 • G5 | Hwy 62 Dispersed

Dispersed sites, No water, No toilets, No tents/RVs: Free, Reservations not accepted, Stay limit: 14 days, Elevation: 952ft/290m. Nearest town: Parker (AZ). GPS: 34.203375, -114.418983

162 • G5 | Midland LTVA

Dispersed sites, No water, No toilets, No tents/RVs: $40, $40 for 2 weeks, $180 for season, Open Sep-Apr, Elevation: 525ft/160m, Telephone: 760-833-7100. Nearest town: Blythe. GPS: 33.727222, -114.658889

163 • G5 | Mojave Preserve – Kelbaker Rd

Dispersed sites, No water, No toilets, Tents only: Free, High-clearance vehicles recommended, Open all year, Reservations not accepted, Elevation: 3544ft/1080m. Nearest town: Needles. GPS: 34.745683, -115.651977

164 • G5 | Snaggletooth Dispersed

Dispersed sites, No water, No toilets, No tents/RVs: Free, Reservations not accepted, Stay limit: 14 days, Elevation: 1946ft/593m, Telephone: 760-326-7000. Nearest town: Needles. GPS: 34.592812, -114.635976

165 • G5 | Summit Dispersed

Dispersed sites, No water, No toilets, Tent & RV camping: Free, Beside RR, Elevation: 1663ft/507m. Nearest town: Desert Center. GPS: 33.603716, -115.532372

166 • G5 | Turtle Mountain Road Dispersed

Dispersed sites, No water, No toilets, Tent & RV camping: Free, Various spots along road, Elevation: 1567ft/478m, Telephone: 760-326-7000. Nearest town: Needles. GPS: 34.469165, -114.814191

167 • G5 | Turtle Mountains Wilderness – Brown's Camp

Dispersed sites, No water, Vault/pit toilet, Tent & RV camping: Free, 4x4 recommended, Elevation: 1831ft/558m, Telephone: 760-326-7000. Nearest town: Needles. GPS: 34.435744, -114.824221

168 • G5 | Turtle Mountains Wilderness – Lisa Dawn Camp

Dispersed sites, No water, Vault/pit toilet, Tent & RV camping: Free, 4x4 recommended, Elevation: 1922ft/586m, Telephone: 760-326-7000. Nearest town: Needles. GPS: 34.427155, -114.824464

169 • G5 | Vidal Junction Dispersed

Dispersed sites, No water, No tents/RVs: Fee unk, Elevation: 922ft/281m. Nearest town: Vidal Junction. GPS: 34.187556, -114.570708

170 • H4 | Anza Borego Desert

Dispersed sites, No water, No toilets, Tent & RV camping: Free, Elevation: 408ft/124m. Nearest town: Salton City. GPS: 33.278953, -116.058357

171 • H4 | Anza Dispersed

Dispersed sites, No water, No toilets, Tent & RV camping: Free, Open all year, Reservations not accepted, Elevation: 423ft/129m. Nearest town: Ocotillo. GPS: 32.717064, -115.911876

172 • H4 | Cottonwood

Total sites: 30, RV sites: 30, No water, Vault/pit toilet, No showers, No RV dump, Tent & RV camping: $6, Reservations not accepted, Stay limit: 14 days, Elevation: 4346ft/1325m, Telephone: 760-337-4400. GPS: 32.800356, -116.338276

173 • H4 | Coyote Dispersed

Dispersed sites, No water, No toilets, Tent & RV camping: Free, Open all year, Reservations not accepted, Elevation: 498ft/152m. Nearest town: Ocotillo. GPS: 32.657673, -115.925652

174 • H4 | Dunaway Dispersed

Dispersed sites, No water, No toilets, Tent & RV camping: Free, Open all year, Reservations not accepted, Elevation: 6ft/2m. Nearest town: Seeley. GPS: 32.766288, -115.791317

175 • H4 | Jacumba Mountains Wilderness

Dispersed sites, No water, No toilets, Tent & RV camping: Free, Elevation: 1158ft/353m, Telephone: 760-337-4400. Nearest town: El Centro. GPS: 32.679676, -116.017718

176 • H4 | Lower Lark Canyon

Total sites: 8, RV sites: 8, No water, Vault/pit toilet, Tent & RV camping: $6, Open all year, Elevation: 3838ft/1170m, Telephone: 760-337-4400. Nearest town: Boulevard. GPS: 32.727888, -116.273628

177 • H4 | Ocotillo Dispersed

Dispersed sites, No toilets, Tent & RV camping: Fee unk, Elevation: 128ft/39m. Nearest town: Ocotillo Wells. GPS: 33.071292, -116.107812

178 • H4 | Overlook Dispersed

Dispersed sites, No water, No toilets, Tent & RV camping: Free, Open all year, Reservations not accepted, Elevation: 260ft/79m. Nearest town: Seeley. GPS: 32.748681, -115.851763

179 • H4 | Plaster City East OHV

Dispersed sites, No toilets, Tent & RV camping: Free, Elevation: 62ft/19m, Telephone: 760-337-4400. Nearest town: Plaster City. GPS: 32.815475, -115.851213

180 • H4 | Plaster City West OHV

Dispersed sites, No toilets, Tent & RV camping: Free, Elevation: 272ft/83m, Telephone: 760-337-4400. Nearest town: Plaster City. GPS: 32.764608, -115.932853

181 • H4 | Shellbeds Dispersed

Dispersed sites, No water, No toilets, Tent & RV camping: Free, Open all year, Reservations not accepted, Elevation: 155ft/47m. Nearest town: Seeley. GPS: 32.745254, -115.828929

182 • H4 | Sunrise Butte Dispersed

Dispersed sites, No water, No toilets, Tent & RV camping: Free, Open all year, Reservations not accepted, Elevation: 372ft/113m. Nearest town: Ocotillo. GPS: 32.658442, -115.843709

183 • H4 | Superstition Mountain OHV

Dispersed sites, No water, No toilets, Tent & RV camping: Free, Elevation: 42ft/13m, Telephone: 760-337-4400. Nearest town: El Centro. GPS: 32.888895, -115.765581

184 • H4 | Upper Lark Canyon

Total sites: 15, RV sites: 7, No water, Vault/pit toilet, Tent & RV camping: $6, Non-potable water, Open all year, Elevation: 3877ft/1182m, Telephone: 760-337-4400. Nearest town: Boulevard. GPS: 32.730394, -116.274909

185 • H4 | Valley of the Moon – Elliot Mine Area

Dispersed sites, No water, No toilets, Tent & RV camping: Free, Elevation: 3852ft/1174m. Nearest town: Jacumba Hot Springs. GPS: 32.625232, -116.081864

186 • H5 | American Girl Mine

Dispersed sites, No water, No toilets, Tent & RV camping: Free, Some land owned by mining company - camping with permission, Open all year, Elevation: 475ft/145m. Nearest town: Yuma. GPS: 32.833258, -114.805396

187 • H5 | Bradshaw Trail Dispersed 1

Dispersed sites, No water, No toilets, Tent & RV camping: Free, Reservations not accepted, Elevation: 2137ft/651m. Nearest town: Desert Center. GPS: 33.525997, -115.452506

188 • H5 | Bradshaw Trail Dispersed 2

Dispersed sites, No water, No toilets, Tent & RV camping: Free, Reservations not accepted, Elevation: 2255ft/687m. Nearest town: Desert Center. GPS: 33.515023, -115.418213

189 • H5 | Bradshaw Trail Dispersed 3

Dispersed sites, No water, No toilets, Tent & RV camping: Free, Beside RR, Reservations not accepted, Elevation: 2380ft/725m. Nearest town: Desert Center. GPS: 33.502239, -115.386376

190 • H5 | Bradshaw Trail Dispersed 4

Dispersed sites, No water, No toilets, Tent & RV camping: Free, Reservations not accepted, Elevation: 2481ft/756m. Nearest town: Desert Center. GPS: 33.494082, -115.339331

191 • H5 | Bradshaw Trail Dispersed 5

Dispersed sites, No water, No toilets, Tent & RV camping: Free, Reservations not accepted, Elevation: 2326ft/709m. Nearest town: Desert Center. GPS: 33.471765, -115.291547

192 • H5 | Bradshaw Trail Dispersed 6

Dispersed sites, No water, No toilets, Tent & RV camping: Free, Reservations not accepted, Elevation: 1971ft/601m. Nearest town: Desert Center. GPS: 33.437309, -115.224258

193 • H5 | Dupont Road Dispersed

Dispersed sites, No water, No toilets, Tents only: Free, 4x4 required, Elevation: 1415ft/431m. Nearest town: Desert Center. GPS: 33.556237, -115.232827

194 • H5 | Fergusen Lake

Dispersed sites, No water, No toilets, Tent & RV camping: Free, Elevation: 177ft/54m, Telephone: 928-317-3200. Nearest town: Yuma, AZ. GPS: 32.969803, -114.497536

195 • H5 | Glamis Dispersed

Dispersed sites, No water, No toilets, No tents/RVs: Free, Elevation: 450ft/137m. Nearest town: Glamis. GPS: 33.014407, -115.039232

196 • H5 | Holtville Hot Springs LTVA

Dispersed sites, No water, No toilets, Tent & RV camping: $40, 15 Sep-15-Apr: $180 entire season/ $80 4-week stay/ $40 2-week stay, 16 Apr-14 Sep: free for 14 days, Stay limit: 210 days, Elevation: 38ft/12m, Telephone: 760-337-4400. Nearest town: Holtville. GPS: 32.768612, -115.269856

197 • H5 | Imperial Dam LTVA

Dispersed sites, No water, No toilets, RV dump, No tents/RVs: $40, $40 - 14 days/$180 - 7 months, Daily fee 15 Sep-15 Apr, Elevation: 161ft/49m, Telephone: 928-317-3200. Nearest town: Yuma, AZ. GPS: 32.870723, -114.466584

198 • H5 | Imperial Dam LTVA – Beehive Mesa

Dispersed sites, No water, No toilets, No tents/RVs: $15, $40 - 14 days/$180 - 7 months, Daily fee 15 Sep-15 Apr, Elevation: 171ft/52m, Telephone: 928-317-3200. Nearest town: Yuma. GPS: 32.867839, -114.49019

199 • H5 | Imperial Dam LTVA – Coyote Ridge

Dispersed sites, No water, No toilets, No tents/RVs: $15, $40 - 14 days/$180 - 7 months, Daily fee 15 Sep-15 Apr, Elevation: 249ft/76m, Telephone: 928-317-3200. Nearest town: Yuma. GPS: 32.857837, -114.507486

200 • H5 | Imperial Dam LTVA – Hurricane Ridge

Dispersed sites, No water, No toilets, No tents/RVs: $15, $40 - 14 days/$180 - 7 months, Daily fee 15 Sep-15 Apr, Elevation: 285ft/87m, Telephone: 928-317-3200. Nearest town: Yuma. GPS: 32.901723, -114.491947

201 • H5 | Imperial Dam LTVA – Kripple Creek

Dispersed sites, No water, RV dump, No tents/RVs: $15, $40 - 14 days/$180 - 7 months, Daily fee 15 Sep-15 Apr, Elevation: 210ft/64m, Telephone: 928-317-3200. Nearest town: Yuma. GPS: 32.889488, -114.486457

202 • H5 | Imperial Dam LTVA – Northwest Territory

Dispersed sites, No toilets, Tent & RV camping: $40, $40 - 14 days/$180 - 7 months, Daily fee 15 Sep-15 Apr, Open all year, Elevation: 315ft/96m, Telephone: 928-317-3200. Nearest town: Yuma, AZ. GPS: 32.902136, -114.503358

203 • H5 | Imperial Dam LTVA – Quail Hill

Dispersed sites, No water, No toilets, No tents/RVs: $15, $40 - 14 days/$180 - 7 months, Daily fee 15 Sep-15 Apr, Elevation: 180ft/55m, Telephone: 928-317-3200. Nearest town: Yuma. GPS: 32.873405, -114.482121

204 • H5 | Imperial Dam LTVA – Skunk Hollow

Dispersed sites, No water, No toilets, No tents/RVs: $15, $40 - 14 days/$180 - 7 months, Daily fee 15 Sep-15 Apr, Elevation: 279ft/85m, Telephone: 928-317-3200. Nearest town: Yuma. GPS: 32.89777, -114.493824

205 • H5 | Imperial Dam LTVA – South Mesa

Dispersed sites, Central water, Flush toilet, Free showers, RV dump, No tents/RVs: $15, Outside showers, Elevation: 282ft/86m, Telephone: 928-317-3200. Nearest town: Yuma. GPS: 32.901015, -114.495866

206 • H5 | Imperial Sand Dunes RA – Buttercup

Dispersed sites, No water, Vault/pit toilet, No tents/RVs: $35, Permit required 1 Oct-15 Apr - $35-$50/week or $150/season, Elevation: 161ft/49m, Telephone: 760-334-3919. Nearest town: Yuma (AZ). GPS: 32.739056, -114.880945

207 • H5 | Imperial Sand Dunes RA – Cement Flats

Dispersed sites, No water, Vault/pit toilet, No tents/RVs: $35, Permit required 1 Oct-15 Apr - $35-$50/week or $150/season, Elevation: 167ft/51m, Telephone: 760-334-3919. Nearest town: Holtville. GPS: 32.974092, -115.176727

208 • H5 | Imperial Sand Dunes RA – Dunebuggy Flats

Dispersed sites, No water, Vault/pit toilet, No tents/RVs: $35, Permit required 1 Oct-15 Apr - $35-$50/week or $150/season, Elevation: 151ft/46m, Telephone: 760-334-3919. Nearest town: Yuma (AZ). GPS: 32.713893, -114.941632

209 • H5 | Imperial Sand Dunes RA – Dunes Vista

Dispersed sites, No water, No toilets, No tents/RVs: $35, Permit required 1 Oct-15 Apr - $35-$50/week or $150/season, Elevation: 226ft/69m, Telephone: 760-334-3919. Nearest town: Yuma (AZ). GPS: 32.764557, -114.836917

210 • H5 | Imperial Sand Dunes RA – Gecko

Dispersed sites, No water, No toilets, No tents/RVs: $35, Permit required 1 Oct-15 Apr - $35-$50/week or $150/season, Elevation: 256ft/78m, Telephone: 760-334-3919. Nearest town: Brawley. GPS: 32.939572, -115.142766

211 • H5 | Imperial Sand Dunes RA – Gecko Loop

Dispersed sites, No water, Vault/pit toilet, No tents/RVs: $35, Permit required 1 Oct-15 Apr - $35-$50/week or $150/season, Elevation: 259ft/79m, Telephone: 760-334-3919. Nearest town: Holtville. GPS: 32.941762, -115.140132

212 • H5 | Imperial Sand Dunes RA – Glamis Flats

Dispersed sites, No water, Vault/pit toilet, No tents/RVs: $35, Permit required 1 Oct-15 Apr - $35-$50/week or $150/season, Elevation: 305ft/93m, Telephone: 760-334-3919. Nearest town: Holtville. GPS: 32.992425, -115.079767

213 • H5 | Imperial Sand Dunes RA – Grays Well

Dispersed sites, No water, No toilets, No tents/RVs: $35, Permit required 1 Oct-15 Apr - $35-$50/week or $150/season, Elevation: 151ft/46m, Telephone: 760-334-3919. Nearest town: Yuma (AZ). GPS: 32.710278, -114.924167

214 • H5 | Imperial Sand Dunes RA – Keyhole

Dispersed sites, No water, No toilets, No tents/RVs: $35, Permit required 1 Oct-15 Apr - $35-$50/week or $150/season, Reservations not accepted, Stay limit: 14 days, Elevation: 243ft/74m, Telephone: 760-334-3919. Nearest town: Holtville. GPS: 32.915276, -115.117301

215 • H5 | Imperial Sand Dunes RA – Midway

Dispersed sites, No water, No toilets, No tents/RVs: $35, Permit required 1 Oct-15 Apr - $35-$50/week or $150/season, Stay limit: 14 days, Elevation: 216ft/66m, Telephone: 760-334-3919. Nearest town: Yuma (AZ). GPS: 32.715833, -114.914722

216 • H5 | Imperial Sand Dunes RA – Ogilby

Dispersed sites, No water, No toilets, No tents/RVs: $35, Permit required 1 Oct-15 Apr - $35-$50/week or $150/season, Elevation: 285ft/87m, Telephone: 760-334-3919. Nearest town: Yuma (AZ). GPS: 32.811098, -114.888426

217 • H5 | Imperial Sand Dunes RA – Osborne Overlook

Dispersed sites, No water, No toilets, No tents/RVs: $35, Permit required 1 Oct-15 Apr - $35-$50/week or $150/ season, Elevation: 459ft/140m, Telephone: 760-334-3919. Nearest town: Holtville. GPS: 32.983056, -115.133056

218 • H5 | Imperial Sand Dunes RA – Pad 1

Dispersed sites, No water, No toilets, No tents/RVs: $35, Permit required 1 Oct-15 Apr - $35-$50/week or $150/ season, Elevation: 226ft/69m, Telephone: 760-334-3919. Nearest town: Holtville. GPS: 32.968029, -115.170833

219 • H5 | Imperial Sand Dunes RA – Pad 1.5

Dispersed sites, No water, No toilets, No tents/RVs: $35, Permit required 1 Oct-15 Apr - $35-$50/week or $150/ season, Elevation: 194ft/59m, Telephone: 760-334-3919. Nearest town: Holtville. GPS: 32.960445, -115.168343

220 • H5 | Imperial Sand Dunes RA – Pad 2

Dispersed sites, No water, No toilets, No tents/RVs: $35, Permit required 1 Oct-15 Apr - $35-$50/week or $150/ season, Elevation: 216ft/66m, Telephone: 760-334-3919. Nearest town: Holtville. GPS: 32.956111, -115.162222

221 • H5 | Imperial Sand Dunes RA – Pad 2.5

Dispersed sites, No water, No toilets, No tents/RVs: $35, Permit required 1 Oct-15 Apr - $35-$50/week or $150/ season, Elevation: 272ft/83m, Telephone: 760-334-3919. Nearest town: Holtville. GPS: 32.944664, -115.146639

222 • H5 | Imperial Sand Dunes RA – Pad 3

Dispersed sites, No water, No toilets, No tents/RVs: $35, Permit required 1 Oct-15 Apr - $35-$50/week or $150/ season, Elevation: 266ft/81m, Telephone: 760-334-3919. Nearest town: Holtville. GPS: 32.934167, -115.136944

223 • H5 | Imperial Sand Dunes RA – Pad 4

Dispersed sites, No water, No toilets, No tents/RVs: $35, Permit required 1 Oct-15 Apr - $35-$50/week or $150/ season, Elevation: 276ft/84m, Telephone: 760-334-3919. Nearest town: Holtville. GPS: 32.921667, -115.122778

224 • H5 | Imperial Sand Dunes RA – Pad 5

Dispersed sites, No water, No toilets, No tents/RVs: $35, Permit required 1 Oct-15 Apr - $35-$50/week or $150/ season, Elevation: 249ft/76m, Telephone: 760-334-3919. Nearest town: Holtville. GPS: 32.932688, -115.135607

225 • H5 | Imperial Sand Dunes RA – Palo Verde Flats

Dispersed sites, No water, No toilets, No tents/RVs: $35, Permit required 1 Oct-15 Apr - $35-$50/week or $150/ season, Elevation: 299ft/91m, Telephone: 760-334-3919. Nearest town: Holtville. GPS: 32.994017, -115.090519

226 • H5 | Imperial Sand Dunes RA – Roadrunner

Dispersed sites, No water, No toilets, No tents/RVs: $35, Permit required 1 Oct-15 Apr - $35-$50/week or $150/ season, Stay limit: 14 days, Elevation: 272ft/83m, Telephone: 760-334-3919. Nearest town: Holtville. GPS: 32.911667, -115.117778

227 • H5 | Imperial Sand Dunes RA – Wash 10

Dispersed sites, No water, Vault/pit toilet, No tents/RVs: $35, Permit required 1 Oct-15 Apr - $35-$50/week or $150/ season, Elevation: 351ft/107m, Telephone: 760-334-3919. Nearest town: Holtville. GPS: 32.980238, -115.046151

228 • H5 | Imperial Sand Dunes RA – Wash 20

Dispersed sites, No water, No toilets, No tents/RVs: $35, Permit required 1 Oct-15 Apr - $35-$50/week or $150/ season, Elevation: 368ft/112m, Telephone: 760-334-3919. Nearest town: Holtville. GPS: 32.954722, -115.014167

229 • H5 | Imperial Sand Dunes RA – Wash 4

Dispersed sites, No water, Vault/pit toilet, No tents/RVs: $35, Permit required 1 Oct-15 Apr - $35-$50/week or $150/ season, Elevation: 341ft/104m, Telephone: 760-334-3919. Nearest town: Holtville. GPS: 32.990833, -115.061389

230 • H5 | Imperial Sand Dunes RA – Wash 6

Dispersed sites, No water, Vault/pit toilet, No tents/RVs: $35, Permit required 1 Oct-15 Apr - $35-$50/week or $150/ season, Elevation: 344ft/105m, Telephone: 760-334-3919. Nearest town: Holtville. GPS: 32.988056, -115.056944

231 • H5 | Indian Pass Wilderness

Dispersed sites, No water, No toilets, Tent & RV camping: Free, Reservations not accepted, Elevation: 854ft/260m, Telephone: 760-337-4400. Nearest town: Yuma, AZ. GPS: 33.025588, -114.769878

232 • H5 | Mule Mountain – Coon Hollow LTVA

Total sites: 29, RV sites: 29, No water, Vault/pit toilet, Tent & RV camping: $40, $40 - 2 weeks, $180 - season, Open all year, Reservations not accepted, Elevation: 653ft/199m, Telephone: 760-833-7100. Nearest town: Blythe. GPS: 33.4475, -114.900278

233 • H5 | Mule Mountain – Wiley's Well LTVA

Total sites: 15, RV sites: 15, No water, Vault/pit toilet, Tent & RV camping: $40, $40 - 2 weeks, $180 - season, Open all year, Reservations not accepted, Stay limit: 14 days, Elevation: 587ft/179m, Telephone: 760-833-7100. Nearest town: Blythe. GPS: 33.493611, -114.887778

234 • H5 | Ogilby Road

Dispersed sites, No water, No toilets, Tent & RV camping: Free, Near RR, Reservations not accepted, Elevation: 371ft/113m. Nearest town: Yuma, AZ. GPS: 32.818195, -114.83765

235 • H5 | Oxbow Lake

Dispersed sites, No water, Vault/pit toilet, Tent & RV camping: $15, Elevation: 223ft/68m, Telephone: 928-317-3200. Nearest town: Blythe. GPS: 33.387659, -114.711933

236 • H5 | Pilot Knob

Dispersed sites, No water, No toilets, No tents/RVs: $40, Fees: Sep 15-Apr 15 $180/$80 4-week stay/$40 2-week stay/14 day camping free Apr 16-Sep 14, Open Sep-Apr, Elevation: 295ft/90m, Telephone: 760-337-4400. Nearest town: Yuma, AZ. GPS: 32.743056, -114.754722

237 • H5 | Powerline

Dispersed sites, No water, No toilets, Tent & RV camping: Free, Reservations not accepted, Stay limit: 14 days, Elevation: 426ft/130m. Nearest town: Yuma (AZ). GPS: 32.838637, -114.640491

238 • H5 | Senator Wash North Shore

Dispersed sites, No water, No toilets, Tent & RV camping: $15, Dump station at South Mesa, Reservations not accepted, Elevation: 275ft/84m, Telephone: 928-317-3200. Nearest town: Yuma (AZ). GPS: 32.907754, -114.495031

239 • H5 | Squaw Lake

Total sites: 200, RV sites: 125, Central water, Flush toilet, Pay showers, No RV dump, Tent & RV camping: $15, Open all year, Stay limit: 14 days, Elevation: 210ft/64m, Telephone: 928-317-3200. Nearest town: Yuma. GPS: 32.903265, -114.476818

240 • H5 | Summit Road Dispersed 1

Dispersed sites, No water, No toilets, Tents only: Free, 4x4 needed, Reservations not accepted, Elevation: 1465ft/447m, Telephone: 760-833-7100. Nearest town: Indo. GPS: 33.562608, -115.589337

241 • H5 | Tamarisk LTVA

Dispersed sites, No water, No toilets, No tents/RVs: Fee unk, $40 - 2 weeks, $180 - season, Open Sep-Apr, Elevation: 112ft/34m, Telephone: 760-337-4400. Nearest town: Holtville. GPS: 32.708056, -115.128056

242 • H5 | Wiley Well District Geode Beds

Dispersed sites, No water, No toilets, Tents only: Free, Road can be very rough, Reservations not accepted, Elevation: 904ft/276m. Nearest town: Blythe. GPS: 33.383857, -114.985172

Colorado

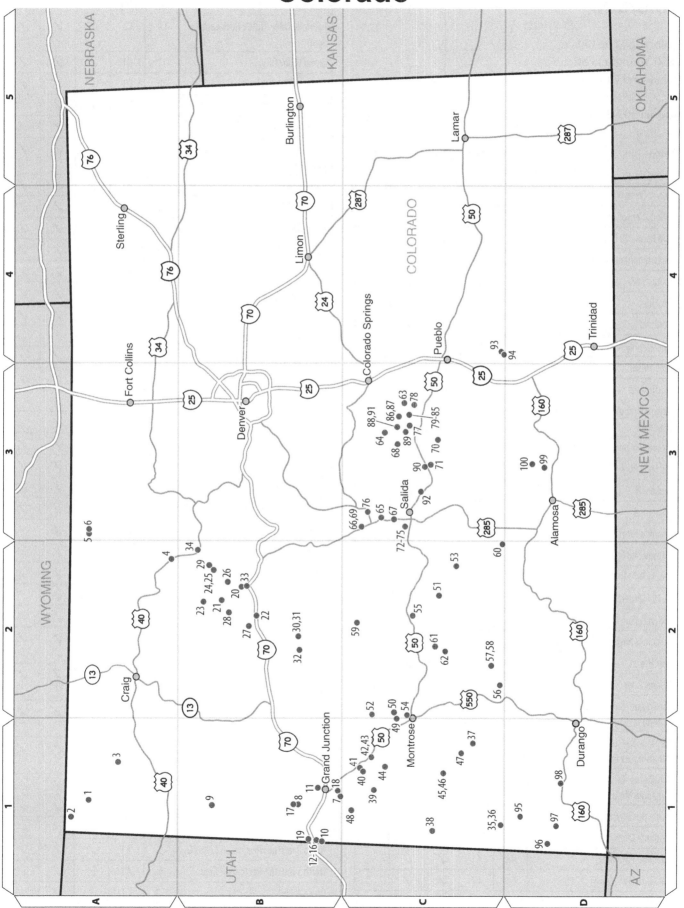

Colorado

Colorado State Office
2850 Youngfield St
Lakewood CO 80215

Phone: 303-239-3600

Name	ID	Map	RVs	Tents	Free
Aggregate	35	C1	✓	✓	✓
Beaver Creek WSA	63	C3	✓	✓	✓
Billings Canyon Dispersed	7	B1	✓		✓
BLM Road 209 Dispersed	8	B1	✓	✓	✓
Bocco Mountain Recreation Area	20	B2	✓	✓	✓
Booger Red	64	C3	✓	✓	✓
Box Elder	36	C1	✓	✓	✓
Bradfield	95	D1	✓	✓	
Browns Canyon WSA	65	C3		✓	✓
Buena Vista	66	C3	✓	✓	✓
Caddiz Flats	37	C1	✓	✓	✓
Canyon Pintado Historic District Dispersed	9	B1	✓	✓	✓
Catamount Bridge	21	B2	✓	✓	✓
Chimney Rock	4	A2	✓	✓	✓
Chukar TH	50	C2		✓	✓
Cochetopa	51	C2	✓	✓	✓
Colorado River – May Flats	10	B1		✓	✓
Cottonwood Grove	52	C2	✓	✓	✓
County Rd 114	53	C2	✓	✓	✓
CR 194 Dispersed	67	C3	✓	✓	✓
Cucharas Canyon – Kenner Ranch	93	C4	✓	✓	✓
Cucharas Canyon – Sheep's Crossing	94	C4	✓	✓	✓
Deer Haven	68	C3	✓	✓	✓
Dolores River – Bedrock Access	38	C1	✓	✓	✓
Dominguez-Escalante NCA – Big Dominguez	39	C1	✓	✓	✓
Dominguez-Escalante NCA – Dominguez Creek	40	C1	✓	✓	✓
Dominguez-Escalante NCA – Triangle Mesa	41	C1	✓	✓	✓
Escalante Canyon Road Dispersed	42	C1	✓	✓	✓
Escalante Canyon Road Dispersed	43	C1	✓	✓	✓
Escalante Pot Holes	44	C1	✓	✓	
Flat-Top OHV	54	C2	✓	✓	✓

Name	ID	Map	RVs	Tents	Free
Fourmile TMA – Turtle Rock Camp Spur	69	C3	✓	✓	✓
Grand Valley ORV	11	B1	✓	✓	✓
Grape Creek WSA	70	C3		✓	✓
Gypsum Recreation Site	22	B2	✓	✓	
Hartman Rocks Rec Area	55	C2	✓	✓	✓
Hovenweep NM – Canyon of the Ancients	96	D1	✓	✓	✓
Irish Canyon	1	A1	✓	✓	✓
King Creek TH	23	B2	✓	✓	✓
Kokopelli's Trail – Castle Rocks	12	B1		✓	✓
Kokopelli's Trail – Jouflas	13	B1		✓	✓
Kokopelli's Trail – Knowles Overlook	14	B1		✓	✓
Kokopelli's Trail – Rabbit Valley	15	B1	✓	✓	✓
Kremmling RMA – Cottonwood	24	B2		✓	✓
Kremmling RMA – Radium	25	B2	✓	✓	✓
Kremmling RMA – Windy Point	26	B2		✓	✓
Lake Como Road Dispersed	99	D3	✓	✓	✓
Ledges Cottonwood	45	C1	✓	✓	
Ledges Rockhouse	46	C1	✓	✓	
Lower Beaver	47	C1	✓	✓	✓
Lyons Gulch	27	B2		✓	✓
Maggie Gulch	56	C2		✓	✓
McElmo Dome Sand Creek Overlook	97	D1		✓	✓
McInnis Canyons NCA – RV Area	16	B1	✓	✓	
McIntyre Hills WSA	71	C3		✓	✓
Mesa Verde Dispersed	98	D1	✓	✓	✓
Mill Creek	57	C2	✓	✓	
Mill Creek Dispersed	58	C2	✓	✓	✓
Mount Shavano Wilderness Preserve Dispersed 1	72	C3	✓	✓	✓
Mount Shavano Wilderness Preserve Dispersed 2	73	C3	✓	✓	✓
Mount Shavano Wilderness Preserve Dispersed 3	74	C3	✓	✓	✓
Mount Shavano Wilderness Preserve Dispersed 4	75	C3	✓	✓	✓
Mud Springs	48	C1	✓	✓	
Mushroom Gulch	76	C3	✓	✓	✓
North Fruita Desert (NFD)	17	B1	✓	✓	
North Sand Hills Rec Area – Sage CG	5	A3	✓	✓	✓
North Sand Hills Recreation Area	6	A3		✓	✓
Oh Be Joyful	59	C2	✓	✓	

Name	ID	Map	RVs	Tents	Free
Oil Well Flat	77	C3	✓	✓	✓
Peach Valley OHV	49	C1	✓	✓	✓
Penitente Canyon	60	C2	✓	✓	
Penrose Common Rec Site	78	C3	✓	✓	✓
Phantom Canyon #1	79	C3	✓	✓	
Phantom Canyon #2	80	C3	✓	✓	
Phantom Canyon #3	81	C3	✓	✓	✓
Phantom Canyon #4	82	C3	✓	✓	✓
Phantom Canyon #5	83	C3	✓	✓	✓
Phantom Canyon #6	84	C3	✓	✓	✓
Phantom Canyon #7	85	C3	✓	✓	✓
Phantom Canyon #8	86	C3	✓	✓	✓
Phantom Canyon #9	87	C3	✓	✓	✓
Pinball Point	28	B2	✓	✓	✓
Pumphouse	29	B2	✓	✓	
Red Bridge	61	C2	✓	✓	
Rocky Reservoir	2	A1	✓	✓	✓
Sand Gulch	88	C3	✓	✓	
Sand Wash Basin	3	A1	✓	✓	✓
Seep Springs WSA	89	C3	✓	✓	✓
Texas Creek	90	C3	✓	✓	✓
The Bank	91	C3	✓	✓	
The Crown SRMA – Prince Creek 1	30	B2	✓	✓	✓
The Crown SRMA – Prince Creek 2	31	B2	✓	✓	✓
The Gate	62	C2	✓	✓	
Third Flats Rd Dispersed	18	B1	✓		✓
Thompson Creek	32	B2	✓	✓	✓
Turkey Rock	92	C3	✓	✓	✓
Walk Through Time	19	B1	✓	✓	✓
Wolcott	33	B2	✓	✓	
Wolford Mountain Recreation Area	34	B2	✓	✓	✓
Zapata Falls	100	D3	✓	✓	

1 • A1 | Irish Canyon

Total sites: 6, RV sites: 6, No water, Vault/pit toilet, Tent & RV camping: Free, Elevation: 6643ft/2025m. Nearest town: Maybell. GPS: 40.829422, -108.735592

2 • A1 | Rocky Reservoir

Total sites: 5, RV sites: 5, No water, Vault/pit toilet, Tent & RV camping: Free, Elevation: 8468ft/2581m. Nearest town: Maybell. GPS: 40.959387, -108.904992

3 • A1 | Sand Wash Basin

Dispersed sites, No water, No toilets, Tent & RV camping: Free, Reservations not accepted, Elevation: 5827ft/1776m, Telephone: 970-826-5000. Nearest town: Maybell. GPS: 40.627231, -108.380918

4 • A2 | Chimney Rock

Dispersed sites, No water, No toilets, Tent & RV camping: Free, More sites further long road, Elevation: 7762ft/2366m. Nearest town: Kremmling. GPS: 40.259787, -106.450365

5 • A3 | North Sand Hills Rec Area – Sage CG

Total sites: 13, RV sites: 13, No water, Vault/pit toilet, Tent & RV camping: Free, Reservations not accepted, Stay limit: 14 days, Elevation: 8309ft/2533m, Telephone: 970-724-3000. Nearest town: Cowdrey. GPS: 40.873462, -106.220487

6 • A3 | North Sand Hills Recreation Area

Dispersed sites, No water, Vault/pit toilet, Tent & RV camping: Free, Reservations not accepted, Stay limit: 14 days, Elevation: 8619ft/2627m, Telephone: 970-724-3000. Nearest town: Cowdrey. GPS: 40.870983, -106.200034

7 • B1 | Billings Canyon Dispersed

Dispersed sites, No water, Vault/pit toilet, No tents/RVs: Free, Reservations not accepted, Elevation: 6160ft/1878m, Telephone: 970-244-3000. Nearest town: Grand Junction. GPS: 38.984101, -108.613183

8 • B1 | BLM Road 209 Dispersed

Total sites: 28, RV sites: 28, No water, No toilets, Tent & RV camping: Free, Sites along 1 mile of road, Firepans required, Reservations not accepted, Elevation: 5071ft/1546m, Telephone: 970-244-3000. Nearest town: Fruita. GPS: 39.305555, -108.704494

9 • B1 | Canyon Pintado Historic District Dispersed

Dispersed sites, No water, No toilets, Tent & RV camping: Free, Elevation: 5796ft/1767m, Telephone: 970-878-3800. Nearest town: Rangely. GPS: 39.925968, -108.737626

10 • B1 | Colorado River – May Flats

Dispersed sites, No water, Tents only: Free, Also boat-in sites, No open fires, Elevation: 4333ft/1321m. Nearest town: Fruita. GPS: 39.116093, -109.043788

11 • B1 | Grand Valley ORV

Dispersed sites, No water, No toilets, Tent & RV camping: Free, Reservations not accepted, Elevation: 4884ft/1489m, Telephone: 970-244-3000. GPS: 39.156361, -108.541565

12 • B1 | Kokopelli's Trail – Castle Rocks

Dispersed sites, No water, Vault/pit toilet, Tents only: Free, Stay limit: 7 days, Elevation: 4492ft/1369m, Telephone: 970-244-3000. Nearest town: Grand Junction. GPS: 39.158598, -109.034096

13 • B1 | Kokopelli's Trail – Jouflas

Total sites: 10, RV sites: 4, No water, No toilets, Tent & RV camping: Free, Reservations not accepted, Stay limit: 14 days, Elevation: 4696ft/1431m, Telephone: 970-244-3000. Nearest town: Grand Junction. GPS: 39.175964, -109.022171

14 • B1 | Kokopelli's Trail – Knowles Overlook

Dispersed sites, No water, Vault/pit toilet, Tents only: Free, Reservations not accepted, Stay limit: 7 days, Elevation: 4652ft/1418m, Telephone: 970-244-3000. Nearest town: Grand Junction. GPS: 39.136795, -109.026938

15 • B1 | Kokopelli's Trail – Rabbit Valley

Dispersed sites, No water, No toilets, Tent & RV camping: Free, Elevation: 4669ft/1423m, Telephone: 970-244-3000. Nearest town: Grand Junction. GPS: 39.179838, -109.021429

16 • B1 | McInnis Canyons NCA – RV Area

Dispersed sites, No water, No toilets, Tent & RV camping: Fee unk, Elevation: 4698ft/1432m, Telephone: 970-244-3000. Nearest town: Grand Junction. GPS: 39.192945, -108.996319

17 • B1 | North Fruita Desert (NFD)

Total sites: 35, RV sites: 35, No water, Vault/pit toilet, Tent & RV camping: $10, Enter at north end of camp road off BLM 18 Road, Sites along 1 mile of road, Open Mar-Nov, Reservations not accepted, Stay limit: 14 days, Elevation: 5328ft/1624m, Telephone: 970-244-3000. Nearest town: Fruita. GPS: 39.327391, -108.703967

18 • B1 | Third Flats Rd Dispersed

Dispersed sites, No water, Vault/pit toilet, No tents/RVs: Free, Reservations not accepted, Elevation: 5202ft/1586m, Telephone: 970-244-3000. Nearest town: Grand Junction. GPS: 39.009631, -108.576072

19 • B1 | Walk Through Time

Dispersed sites, No water, No toilets, Tent & RV camping: Free, Steep road, RVs beware, Elevation: 4972ft/1515m, Telephone: 970-244-3000. Nearest town: Grand Junction. GPS: 39.193168, -109.027405

20 • B2 | Bocco Mountain Recreation Area

Dispersed sites, No water, Vault/pit toilet, Tent & RV camping: Free, Reservations not accepted, Elevation: 7525ft/2294m, Telephone: 970-876-9000. Nearest town: Wolcott. GPS: 39.742715, -106.705977

21 • B2 | Catamount Bridge

Total sites: 5, RV sites: 5, No water, Vault/pit toilet, Tent & RV camping: Free, Near RR, Open all year, Elevation: 6581ft/2006m, Telephone: 970-876-9000. Nearest town: Eagle. GPS: 39.890591, -106.832303

22 • B2 | Gypsum Recreation Site

Total sites: 8, RV sites: 8, No water, Vault/pit toilet, Tent & RV camping: $10, Open May-Nov, Stay limit: 14 days, Elevation: 6273ft/1912m, Telephone: 970-876-9000. Nearest town: Gypsum. GPS: 39.655136, -106.975603

23 • B2 | King Creek TH

Dispersed sites, No water, No toilets, Tent & RV camping: Free, Reservations not accepted, Stay limit: 14 days, Elevation: 8393ft/2558m, Telephone: 970-876-9000. Nearest town: Toponas. GPS: 40.030305, -106.846861

24 • B2 | Kremmling RMA – Cottonwood

Dispersed sites, No water, No toilets, Tents only: Free, Also boat-in sites, 4x4 recommended, Elevation: 6893ft/2101m, Telephone: 970-724-3000. GPS: 39.958819, -106.549789

25 • B2 | Kremmling RMA – Radium

Total sites: 9, RV sites: 9, No water, Vault/pit toilet, Tent & RV camping: $6, Group site: $30, Open May-Oct, Stay limit: 14 days, Elevation: 6900ft/2103m, Telephone: 970-724-3000. Nearest town: Kremmling. GPS: 39.950241, -106.556214

26 • B2 | Kremmling RMA – Windy Point

Dispersed sites, No water, No toilets, Tents only: Free, Elevation: 6741ft/2055m, Telephone: 970-724-3000. GPS: 39.854666, -106.662872

27 • B2 | Lyons Gulch

Total sites: 4, No water, Vault/pit toilet, Tents only: Free, Group site available, Open all year, Reservations not accepted, Elevation: 6214ft/1894m, Telephone: 970-876-9000. Nearest town: Dotsero. GPS: 39.698597, -107.072331

28 • B2 | Pinball Point

Total sites: 1, No water, Vault/pit toilet, Tent & RV camping: Free, Open all year, Elevation: 6463ft/1970m. Nearest town: McCoy. GPS: 39.841852, -106.940927

29 • B2 | Pumphouse

Total sites: 18, RV sites: 18, No toilets, Tent & RV camping: $10, Open all year, Reservations not accepted, Stay limit: 14 days, Elevation: 6965ft/2123m, Telephone: 970-724-3000. Nearest town: Kremmling. GPS: 39.985379, -106.513173

30 • B2 | The Crown SRMA – Prince Creek 1

Total sites: 5, RV sites: 5, No water, Vault/pit toilet, Tent & RV camping: Free, Group site available, Reservations not accepted, Elevation: 7187ft/2191m, Telephone: 970-876-9000. Nearest town: Carbondale. GPS: 39.339897, -107.159602

31 • B2 | The Crown SRMA – Prince Creek 2

Dispersed sites, No water, Vault/pit toilet, Tent & RV camping: Free, Group site available, Reservations not accepted, Elevation: 7466ft/2276m, Telephone: 970-876-9000. Nearest town: Carbondale. GPS: 39.332441, -107.151558

32 • B2 | Thompson Creek

Total sites: 4, RV sites: 4, No water, No toilets, Tent & RV camping: Free, Open Jun, Reservations not accepted, Stay limit: 14 days, Elevation: 7264ft/2214m, Telephone: 970-876-9000. Nearest town: Carbondale. GPS: 39.322026, -107.281745

33 • B2 | Wolcott

Total sites: 6, RV sites: 6, No water, Vault/pit toilet, Tent & RV camping: $10, Open May-Nov, Reservations not accepted, Elevation: 6968ft/2124m, Telephone: 970-876-9000. Nearest town: Dotsero. GPS: 39.712434, -106.696491

34 • B2 | Wolford Mountain Recreation Area

Dispersed sites, No water, No toilets, Tent & RV camping: Free, Elevation: 7412ft/2259m, Telephone: 970-724-3000. Nearest town: Kremmling. GPS: 40.073309, -106.367377

35 • C1 | Aggregate

Dispersed sites, No water, No toilets, Tent & RV camping: Free, 4x4 or high-clearance required, Reservations not accepted, Elevation: 6087ft/1855m. Nearest town: Dove Creek. GPS: 37.804294, -108.818986

36 • C1 | Box Elder

Total sites: 11, RV sites: 11, No water, Vault/pit toilet, Tent & RV camping: Free, Reservations not accepted, Elevation: 6087ft/1855m, Telephone: 970-882-7296. Nearest town: Dove Creek. GPS: 37.801119, -108.824266

37 • C1 | Caddiz Flats

Total sites: 3, RV sites: 3, No water, Vault/pit toilet, Tent & RV camping: Free, Reservations not accepted, Elevation: 7303ft/2226m, Telephone: 970-240-5300. Nearest town: Placerville. GPS: 38.027246, -108.092968

38 • C1 | Dolores River – Bedrock Access

Total sites: 4, RV sites: 4, No water, No toilets, Tent & RV camping: Free, Also a large flat area for dispersed camping, Reservations not accepted, Elevation: 4967ft/1514m, Telephone: 970-240-5300. Nearest town: Naturita. GPS: 38.304135, -108.895086

39 • C1 | Dominguez-Escalante NCA – Big Dominguez

Total sites: 9, RV sites: 9, No water, Vault/pit toilet, Tent & RV camping: Free, Open May-Oct, Elevation: 7136ft/2175m, Telephone: 970-244-3000. Nearest town: Grand Junction. GPS: 38.745, -108.55

40 • C1 | Dominguez-Escalante NCA – Dominguez Creek

Dispersed sites, No water, Vault/pit toilet, Tent & RV camping: Free, Also boat-in sites, Elevation: 4765ft/1452m, Telephone: 970-244-3000. Nearest town: Grand Junction. GPS: 38.829413, -108.379162

41 • C1 | Dominguez-Escalante NCA – Triangle Mesa

Dispersed sites, No water, Vault/pit toilet, Tent & RV camping: Free, Reservations not accepted, Elevation: 4963ft/1513m, Telephone: 970-244-3000. Nearest town: Grand Junction. GPS: 38.852875, -108.348021

42 • C1 | Escalante Canyon Road Dispersed

Dispersed sites, No water, No toilets, Tent & RV camping: Free, Reservations not accepted, Elevation: 4961ft/1512m, Telephone: 970-244-3000. Nearest town: Delta. GPS: 38.763711, -108.244987

43 • C1 | Escalante Canyon Road Dispersed

Dispersed sites, No water, No toilets, Tent & RV camping: Free, Reservations not accepted, Elevation: 5293ft/1613m, Telephone: 970-244-3000. Nearest town: Delta. GPS: 38.778569, -108.250816

44 • C1 | Escalante Pot Holes

Total sites: 4, RV sites: 4, No water, Vault/pit toilet, Tent & RV camping: Fee unk, Reservations not accepted, Elevation: 5551ft/1692m, Telephone: 970-244-3000. Nearest town: Delta. GPS: 38.669734, -108.327939

45 • C1 | Ledges Cottonwood

Total sites: 14, RV sites: 14, No water, Vault/pit toilet, Tent & RV camping: $5-20, Reservations not accepted, Stay limit: 14 days, Elevation: 6181ft/1884m, Telephone: 970-240-5300. Nearest town: Naturita. GPS: 38.247088, -108.381217

46 • C1 | Ledges Rockhouse

Total sites: 14, RV sites: 14, No water, Vault/pit toilet, Tent & RV camping: $5-20, Reservations not accepted, Stay limit: 14 days, Elevation: 6102ft/1860m, Telephone: 970-240-5300. Nearest town: Naturita. GPS: 38.235302, -108.369345

47 • C1 | Lower Beaver

Total sites: 5, RV sites: 2, No water, Vault/pit toilet, Tent & RV camping: Free, Reservations not accepted, Stay limit: 14 days, Elevation: 6696ft/2041m, Telephone: 970-240-5300. Nearest town: Norwood. GPS: 38.109524, -108.188844

48 • C1 | Mud Springs

Total sites: 14, RV sites: 14, Central water, Vault/pit toilet, No showers, No RV dump, Tent & RV camping: $10, Spring water available, Open May-Nov, Elevation: 8527ft/2599m, Telephone: 970-244-3000. Nearest town: Glade Park. GPS: 38.905091, -108.739038

49 • C1 | Peach Valley OHV

Dispersed sites, No water, Vault/pit toilet, Tent & RV camping: Free, Reservations not accepted, Elevation: 5630ft/1716m, Telephone: 970-240-5300. Nearest town: Montrose. GPS: 38.595108, -107.889987

50 • C2 | Chukar TH

Total sites: 4, RV sites: 0, No water, Vault/pit toilet, Tents only: Free, High-clearance 4WD required, Elevation: 5932ft/1808m, Telephone: 970-240-5300. Nearest town: Montrose. GPS: 38.613069, -107.835763

51 • C2 | Cochetopa

Total sites: 14, RV sites: 14, No water, Vault/pit toilet, Tent & RV camping: Free, Other sites along 4-mile stretch of road, Reservations not accepted, Stay limit: 14 days, Elevation: 8819ft/2688m, Telephone: 970-642-4940. Nearest town: Gunnison. GPS: 38.306703, -106.763899

52 • C2 | Cottonwood Grove

Total sites: 6, RV sites: 6, No water, Vault/pit toilet, Tent & RV camping: Free, Stay limit: 14 days, Elevation: 5125ft/ 1562m, Telephone: 970-240-5300. Nearest town: Delta. GPS: 38.779104, -107.853145

53 • C2 | County Rd 114

Dispersed sites, No water, No toilets, Tent & RV camping: Free, Elevation: 8800ft/2682m. Nearest town: Saguache. GPS: 38.185974, -106.488544

54 • C2 | Flat-Top OHV

Dispersed sites, No water, Vault/pit toilet, Tent & RV camping: Free, Reservations not accepted, Stay limit: 14 days, Elevation: 5900ft/1798m, Telephone: 970-240-5300. Nearest town: Montrose. GPS: 38.521346, -107.859268

55 • C2 | Hartman Rocks Rec Area

Dispersed sites, No water, No toilets, Tent & RV camping: Free, Camping only in designated dispersed sites, Rough roads, Reservations not accepted, Stay limit: 14 days, Elevation: 8146ft/2483m, Telephone: 970-642-4940. Nearest town: Gunnison. GPS: 38.496697, -106.945371

56 • C2 | Maggie Gulch

Dispersed sites, No water, No toilets, Tents only: Free, Elevation: 10416ft/3175m. Nearest town: Silverton. GPS: 37.844401, -107.557967

57 • C2 | Mill Creek

Total sites: 23, RV sites: 23, Central water, Vault/pit toilet, No showers, No RV dump, Tent & RV camping: $7, Reservations not accepted, Stay limit: 14 days, Elevation: 9465ft/2885m, Telephone: 970-642-4940. Nearest town: Carson. GPS: 37.906615, -107.390239

58 • C2 | Mill Creek Dispersed

Dispersed sites, No water, No toilets, Tent & RV camping: Free, Elevation: 9414ft/2869m. Nearest town: Lake City. GPS: 37.906254, -107.380846

59 • C2 | Oh Be Joyful

Total sites: 30, RV sites: 12, No water, Vault/pit toilet, Tent & RV camping: $5-10, Open May-Sep, Reservations accepted, Elevation: 9024ft/2751m, Telephone: 970-642-4940. Nearest town: Crested Butte. GPS: 38.908417, -107.025476

60 • C2 | Penitente Canyon

Total sites: 13, RV sites: 4, Central water, Vault/pit toilet, No showers, No RV dump, Tent & RV camping: $11, Also walk-to/group sites, Group site $20, Generator hours: 0700-2200, Open all year, Reservations not accepted, Stay limit: 14 days, Elevation: 7972ft/2430m, Telephone: 719-852-7074. Nearest town: La Garita. GPS: 37.842675, -106.282365

61 • C2 | Red Bridge

Total sites: 7, RV sites: 7, No water, Vault/pit toilet, Tent & RV camping: $5, Open May-Sep, Reservations not accepted, Elevation: 7940ft/2420m, Telephone: 970-641-0471. Nearest town: Lake City. GPS: 38.324252, -107.226904

62 • C2 | The Gate

Total sites: 8, RV sites: 8, Central water, Vault/pit toilet, No showers, No RV dump, Tent & RV camping: $5, Reservations not accepted, Stay limit: 14 days, Elevation: 8045ft/2452m, Telephone: 970-641-0471. Nearest town: Lake City. GPS: 38.246453, -107.259747

63 • C3 | Beaver Creek WSA

Dispersed sites, No water, No toilets, Tent & RV camping: Free, Elevation: 6134ft/1870m. Nearest town: Canon City. GPS: 38.570444, -105.012282

64 • C3 | Booger Red

Dispersed sites, No water, No toilets, Tent & RV camping: Free, High-clearance vehicles recommended, Open Apr-Nov, Elevation: 7807ft/2380m, Telephone: 719-269-8500. Nearest town: Canon City. GPS: 38.708975, -105.275732

65 • C3 | Browns Canyon WSA

Dispersed sites, No water, No toilets, Tents only: Free, Elevation: 7722ft/2354m. Nearest town: Nathrop. GPS: 38.734892, -106.057523

66 • C3 | Buena Vista

Dispersed sites, No water, No toilets, Tent & RV camping: Free, Several sites along road, Elevation: 8070ft/2460m. Nearest town: Buena Vista. GPS: 38.872347, -106.147037

67 • C3 | CR 194 Dispersed

Dispersed sites, No water, No toilets, Tent & RV camping: Free, Reservations not accepted, Elevation: 7557ft/2303m. Nearest town: Salida. GPS: 38.638765, -106.076023

68 • C3 | Deer Haven

Dispersed sites, No water, No toilets, Tent & RV camping: Free, Open Apr-Oct, Elevation: 8236ft/2510m. Nearest town: Canon City. GPS: 38.623232, -105.385823

69 • C3 | Fourmile TMA – Turtle Rock Camp Spur

Total sites: 20, RV sites: 20, No water, No toilets, Tent & RV camping: Free, Elevation: 8298ft/2529m. Nearest town: Buena Vista. GPS: 38.881897, -106.144801

70 • C3 | Grape Creek WSA

Dispersed sites, No water, No toilets, Tents only: Free, Elevation: 6813ft/2077m. Nearest town: Canon City. GPS: 38.323325, -105.345579

71 • C3 | McIntyre Hills WSA

Dispersed sites, No water, No toilets, Tents only: Free, Reservations not accepted, Elevation: 6530ft/1990m. Nearest town: Canon City. GPS: 38.392217, -105.576467

72 • C3 | Mount Shavano Wilderness Preserve Dispersed 1

Dispersed sites, No water, No toilets, Tent & RV camping: Free, Large area with many sites, Reservations not accepted, Elevation: 8189ft/2496m. Nearest town: Poncha Springs. GPS: 38.554285, -106.115969

73 • C3 | Mount Shavano Wilderness Preserve Dispersed 2

Dispersed sites, No water, No toilets, Tent & RV camping: Free, Reservations not accepted, Elevation: 8592ft/2619m. Nearest town: Poncha Springs. GPS: 38.565766, -106.138549

74 • C3 | Mount Shavano Wilderness Preserve Dispersed 3

Dispersed sites, No water, No toilets, Tent & RV camping: Free, Reservations not accepted, Elevation: 8772ft/2674m. Nearest town: Poncha Springs. GPS: 38.565248, -106.154139

75 • C3 | Mount Shavano Wilderness Preserve Dispersed 4

Dispersed sites, No water, No toilets, Tent & RV camping: Free, Reservations not accepted, Elevation: 8848ft/2697m. Nearest town: Poncha Springs. GPS: 38.570103, -106.156511

76 • C3 | Mushroom Gulch

Dispersed sites, No water, No toilets, Tent & RV camping: Free, Elevation: 8702ft/2652m, Telephone: 719-539-3591. Nearest town: Buena Vista. GPS: 38.837947, -106.002183

77 • C3 | Oil Well Flat

Dispersed sites, No water, No toilets, Tent & RV camping: Free, Open Oct-May, Reservations not accepted, Elevation: 6007ft/1831m, Telephone: 719-269-8500. Nearest town: Canon City. GPS: 38.535786, -105.215457

78 • C3 | Penrose Common Rec Site

Dispersed sites, No water, No toilets, Tent & RV camping: Free, Open Sep-May, Stay limit: 14 days, Elevation: 5817ft/ 1773m, Telephone: 719-269-8500. Nearest town: Canon City. GPS: 38.493347, -105.031589

79 • C3 | Phantom Canyon #1

Dispersed sites, No water, No toilets, Tent & RV camping: Fee unk, No large RVs, Elevation: 5951ft/1814m. Nearest town: Canon city. GPS: 38.512896, -105.114352

80 • C3 | Phantom Canyon #2

Dispersed sites, No water, No toilets, Tent & RV camping: Fee unk, No large RVs, Elevation: 5985ft/1824m. Nearest town: Canon city. GPS: 38.513627, -105.116388

81 • C3 | Phantom Canyon #3

Dispersed sites, No water, No toilets, Tent & RV camping: Free, No large RVs, Elevation: 6088ft/1856m. Nearest town: Canon city. GPS: 38.520213, -105.121709

82 • C3 | Phantom Canyon #4

Dispersed sites, No water, No toilets, Tent & RV camping: Free, No large RVs, Elevation: 6097ft/1858m. Nearest town: Canon city. GPS: 38.519436, -105.123928

83 • C3 | Phantom Canyon #5

Dispersed sites, No water, No toilets, Tent & RV camping: Free, No large RVs, Elevation: 6512ft/1985m. Nearest town: Canon city. GPS: 38.536596, -105.118141

84 • C3 | Phantom Canyon #6

Dispersed sites, No water, No toilets, Tent & RV camping: Free, No large RVs, Elevation: 6854ft/2089m. Nearest town: Canon city. GPS: 38.552323, -105.095887

85 • C3 | Phantom Canyon #7

Dispersed sites, No water, No toilets, Tent & RV camping: Free, No large RVs, Elevation: 6890ft/2100m. Nearest town: Canon city. GPS: 38.556567, -105.092786

86 • C3 | Phantom Canyon #8

Dispersed sites, No water, No toilets, Tent & RV camping: Free, No large RVs, Elevation: 7978ft/2432m. Nearest town: Canon city. GPS: 38.602008, -105.123676

87 • C3 | Phantom Canyon #9

Dispersed sites, No water, No toilets, Tent & RV camping: Free, No large RVs, Elevation: 8109ft/2472m. Nearest town: Canon city. GPS: 38.610112, -105.132594

88 • C3 | Sand Gulch

Total sites: 16, RV sites: 4, No water, Vault/pit toilet, Tent & RV camping: $7, Group site: $14, Trailers not recommended, Reservations not accepted, Stay limit: 14 days, Elevation: 6463ft/1970m, Telephone: 719-269-8500. Nearest town: Canon City. GPS: 38.617709, -105.229534

89 • C3 | Seep Springs WSA

Dispersed sites, No water, No toilets, Tent & RV camping: Free, Open Sep-Jun, Elevation: 6332ft/1930m. Nearest town: Canon City. GPS: 38.557221, -105.271448

90 • C3 | Texas Creek

Dispersed sites, No water, No toilets, Tent & RV camping: Free, Open Sep-May, Elevation: 6291ft/1917m, Telephone: 719-269-8500. Nearest town: Canon City. GPS: 38.415728, -105.586324

91 • C3 | The Bank

Total sites: 13, RV sites: 4, No water, Vault/pit toilet, Tent & RV camping: $7, Trailers not recommended, Reservations not accepted, Stay limit: 14 days, Elevation: 6795ft/2071m, Telephone: 719-269-8500. Nearest town: Canon City. GPS: 38.629015, -105.227119

92 • C3 | Turkey Rock

Dispersed sites, No water, No toilets, Tent & RV camping: Free, Reservations not accepted, Elevation: 6794ft/2071m. Nearest town: Howard. GPS: 38.443108, -105.820964

93 • C4 | Cucharas Canyon – Kenner Ranch

Dispersed sites, No water, No toilets, Tent & RV camping: Free, Elevation: 5978ft/1822m. Nearest town: Walsenburg. GPS: 37.844782, -104.550094

94 • C4 | Cucharas Canyon – Sheep's Crossing

Dispersed sites, No water, No toilets, Tent & RV camping: Free, Elevation: 5884ft/1793m. Nearest town: Walsenburg. GPS: 37.829964, -104.571211

95 • D1 | Bradfield

Total sites: 17, RV sites: 17, Central water, Vault/pit toilet, No showers, No RV dump, Tent & RV camping: $8, Hand water pumps, No services in winter, Open all year, Reservations not accepted, Elevation: 6466ft/1971m, Telephone: 970-247-4874. Nearest town: Cortez . GPS: 37.658322, -108.737422

96 • D1 | Hovenweep NM – Canyon of the Ancients

Dispersed sites, No water, No toilets, Tent & RV camping: Free, Camp no closer than 300' to ruins, Elevation: 6878ft/

2096m, Telephone: 970-882-5600. Nearest town: Pleasant View. GPS: 37.44563, -108.973315

97 • D1 | McElmo Dome Sand Creek Overlook

Dispersed sites, No water, No toilets, Tents only: Free, Rough road, Elevation: 7054ft/2150m. Nearest town: Cortez. GPS: 37.383253, -108.803658

98 • D1 | Mesa Verde Dispersed

Total sites: 13, RV sites: 13, No water, No toilets, Tent & RV camping: Free, Elevation: 6707ft/2044m. Nearest town: Cortez. GPS: 37.360258, -108.426089

99 • D3 | Lake Como Road Dispersed

Dispersed sites, No water, No toilets, Tent & RV camping: Free, Elevation: 7689ft/2344m. Nearest town: Alamosa. GPS: 37.526988, -105.593546

100 • D3 | Zapata Falls

Total sites: 23, RV sites: 23, No water, Vault/pit toilet, Tent & RV camping: $11, Access may be limited in winter, Generator hours: 0700-2200, Open all year, Reservations not accepted, Elevation: 9147ft/2788m, Telephone: 719-852-7074. Nearest town: Alamosa. GPS: 37.619058, -105.560089

Idaho

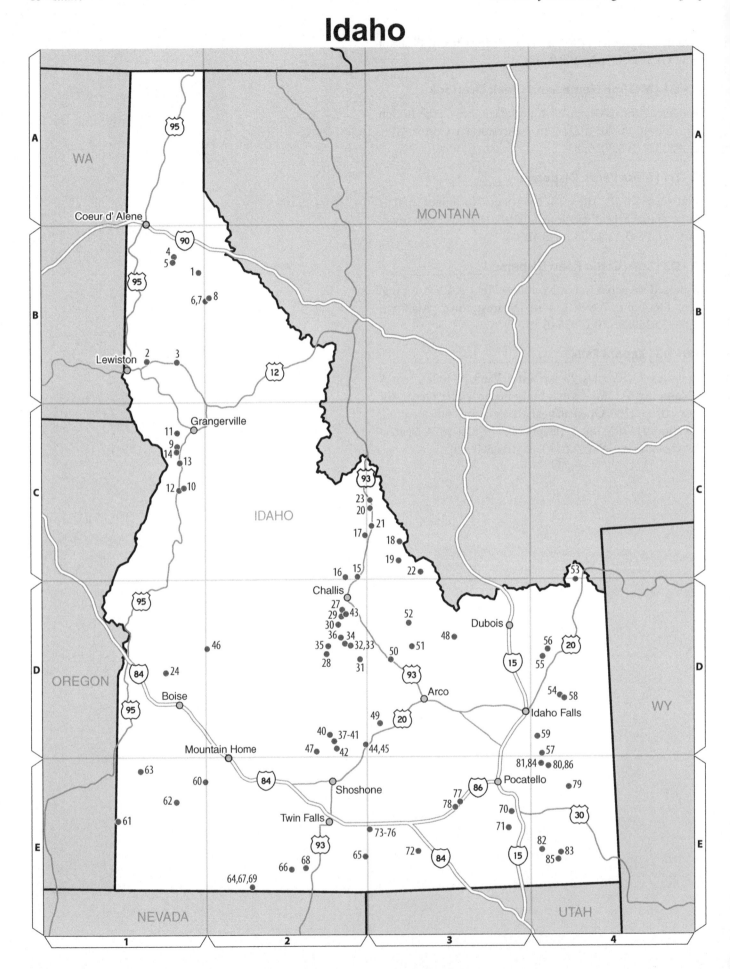

Idaho

Idaho State Office
1387 S Vinnell Way
Boise ID 83709

Phone: 208-373-4000

Name	ID	Map	RVs	Tents	Free
Agency Creek	18	C3	✓	✓	✓
Bayhorse	27	D2	✓	✓	
Big Cottonwood	64	E2	✓	✓	✓
Big Cottonwood Creek TH	65	E2	✓	✓	✓
Birch Creek	48	D3	✓	✓	
Blackfoot Reservoir	79	E4	✓	✓	
Boulder White Clouds	28	D2	✓	✓	✓
Cedar Creek Reservoir	66	E2	✓	✓	✓
Cottonwood	15	C2	✓	✓	
Cove	60	E1	✓	✓	
Crater Lake	6	B2		✓	✓
Crater Peak	7	B2		✓	✓
Cutthroat Trout	80	E4	✓	✓	✓
Deadman Hole	29	D2	✓	✓	✓
East Fork	30	D2	✓	✓	
Fish Creek Reservoir	49	D3	✓	✓	✓
Garden Creek	31	D2	✓	✓	✓
Goodenough Creek	70	E3	✓	✓	✓
Graves Creek	81	E4	✓	✓	✓
Hammer Creek	9	C1	✓	✓	
Hawkins Reservoir	71	E3	✓	✓	✓
Heart Mountain Springs	82	E4	✓	✓	✓
Henrys Lake South Shore Access	53	D4	✓	✓	✓
Herd Lake	32	D2		✓	✓
Herd Lake Overlook	33	D2		✓	✓
Huckleberry	1	B1	✓	✓	
Island Bar	10	C1	✓	✓	✓
Joseph T. Fallini (McKay Reservoir)	50	D3	✓	✓	
Juniper Grove	67	E2	✓	✓	✓
Kelly's Island	54	D4	✓	✓	
Lake Creek TH	34	D2		✓	✓
Little Boulder	35	D2	✓	✓	✓
Little Gem Cycle Park	24	D1	✓	✓	✓
Lower Herd Creek TH	36	D2	✓	✓	✓

Name	ID	Map	RVs	Tents	Free
Lud Drexler	68	E2	✓	✓	
Magic Reservoir – Lava Cove	37	D2	✓	✓	✓
Magic Reservoir – Lava Creek	38	D2	✓	✓	✓
Magic Reservoir – Magic Dam	39	D2	✓	✓	✓
Magic Reservoir – Moonstone Access	40	D2	✓	✓	✓
Magic Reservoir – Myrtle Point	41	D2	✓	✓	✓
Magic Reservoir – Richfield Diversion	42	D2	✓	✓	✓
Malm Gulch TH	43	D2		✓	✓
Maple Grove	83	E4	✓	✓	
McClendon Spring	72	E3	✓	✓	✓
McFarland	19	C3	✓	✓	
McKay's Bend	2	B1	✓	✓	
Milner Reservoir #1	73	E3	✓	✓	
Milner Reservoir #2	74	E3	✓	✓	
Milner Reservoir #3	75	E3	✓	✓	
Milner Reservoir #4	76	E3		✓	
Morgan Bar	20	C3	✓	✓	
Morgan Creek	16	C2	✓	✓	✓
Morgans Bridge	84	E4	✓	✓	✓
North Fork Owyhee River	61	E1	✓	✓	✓
Orphan Point Saddle	8	B2		✓	✓
Pass Creek	51	D3	✓	✓	✓
Pine Bar	11	C1	✓	✓	
Pink House	3	B1	✓	✓	
Pipeline	77	E3	✓	✓	✓
Poison Creek	62	E1	✓	✓	✓
Redpoint	85	E4	✓	✓	
Sage Hen Flats	86	E4	✓	✓	✓
Sheep Springs	4	B1	✓	✓	✓
Shorts Bar	12	C1	✓	✓	✓
Shoup Bridge Recreation Site	21	C3	✓	✓	
Silver City	63	E1	✓	✓	✓
Silver Creek North	44	D2	✓	✓	✓
Silver Creek South	45	D2	✓	✓	✓
Slate Creek	13	C1	✓	✓	
Smokey Cubs	22	C3	✓	✓	✓
Snake River Vista	78	E3	✓	✓	✓
South Fork Payette River	46	D2	✓	✓	
St Anthony Dunes – Egin Lakes	55	D4	✓	✓	
St Anthony Dunes – Red Road	56	D4	✓	✓	✓

Name	ID	Map	RVs	Tents	Free
Steck Park	25	D1	✓	✓	
Summit Creek	52	D3	✓	✓	✓
The Forks	69	E2	✓	✓	✓
Thorn Creek Reservoir	47	D2	✓	✓	✓
Tingley Spring	5	B1		✓	✓
Tower Rock	23	C3	✓	✓	
Trail Creek Bridge	57	D4	✓	✓	✓
Weiser Sand Dunes OHV	26	D1	✓	✓	✓
White Bird Gravel Pit	14	C1	✓	✓	✓
Williams Lake	17	C2	✓	✓	
Wolf Flats	58	D4	✓	✓	✓
Wolverine Canyon	59	D4	✓	✓	✓

1 • B1 | Huckleberry

Total sites: 30, RV sites: 30, Electric sites: 30, Water at site, Vault/pit toilet, No showers, RV dump, Tent & RV camping: $23, No water in winter, 3 group sites with electric and water, Open all year, Reservations accepted, Elevation: 2247ft/685m, Telephone: 208-769-5000. Nearest town: St. Maries. GPS: 47.268711, -116.086204

2 • B1 | McKay's Bend

Total sites: 17, RV sites: 15, Electric sites: 15, Water at site, Flush toilet, Free showers, No RV dump, Tents: $10/RVs: $18, 14 FHU, Open all year, Reservations not accepted, Elevation: 854ft/260m, Telephone: 208-962-3245. Nearest town: Lewiston. GPS: 46.497823, -116.727275

3 • B1 | Pink House

Total sites: 18, RV sites: 15, Electric sites: 15, Water at site, Flush toilet, No showers, RV dump, Tents: $10/RVs: $18, 15 FHU, Open all year, Reservations not accepted, Elevation: 971ft/296m, Telephone: 208-962-3245. Nearest town: Lewiston. GPS: 46.503036, -116.348075

4 • B1 | Sheep Springs

Total sites: 3, RV sites: 3, No water, Vault/pit toilet, Tent & RV camping: Free, Narrow steep rough road, Elevation: 5469ft/1667m, Telephone: 208-769-5000. Nearest town: St Maries. GPS: 47.388432, -116.401522

5 • B1 | Tingley Spring

Total sites: 6, RV sites: 0, No water, Vault/pit toilet, Tents only: Free, Access road is narrow/steep/rough, Open Jun-Sep, Reservations not accepted, Elevation: 5050ft/1539m, Telephone: 208-769-5000. Nearest town: St Maries. GPS: 47.357848, -116.413052

6 • B2 | Crater Lake

Dispersed sites, No water, Vault/pit toilet, Tents only: Free, Open Jul-Sep, Reservations not accepted, Stay limit: 14 days, Elevation: 6255ft/1907m, Telephone: 208-769-5000. Nearest town: Clarkia. GPS: 47.034496, -115.977257

7 • B2 | Crater Peak

Dispersed sites, No water, Vault/pit toilet, Tents only: Free, Reservations not accepted, Elevation: 6271ft/1911m, Telephone: 208-769-5000. Nearest town: Clarkia. GPS: 47.028456, -115.984142

8 • B2 | Orphan Point Saddle

Dispersed sites, No water, Vault/pit toilet, Tents only: Free, Open Jul-Sep, Reservations not accepted, Elevation: 5954ft/1815m, Telephone: 208-769-5000. Nearest town: Clarkia. GPS: 47.044825, -115.944908

9 • C1 | Hammer Creek

Total sites: 12, RV sites: 12, Central water, Vault/pit toilet, No showers, RV dump, Tent & RV camping: $10, Open all year, Reservations not accepted, Elevation: 1424ft/434m, Telephone: 208-962-3245. Nearest town: White Bird. GPS: 45.765102, -116.325269

10 • C1 | Island Bar

Dispersed sites, No water, Vault/pit toilet, Tent & RV camping: Free, Open all year, Reservations not accepted, Elevation: 1818ft/554m, Telephone: 208-962-3245. Nearest town: Riggins. GPS: 45.41795, -116.261151

11 • C1 | Pine Bar

Total sites: 6, RV sites: 6, Central water, Vault/pit toilet, No showers, No RV dump, Tent & RV camping: $7, Open all year, Reservations not accepted, Elevation: 1444ft/440m, Telephone: 208-962-3245. Nearest town: Cottonwood. GPS: 45.891215, -116.332572

12 • C1 | Shorts Bar

Dispersed sites, No water, Vault/pit toilet, Tent & RV camping: Free, Open all year, Reservations not accepted, Elevation: 1749ft/533m, Telephone: 208-962-3245. Nearest town: Riggins. GPS: 45.414227, -116.301712

13 • C1 | Slate Creek

Total sites: 5, RV sites: 5, Central water, Vault/pit toilet, No showers, RV dump, Tent & RV camping: $10, Reservations not accepted, Elevation: 1608ft/490m, Telephone: 208-

962-3245. Nearest town: White Bird. GPS: 45.646419, -116.293016

14 • C1 | White Bird Gravel Pit

Dispersed sites, No water, Vault/pit toilet, Tent & RV camping: Free, Reservations not accepted, Elevation: 1493ft/455m, Telephone: 208-962-3245. Nearest town: White Bird. GPS: 45.743659, -116.324746

15 • C2 | Cottonwood

Total sites: 15, RV sites: 15, Central water, Vault/pit toilet, No showers, RV dump, Tent & RV camping: $10, Open all year, Reservations not accepted, Elevation: 4695ft/1431m, Telephone: 208-879-6200. Nearest town: Challis. GPS: 44.668745, -114.078215

16 • C2 | Morgan Creek

Total sites: 4, RV sites: 4, Central water, Vault/pit toilet, No showers, No RV dump, Tent & RV camping: Free, Open May-Oct, Reservations not accepted, Stay limit: 14 days, Elevation: 5545ft/1690m, Telephone: 208-879-6200. Nearest town: Challis. GPS: 44.667956, -114.229757

17 • C2 | Williams Lake

Total sites: 11, RV sites: 11, Central water, Vault/pit toilet, No showers, No RV dump, Tent & RV camping: $5, Reservations not accepted, Stay limit: 14 days, Elevation: 5474ft/1668m, Telephone: 208-756-5400. Nearest town: Salmon. GPS: 45.020588, -113.968942

18 • C3 | Agency Creek

Total sites: 4, RV sites: 4, No toilets, Tent & RV camping: Free, Reservations not accepted, Elevation: 5430ft/1655m, Telephone: 208-756-5400. Nearest town: Tendoy. GPS: 44.961238, -113.542103

19 • C3 | McFarland

Total sites: 10, RV sites: 10, Central water, Vault/pit toilet, No showers, No RV dump, Tent & RV camping: $5, Open May-Sep, Reservations not accepted, Elevation: 5381ft/1640m, Telephone: 208-756-5400. Nearest town: Leadore. GPS: 44.802342, -113.566311

20 • C3 | Morgan Bar

Total sites: 8, RV sites: 8, Central water, Vault/pit toilet, No showers, No RV dump, Tent & RV camping: $5, Open May-Sep, Reservations not accepted, Elevation: 3842ft/1171m, Telephone: 208-756-5400. Nearest town: Salmon. GPS: 45.253518, -113.907191

21 • C3 | Shoup Bridge Recreation Site

Total sites: 5, RV sites: 5, Central water, Vault/pit toilet, Tent & RV camping: $5, Open Apr-Oct, Reservations not accepted, Stay limit: 14 days, Elevation: 4049ft/1234m, Telephone: 208-756-5400. Nearest town: Salmon. GPS: 45.098012, -113.893266

22 • C3 | Smokey Cubs

Total sites: 8, RV sites: 8, No water, Vault/pit toilet, No showers, No RV dump, Tent & RV camping: Free, Open May-Oct, Reservations not accepted, Stay limit: 14 days, Elevation: 6273ft/1912m, Telephone: 208-756-5400. Nearest town: Leadore. GPS: 44.703085, -113.293962

23 • C3 | Tower Rock

Total sites: 6, RV sites: 6, No water, Vault/pit toilet, Tent & RV camping: $5, Reservations not accepted, Stay limit: 14 days, Elevation: 3766ft/1148m, Telephone: 208-756-5400. Nearest town: Salmon. GPS: 45.312093, -113.906675

24 • D1 | Little Gem Cycle Park

Dispersed sites, No water, No toilets, Tent & RV camping: Free, Reservations not accepted, Elevation: 2776ft/846m, Telephone: 208-384-3300. Nearest town: Emmett. GPS: 43.855286, -116.442303

25 • D1 | Steck Park

Total sites: 46, RV sites: 41, Central water, Vault/pit toilet, No showers, RV dump, Tents: $5/RVs: $8, Open Apr-Oct, Reservations not accepted, Elevation: 2149ft/655m, Telephone: 208-384-3300. Nearest town: Weiser. GPS: 44.365407, -117.217822

26 • D1 | Weiser Sand Dunes OHV

Dispersed sites, No water, Vault/pit toilet, Tent & RV camping: Free, Reservations not accepted, Elevation: 2167ft/661m, Telephone: 208-384-3300. Nearest town: Weiser. GPS: 44.297578, -117.208388

27 • D2 | Bayhorse

Total sites: 11, RV sites: 11, Central water, Vault/pit toilet, No showers, No RV dump, Tent & RV camping: $10, Open all year, Reservations not accepted, Stay limit: 14 days, Elevation: 5262ft/1604m, Telephone: 208-879-6200. Nearest town: Challis. GPS: 44.385737, -114.261527

28 • D2 | Boulder White Clouds

Dispersed sites, No water, No toilets, Tent & RV camping: Free, Reservations not accepted, Elevation: 6425ft/1958m, Telephone: 208-879-6200. Nearest town: Challis. GPS: 44.027199, -114.465425

29 • D2 | Deadman Hole

Total sites: 5, RV sites: 5, Central water, Vault/pit toilet, Tent & RV camping: Free, Open all year, Reservations not accepted, Stay limit: 14 days, Elevation: 5233ft/1595m, Telephone: 208-879-6200. Nearest town: Challis. GPS: 44.344377, -114.269932

30 • D2 | East Fork

Total sites: 10, RV sites: 8, Central water, Vault/pit toilet, No showers, No RV dump, Tent & RV camping: $10, Reservations not accepted, Elevation: 5364ft/1635m, Telephone: 208-879-6200. Nearest town: Challis. GPS: 44.267397, -114.326676

31 • D2 | Garden Creek

Total sites: 5, RV sites: 5, No water, Vault/pit toilet, Tent & RV camping: Free, Open May-Oct, Reservations not accepted, Elevation: 6795ft/2071m, Telephone: 208-879-6200. Nearest town: Arco. GPS: 43.976459, -114.064557

32 • D2 | Herd Lake

Total sites: 1, RV sites: 0, No water, Vault/pit toilet, Tents only: Free, Open May-Oct, Reservations not accepted, Elevation: 6957ft/2120m, Telephone: 208-879-6200. Nearest town: Challis. GPS: 44.09489, -114.181694

33 • D2 | Herd Lake Overlook

Dispersed sites, No water, Vault/pit toilet, Tents only: Free, Reservations not accepted, Elevation: 7330ft/2234m. Nearest town: Challis. GPS: 44.092512, -114.175751

34 • D2 | Lake Creek TH

Dispersed sites, No water, No toilets, Tents only: Free, Reservations not accepted, Elevation: 6170ft/1881m, Telephone: 208-732-7200. GPS: 44.105738, -114.242884

35 • D2 | Little Boulder

Total sites: 3, RV sites: 3, Central water, Vault/pit toilet, No showers, No RV dump, Tent & RV camping: Free, Reservations not accepted, Stay limit: 14 days, Elevation: 6177ft/1883m, Telephone: 208-879-6200. Nearest town: Challis. GPS: 44.088561, -114.445017

36 • D2 | Lower Herd Creek TH

Dispersed sites, No water, No toilets, Tent & RV camping: Free, Reservations not accepted, Elevation: 5795ft/1766m. Nearest town: Challis. GPS: 44.150721, -114.296288

37 • D2 | Magic Reservoir – Lava Cove

Dispersed sites, No water, Tent & RV camping: Free, Reservations not accepted, Stay limit: 14 days, Elevation: 4807ft/1465m. Nearest town: Fairfield. GPS: 43.289604, -114.397215

38 • D2 | Magic Reservoir – Lava Creek

Total sites: 9, RV sites: 9, No water, Vault/pit toilet, Tent & RV camping: Free, Reservations not accepted, Stay limit: 14 days, Elevation: 4808ft/1465m, Telephone: 208-732-7200. Nearest town: Fairfield. GPS: 43.290437, -114.389114

39 • D2 | Magic Reservoir – Magic Dam

Dispersed sites, No water, Tent & RV camping: Free, Reservations not accepted, Stay limit: 14 days, Elevation: 4808ft/1465m. Nearest town: Fairfield. GPS: 43.256588, -114.353426

40 • D2 | Magic Reservoir – Moonstone Access

Dispersed sites, No water, Vault/pit toilet, Tent & RV camping: Free, Open all year, Reservations not accepted, Stay limit: 14 days, Elevation: 4816ft/1468m, Telephone: 208-334-3700. Nearest town: Fairfield. GPS: 43.335703, -114.432869

41 • D2 | Magic Reservoir – Myrtle Point

Total sites: 1, RV sites: 1, No water, Vault/pit toilet, Tent & RV camping: Free, Reservations not accepted, Stay limit: 14 days, Elevation: 4784ft/1458m, Telephone: 208-732-7200. Nearest town: Fairfield. GPS: 43.266233, -114.377155

42 • D2 | Magic Reservoir – Richfield Diversion

Dispersed sites, No water, Tent & RV camping: Free, Reservations not accepted, Stay limit: 14 days, Elevation: 4690ft/1430m. Nearest town: Fairfield. GPS: 43.220653, -114.357019

43 • D2 | Malm Gulch TH

Dispersed sites, No water, No toilets, Tents only: Free, Reservations not accepted, Elevation: 5473ft/1668m. Nearest town: Challis. GPS: 44.352016, -114.250023

44 • D2 | Silver Creek North

Total sites: 1, RV sites: 1, No water, Vault/pit toilet, Tent & RV camping: Free, Open Apr-Nov, Reservations not accepted, Elevation: 4722ft/1439m, Telephone: 208-732-7200. Nearest town: Carey. GPS: 43.250552, -113.996463

45 • D2 | Silver Creek South

Total sites: 2, RV sites: 2, No water, Vault/pit toilet, Tent & RV camping: Free, Open Apr-Nov, Reservations not accepted, Elevation: 4706ft/1434m, Telephone: 208-732-7200. Nearest town: Carey. GPS: 43.245947, -113.995983

46 • D2 | South Fork Payette River

Dispersed sites, No water, No toilets, Tent & RV camping: $3, Reservations not accepted, Elevation: 3090ft/942m, Telephone: 208-384-3300. Nearest town: Garden Valley. GPS: 44.06675, -115.939983

47 • D2 | Thorn Creek Reservoir

Dispersed sites, No water, Vault/pit toilet, Tent & RV camping: Free, Reservations not accepted, Elevation: 5532ft/1686m, Telephone: 208-732-7200. Nearest town: Shoshone. GPS: 43.192772, -114.595757

48 • D3 | Birch Creek

Total sites: 25, RV sites: 25, Central water, Vault/pit toilet, Tent & RV camping: Donation, 4 group sites: $35, Open May-Nov, Reservations not accepted, Elevation: 6023ft/1836m, Telephone: 208-524-7500. Nearest town: Mud Lake. GPS: 44.139206, -112.899933

49 • D3 | Fish Creek Reservoir

Total sites: 1, RV sites: 1, No water, Vault/pit toilet, Tent & RV camping: Free, Stay limit: 14 days, Elevation: 5338ft/1627m, Telephone: 208-732-7200. Nearest town: Carey. GPS: 43.432048, -113.824136

50 • D3 | Joseph T. Fallini (McKay Reservoir)

Total sites: 26, RV sites: 22, Electric sites: 22, Water at site, Vault/pit toilet, No showers, RV dump, Tents: $6/RVs: $10-14, Reservations not accepted, Stay limit: 14 days, Elevation: 6109ft/1862m, Telephone: 208-756-5400. Nearest town: Challis. GPS: 43.960361, -113.679859

51 • D3 | Pass Creek

Dispersed sites, No water, No toilets, Tent & RV camping: Free, Reservations not accepted, Elevation: 6869ft/2094m. Nearest town: Mackay. GPS: 44.066308, -113.421645

52 • D3 | Summit Creek

Total sites: 7, RV sites: 7, No water, Vault/pit toilet, Tent & RV camping: Free, Open May-Oct, Reservations not accepted, Elevation: 6414ft/1955m, Telephone: 208-879-6200. Nearest town: Howe. GPS: 44.272368, -113.449167

53 • D4 | Henrys Lake South Shore Access

Dispersed sites, No water, Vault/pit toilet, Tent & RV camping: Free, Reservations not accepted, Elevation: 6492ft/1979m, Telephone: 208-524-7500. Nearest town: Island Park. GPS: 44.615644, -111.417305

54 • D4 | Kelly's Island

Total sites: 14, RV sites: 14, Central water, Vault/pit toilet, No showers, No RV dump, Tent & RV camping: $10, 1 reservable group site, Open May-Sep, Reservations not accepted, Elevation: 5026ft/1532m, Telephone: 208-524-7500. Nearest town: Idaho Falls. GPS: 43.623848, -111.663093

55 • D4 | St Anthony Dunes – Egin Lakes

Total sites: 48, RV sites: 48, Electric sites: 48, Central water, Flush toilet, No showers, RV dump, Tents: $12/RVs: $12-30, $10 dump fee, Generator hours: 0700-2300, Open May-Oct, Reservations not accepted, Elevation: 4889ft/1490m, Telephone: 208-524-7500. Nearest town: Rexburg. GPS: 43.962303, -111.853353

56 • D4 | St Anthony Dunes – Red Road

Dispersed sites, No water, Vault/pit toilet, Tent & RV camping: Free, Generator hours: 0700-2300, Reservations not accepted, Elevation: 5015ft/1529m, Telephone: 208-524-7500. Nearest town: Rexburg. GPS: 44.015367, -111.788165

57 • D4 | Trail Creek Bridge

Total sites: 6, RV sites: 6, No water, Vault/pit toilet, Tent & RV camping: Free, Reservations not accepted, Elevation: 5568ft/1697m, Telephone: 208-478-6340. Nearest town: Pocatello. GPS: 43.131645, -111.912332

58 • D4 | Wolf Flats

Dispersed sites, No water, Vault/pit toilet, Tent & RV camping: Free, 25 dispersed sites, Reservations not accepted, Stay limit: 14 days, Elevation: 5065ft/1544m, Telephone: 208-524-7500. Nearest town: Idaho Falls. GPS: 43.598867, -111.610709

59 • D4 | Wolverine Canyon

Dispersed sites, No water, No toilets, Tent & RV camping: Free, Reservations not accepted, Elevation: 5399ft/1646m. Nearest town: Shelley. GPS: 43.279763, -111.958033

60 • E1 | Cove

Total sites: 23, RV sites: 23, Central water, Vault/pit toilet, No showers, No RV dump, Tents: $5/RVs: $12, Reservations not accepted, Stay limit: 14 days, Elevation: 2457ft/749m, Telephone: 208-384-3300. Nearest town: Bruneau. GPS: 42.936713, -115.949546

61 • E1 | North Fork Owyhee River

Total sites: 5, RV sites: 5, No toilets, Tent & RV camping: Free, Elevation: 4836ft/1474m, Telephone: 208-384-3300. Nearest town: Triangle. GPS: 42.59256, -116.98166

62 • E1 | Poison Creek

Total sites: 4, RV sites: 1, No water, Vault/pit toilet, Tent & RV camping: Free, Reservations not accepted, Elevation: 4483ft/1366m, Telephone: 208-384-3300. Nearest town: Bruneau. GPS: 42.757332, -116.297255

63 • E1 | Silver City

Total sites: 6, RV sites: 6, No water, Vault/pit toilet, Tent & RV camping: Free, No road access in winter, Contaminated water, Open May-Nov, Reservations not accepted, Elevation: 6225ft/1897m, Telephone: 208-896-5912. Nearest town: Murphy. GPS: 43.015331, -116.731049

64 • E2 | Big Cottonwood

Total sites: 2, RV sites: 2, No water, Vault/pit toilet, Tent & RV camping: Free, Reservations not accepted, Elevation: 5138ft/1566m, Telephone: 208-735-2060. Nearest town: Murphy Hot Springs. GPS: 42.031336, -115.367297

65 • E2 | Big Cottonwood Creek TH

Total sites: 3, RV sites: 3, No water, No toilets, Tent & RV camping: Free, Nothing larger than van/pu, Reservations not accepted, Elevation: 4728ft/1441m. Nearest town: Oakley. GPS: 42.301754, -114.020561

66 • E2 | Cedar Creek Reservoir

Dispersed sites, No water, No toilets, Tent & RV camping: Free, Reservations not accepted, Elevation: 5255ft/1602m, Telephone: 208-735-2060. Nearest town: Rogerson. GPS: 42.198674, -114.903865

67 • E2 | Juniper Grove

Total sites: 3, RV sites: 3, No water, Vault/pit toilet, No showers, No RV dump, Tent & RV camping: Free, Reservations not accepted, Stay limit: 14 days, Elevation: 5102ft/1555m, Telephone: 208-735-2060. Nearest town: Murphy Hot Springs. GPS: 42.035844, -115.372798

68 • E2 | Lud Drexler

Total sites: 20, RV sites: 20, Central water, Vault/pit toilet, No showers, RV dump, Tent & RV camping: $5, Open all year, Reservations not accepted, Stay limit: 14 days, Elevation: 5046ft/1538m, Telephone: 208-677-6664. Nearest town: Rogerson. GPS: 42.210995, -114.730424

69 • E2 | The Forks

Total sites: 4, RV sites: 4, No water, No toilets, Tent & RV camping: Free, Reservations not accepted, Stay limit: 14 days, Elevation: 5997ft/1828m, Telephone: 208-735-2060. Nearest town: Murphy Hot Springs. GPS: 42.049133, -115.390358

70 • E3 | Goodenough Creek

Total sites: 13, RV sites: 13, No water, Vault/pit toilet, Tent & RV camping: Free, Open May-Nov, Reservations not accepted, Elevation: 5517ft/1682m, Telephone: 208-478-6340. Nearest town: McCammon. GPS: 42.654382, -112.285813

71 • E3 | Hawkins Reservoir

Total sites: 10, RV sites: 10, No water, Vault/pit toilet, Tent & RV camping: Free, Open May-Oct, Reservations not accepted, Stay limit: 14 days, Elevation: 5223ft/1592m, Telephone: 208-373-4000. Nearest town: Virginia. GPS: 42.512699, -112.332738

72 • E3 | McClendon Spring

Dispersed sites, No water, Vault/pit toilet, Tent & RV camping: Free, Reservations not accepted, Stay limit: 14 days, Elevation: 4839ft/1475m, Telephone: 208-677-6600. Nearest town: Albion. GPS: 42.335987, -113.407394

73 • E3 | Milner Reservoir #1

Total sites: 6, RV sites: 6, Vault/pit toilet, Tent & RV camping: $5, Reservations not accepted, Elevation: 4131ft/1259m, Telephone: 208-677-6600. Nearest town: Murtaugh. GPS: 42.525305, -114.004987

74 • E3 | Milner Reservoir #2

Total sites: 5, RV sites: 5, No water, Vault/pit toilet, Tent & RV camping: $5, Reservations not accepted, Elevation: 4160ft/1268m, Telephone: 208-677-6600. Nearest town: Murtaugh. GPS: 42.529573, -113.990865

75 • E3 | Milner Reservoir #3

Total sites: 3, RV sites: 3, No water, Vault/pit toilet, Tent & RV camping: $5, Reservations not accepted, Elevation: 4142ft/1262m, Telephone: 208-677-6600. Nearest town: Murtaugh. GPS: 42.530938, -113.959969

76 • E3 | Milner Reservoir #4

Total sites: 1, RV sites: 0, No water, No toilets, Tents only: $5, Reservations not accepted, Elevation: 4144ft/1263m, Telephone: 208-677-6600. Nearest town: Murtaugh. GPS: 42.532121, -113.940645

77 • E3 | Pipeline

Total sites: 8, RV sites: 8, No water, Vault/pit toilet, Tent & RV camping: Free, Reservations not accepted, Elevation: 4268ft/1301m, Telephone: 208-478-6340. Nearest town: American Falls. GPS: 42.741446, -112.899545

78 • E3 | Snake River Vista

Total sites: 2, RV sites: 2, No water, No toilets, Tent & RV camping: Free, Reservations not accepted, Elevation: 4319ft/1316m, Telephone: 208-677-6600. Nearest town: American Falls. GPS: 42.708672, -112.945489

79 • E4 | Blackfoot Reservoir

Total sites: 28, RV sites: 16, Electric sites: 16, Central water, Vault/pit toilet, No showers, RV dump, Tents: $10/RVs: $15, Open May-Oct, Reservations not accepted, Elevation: 6129ft/1868m, Telephone: 208-478-6340. Nearest town: Soda Springs. GPS: 42.843792, -111.603963

80 • E4 | Cutthroat Trout

Total sites: 3, RV sites: 3, No water, Vault/pit toilet, Tent & RV camping: Free, Reservations not accepted, Stay limit: 14 days, Elevation: 5876ft/1791m, Telephone: 208-478-6340. Nearest town: Pocatello. GPS: 43.039654, -111.856104

81 • E4 | Graves Creek

Total sites: 5, RV sites: 5, No water, Vault/pit toilet, Tent & RV camping: Free, Reservations not accepted, Elevation: 5833ft/1778m, Telephone: 208-478-6340. Nearest town: Blackfoot. GPS: 43.043836, -111.911149

82 • E4 | Heart Mountain Springs

Total sites: 4, RV sites: 4, No water, No toilets, Tent & RV camping: Free, Reservations not accepted, Stay limit: 14 days, Elevation: 5279ft/1609m, Telephone: 208-478-6340. Nearest town: Swanlake. GPS: 42.322448, -111.946742

83 • E4 | Maple Grove

Total sites: 12, RV sites: 12, No water, Vault/pit toilet, Tent & RV camping: $5, Reservations not accepted, Stay limit: 14 days, Elevation: 4903ft/1494m, Telephone: 208-478-6340. Nearest town: Preston. GPS: 42.284717, -111.731552

84 • E4 | Morgans Bridge

Total sites: 12, RV sites: 10, No water, Vault/pit toilet, Tent & RV camping: Free, Also walk-to sites, Open May-Oct, Reservations not accepted, Stay limit: 14 days, Elevation: 5820ft/1774m, Telephone: 208-478-6340. Nearest town: Soda Springs. GPS: 43.058103, -111.923338

85 • E4 | Redpoint

Total sites: 10, RV sites: 10, No water, Vault/pit toilet, Tent & RV camping: $5, Reservations not accepted, Stay limit: 14 days, Elevation: 4699ft/1432m, Telephone: 208-478-6340. Nearest town: Preston. GPS: 42.233971, -111.759086

86 • E4 | Sage Hen Flats

Total sites: 5, RV sites: 5, No water, Vault/pit toilet, Tent & RV camping: Free, Elevation: 5909ft/1801m, Telephone: 208-478-6340. Nearest town: Soda Springs. GPS: 43.020141, -111.826438

Montana

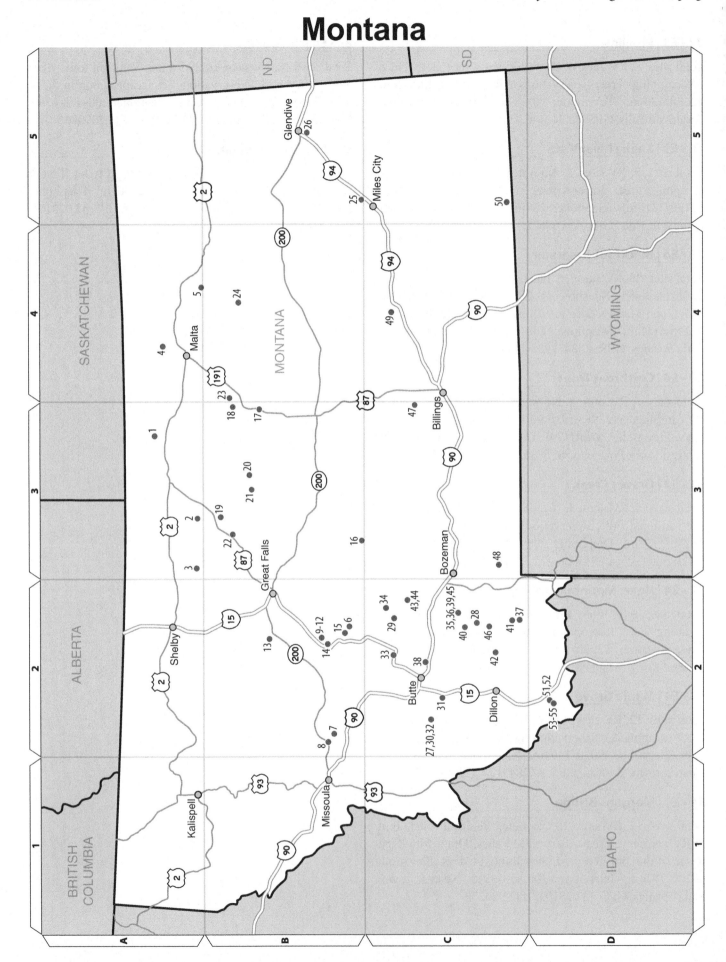

Montana

Montana/Dakotas State Office
5001 Southgate Dr
Billings MT 59101

Phone: 406-896-5004

Name	ID	Map	RVs	Tents	Free
Acton	47	C3	✓	✓	✓
Bair Reservoir Dispersed	16	B3	✓	✓	✓
Big Sheep Creek Dispersed 1	51	D2	✓	✓	✓
Big Sheep Creek Dispersed 2	52	D2	✓	✓	✓
Big Sheep Creek Dispersed 3	53	D2		✓	✓
Big Sheep Creek Dispersed 4	54	D2	✓	✓	✓
BR-12 Prairie Marsh	1	A3	✓	✓	✓
Bryant Creek	27	C2	✓	✓	✓
Camp Creek	23	B4	✓	✓	
Carbella	48	C3	✓	✓	✓
Clute's Landing	28	C2	✓		✓
Cottonwood Rec Area	4	A4	✓	✓	✓
Crow Creek	29	C2	✓	✓	✓
Deadwood Gulch	55	D2	✓	✓	✓
Devils Elbow	6	B2	✓	✓	
Dickie Bridge	30	C2	✓	✓	✓
Divide Bridge	31	C2	✓	✓	
East Bank	32	C2	✓	✓	✓
Galena Gulch	33	C2	✓	✓	✓
Garnet Ghost Town Dispersed	7	B2	✓	✓	✓
Garnet Rd	8	B2	✓	✓	✓
Holter Lake – Departure Point	9	B2	✓	✓	
Holter Lake – Holter Dam	10	B2	✓	✓	
Holter Lake – Holter Lake	11	B2	✓	✓	
Holter Lake – Log Gulch	12	B2	✓	✓	
Indian Road	34	C2	✓	✓	
James Kipp	17	B3	✓	✓	
Lonesome Lake Watchable Wildlife Area	2	A3		✓	✓
Lower Madison #1	35	C2	✓	✓	
Lower Madison #2	36	C2	✓	✓	
Lowry Bridge	13	B2	✓	✓	✓
Mathews Rec Area	25	B5	✓	✓	✓
Moffat Bridge Rec Area	3	A3	✓	✓	✓

Name	ID	Map	RVs	Tents	Free
Montana Gulch	18	B3	✓	✓	
Moorhead Recreation Site	50	C5	✓	✓	✓
Myers Bridge/Howrey Island	49	C4	✓	✓	✓
Palisades	37	C2	✓	✓	
Paulo Reservoir	5	A4	✓	✓	✓
Pipestone TMA Dispersed	38	C2	✓	✓	✓
Red Mountain	39	C2	✓	✓	
Revenue Flats	40	C2	✓	✓	✓
Ruby Creek	41	C2	✓	✓	
Ruby Reservoir	42	C2	✓	✓	
Short Pine ORV Area	26	B5	✓	✓	✓
Sleeping Giant WSA	14	B2		✓	✓
Toston Dam Lower	43	C2	✓	✓	✓
Toston Dam Upper	44	C2	✓	✓	✓
Trapper Springs	45	C2	✓	✓	
Troika Reservoir	24	B4	✓	✓	✓
Upper Missouri River Breaks NM – Coal Banks Landing	19	B3	✓	✓	
Upper Missouri River Breaks NM – Judith Landing	20	B3	✓	✓	
Upper Missouri River Breaks NM – Slaughter River	21	B3		✓	✓
Upper Missouri River Breaks NM – Wood Bottom	22	B3	✓	✓	✓
West Madison	46	C2	✓	✓	
White Sandy	15	B2	✓	✓	

1 • A3 | BR-12 Prairie Marsh

Dispersed sites, No water, No toilets, Tent & RV camping: Free, Reservations not accepted, Elevation: 2727ft/831m, Telephone: 406-262-2820. Nearest town: Zurich. GPS: 48.701212, -109.039178

2 • A3 | Lonesome Lake Watchable Wildlife Area

Dispersed sites, No water, Tents only: Free, 4x4 recommended, Elevation: 2772ft/845m, Telephone: 406-262-2820. Nearest town: Big Sandy. GPS: 48.268446, -110.264508

3 • A3 | Moffat Bridge Rec Area

Dispersed sites, No water, Vault/pit toilet, Tent & RV camping: Free, 3-night limit, Open Apr-Aug, Reservations not accepted, Elevation: 2791ft/851m, Telephone: 406-262-2820. Nearest town: Chester. GPS: 48.265736, -110.993152

4 • A4 | Cottonwood Rec Area

Dispersed sites, No water, Vault/pit toilet, Tent & RV camping: Free, Open all year, Reservations not accepted, Elevation: 2205ft/672m, Telephone: 406-654-5100. Nearest town: Malta. GPS: 48.584176, -107.718963

5 • A4 | Paulo Reservoir

Dispersed sites, No water, Vault/pit toilet, Tent & RV camping: Free, Open all year, Reservations not accepted, Elevation: 2240ft/683m, Telephone: 406-228-3750. Nearest town: Glasgow. GPS: 48.171759, -106.870985

6 • B2 | Devils Elbow

Total sites: 42, RV sites: 42, Central water, No toilets, No showers, No RV dump, Tent & RV camping: $15, Open all year, Reservations not accepted, Stay limit: 14 days, Elevation: 3661ft/1116m, Telephone: 406-227-3570. Nearest town: Helena. GPS: 46.699981, -111.805066

7 • B2 | Garnet Ghost Town Dispersed

Dispersed sites, Central water, Vault/pit toilet, No showers, No RV dump, Tent & RV camping: Free, No camping within 1/2 mile of town, Reservations not accepted, Elevation: 6040ft/1841m, Telephone: 406-329-3914. Nearest town: Missoula. GPS: 46.824674, -113.335168

8 • B2 | Garnet Rd

Dispersed sites, No water, No toilets, Tent & RV camping: Free, Elevation: 4166ft/1270m. Nearest town: Missoula. GPS: 46.885031, -113.463337

9 • B2 | Holter Lake – Departure Point

Total sites: 6, RV sites: 6, Central water, Vault/pit toilet, No showers, No RV dump, Tent & RV camping: $15, Free mid-Oct through Apr, Open all year, Reservations not accepted, Stay limit: 14 days, Elevation: 3668ft/1118m, Telephone: 406-533-7600. Nearest town: Holter Lake. GPS: 46.955977, -111.940271

10 • B2 | Holter Lake – Holter Dam

Total sites: 15, RV sites: 15, Central water, Vault/pit toilet, No showers, No RV dump, Tent & RV camping: $15, Open all year, Reservations not accepted, Elevation: 3455ft/1053m, Telephone: 406-533-7600. Nearest town: Helena. GPS: 46.994279, -112.011409

11 • B2 | Holter Lake – Holter Lake

Total sites: 50, RV sites: 50, Central water, Vault/pit toilet, No showers, No RV dump, Tent & RV camping: $15, Reservations not accepted, Stay limit: 14 days, Elevation: 3638ft/1109m, Telephone: 406-533-7600. Nearest town: Helena. GPS: 46.992826, -111.988889

12 • B2 | Holter Lake – Log Gulch

Total sites: 72, RV sites: 70, Central water, Vault/pit toilet, No showers, No RV dump, Tent & RV camping: $15, Generator hours: 0700-2200, Reservations not accepted, Stay limit: 7 days, Elevation: 3645ft/1111m, Telephone: 406-533-7600. Nearest town: Helena. GPS: 46.962608, -111.941963

13 • B2 | Lowry Bridge

Total sites: 5, RV sites: 5, No water, Vault/pit toilet, No showers, No RV dump, Tent & RV camping: Free, Reservations not accepted, Elevation: 3628ft/1106m, Telephone: 406-538-1900. Nearest town: Simms. GPS: 47.513135, -112.007986

14 • B2 | Sleeping Giant WSA

Dispersed sites, No water, No toilets, Tents only: Free, Open Jun-Nov, Elevation: 6332ft/1930m, Telephone: 406-533-7600. Nearest town: Helena. GPS: 46.925873, -112.069046

15 • B2 | White Sandy

Total sites: 32, RV sites: 32, Central water, Vault/pit toilet, No showers, No RV dump, Tent & RV camping: $15, Group site: $140, Generator hours: 0700-2200, Reservations not accepted, Elevation: 3681ft/1122m, Telephone: 406-458-4744. Nearest town: Helena. GPS: 46.740387, -111.888515

16 • B3 | Bair Reservoir Dispersed

Dispersed sites, No water, Vault/pit toilet, Tent & RV camping: Free, Reservations not accepted, Elevation: 5338ft/1627m. Nearest town: White Sulphur Springs. GPS: 46.581875, -110.569018

17 • B3 | James Kipp

Total sites: 34, RV sites: 34, Central water, Vault/pit toilet, No showers, RV dump, Tent & RV camping: $12, Dump fee $10, No water Nov-Apr, Open Apr-Nov, Reservations not accepted, Stay limit: 14 days, Elevation: 2274ft/693m, Telephone: 406-538-1900. Nearest town: Roy. GPS: 47.625749, -108.681763

18 • B3 | Montana Gulch

Total sites: 10, RV sites: 10, No water, Vault/pit toilet, No showers, No RV dump, Tent & RV camping: $8, Open all year, Reservations not accepted, Stay limit: 14 days, Elevation: 4029ft/1228m, Telephone: 406-654-5100. Nearest town: Landusky. GPS: 47.898193, -108.632568

19 • B3 | Upper Missouri River Breaks NM – Coal Banks Landing

Total sites: 13, RV sites: 13, Central water, Vault/pit toilet, Tent & RV camping: $10, No water Nov - Apr, Open all year, Reservations not accepted, Stay limit: 14 days, Elevation: 2536ft/773m, Telephone: 406-622-4000. Nearest town: Fort Benton. GPS: 48.031638, -110.237488

20 • B3 | Upper Missouri River Breaks NM – Judith Landing

Total sites: 8, RV sites: 8, Central water, Vault/pit toilet, No showers, No RV dump, Tent & RV camping: $5, Open May-Oct, Reservations not accepted, Elevation: 2434ft/742m, Telephone: 406-622-4000. Nearest town: Winifred. GPS: 47.740531, -109.629016

21 • B3 | Upper Missouri River Breaks NM – Slaughter River

Dispersed sites, No water, Vault/pit toilet, Tents only: Free, Also boat-in sites, Reservations not accepted, Elevation: 2441ft/744m, Telephone: 406-622-4000. GPS: 47.717212, -109.848774

22 • B3 | Upper Missouri River Breaks NM – Wood Bottom

Total sites: 4, RV sites: 4, No water, Vault/pit toilet, Tent & RV camping: Free, Open all year, Elevation: 2562ft/781m, Telephone: 406-622-4000. Nearest town: Loma. GPS: 47.911308, -110.493271

23 • B4 | Camp Creek

Total sites: 20, RV sites: 20, Central water, Vault/pit toilet, No showers, No RV dump, Tent & RV camping: $10, Open all year, Reservations not accepted, Elevation: 4078ft/1243m, Telephone: 406-654-5100. Nearest town: Malta. GPS: 47.924935, -108.503594

24 • B4 | Troika Reservoir

Dispersed sites, No water, Vault/pit toilet, Tent & RV camping: Free, Open all year, Reservations not accepted, Elevation: 2545ft/776m, Telephone: 406-228-3750. Nearest town: Glasgow. GPS: 47.811969, -107.123725

25 • B5 | Mathews Rec Area

Dispersed sites, No water, Vault/pit toilet, Tent & RV camping: Free, Beside RR, Open all year, Elevation: 2322ft/708m, Telephone: 406-233-2800. Nearest town: Miles City. GPS: 46.501486, -105.734547

26 • B5 | Short Pine ORV Area

Dispersed sites, No water, No toilets, Tent & RV camping: Free, Open all year, Elevation: 2146ft/654m, Telephone: 406-233-2831. Nearest town: Glendive. GPS: 47.017726, -104.726687

27 • C2 | Bryant Creek

Dispersed sites, No water, No toilets, Tent & RV camping: Free, Elevation: 5759ft/1755m, Telephone: 406-533-7600. Nearest town: Wise River. GPS: 45.858436, -113.085386

28 • C2 | Clute's Landing

Total sites: 2, RV sites: 2, No water, Vault/pit toilet, No tents/RVs: Free, Reservations not accepted, Stay limit: 14 days, Elevation: 4891ft/1491m, Telephone: 406-683-8000. Nearest town: Ennis. GPS: 45.420583, -111.712083

29 • C2 | Crow Creek

Total sites: 8, RV sites: 8, No water, Vault/pit toilet, Tent & RV camping: Free, Open all year, Reservations not accepted, Stay limit: 14 days, Elevation: 4741ft/1445m, Telephone: 406-533-7600. Nearest town: Radersburg. GPS: 46.250852, -111.673494

30 • C2 | Dickie Bridge

Total sites: 10, RV sites: 10, No water, Vault/pit toilet, Tent & RV camping: Free, Open all year, Reservations not accepted, Elevation: 5722ft/1744m, Telephone: 406-533-7600. Nearest town: Divide. GPS: 45.849751, -113.068533

31 • C2 | Divide Bridge

Total sites: 21, RV sites: 21, Central water, Vault/pit toilet, No showers, No RV dump, Tent & RV camping: $10, Open all year, Reservations not accepted, Elevation: 5407ft/1648m, Telephone: 406-533-7600. Nearest town: Divide. GPS: 45.753282, -112.774363

32 • C2 | East Bank

Total sites: 9, RV sites: 9, No water, Vault/pit toilet, Tent & RV camping: Free, Open all year, Reservations not accepted, Elevation: 5751ft/1753m, Telephone: 406-533-7600. Nearest town: Wise River. GPS: 45.856963, -113.083996

33 • C2 | Galena Gulch

Total sites: 9, RV sites: 9, Central water, Vault/pit toilet, No showers, No RV dump, Tent & RV camping: Free, Open all year, Elevation: 5062ft/1543m, Telephone: 406-533-7600. Nearest town: Basin. GPS: 46.254304, -112.183717

34 • C2 | Indian Road

Total sites: 25, RV sites: 25, Central water, Vault/pit toilet, No showers, No RV dump, Tent & RV camping: Fee unk, Elevation: 3809ft/1161m, Telephone: 406-475-3921. Nearest town: Townsend. GPS: 46.334023, -111.528155

35 • C2 | Lower Madison #1

Dispersed sites, No water, No toilets, Tent & RV camping: $8, Reservations not accepted, Elevation: 4458ft/1359m. GPS: 45.609383, -111.574459

36 • C2 | Lower Madison #2

Dispersed sites, No water, No toilets, Tent & RV camping: $8, Reservations not accepted, Elevation: 4457ft/1358m. GPS: 45.612904, -111.571678

37 • C2 | Palisades

Total sites: 10, RV sites: 10, Central water, Vault/pit toilet, No showers, No RV dump, Tent & RV camping: $8, Reservations not accepted, Elevation: 5668ft/1728m, Telephone: 406-683-8000. Nearest town: Ennis. GPS: 44.996378, -111.659796

38 • C2 | Pipestone TMA Dispersed

Dispersed sites, No water, No toilets, Tent & RV camping: Free, Open all year, Reservations not accepted, Stay limit: 14 days, Elevation: 5064ft/1544m, Telephone: 406-533-7600. Nearest town: Butte. GPS: 45.923158, -112.269821

39 • C2 | Red Mountain

Total sites: 19, RV sites: 19, Central water, Vault/pit toilet, No showers, No RV dump, Tent & RV camping: $12, Open May-Sep, Reservations accepted, Elevation: 4492ft/1369m, Telephone: 406-682-4082. Nearest town: Bozeman. GPS: 45.61131, -111.56887

40 • C2 | Revenue Flats

Dispersed sites, No water, Vault/pit toilet, Tent & RV camping: Free, Open all year, Reservations not accepted, Elevation: 5592ft/1704m, Telephone: 406-683-8000. Nearest town: Ennis. GPS: 45.544456, -111.770983

41 • C2 | Ruby Creek

Total sites: 22, RV sites: 22, Central water, Vault/pit toilet, No showers, No RV dump, Tent & RV camping: $8, Open May-Nov, Reservations not accepted, Elevation: 5536ft/1687m, Telephone: 406-683-8000. Nearest town: Ennis. GPS: 45.059988, -111.665468

42 • C2 | Ruby Reservoir

Dispersed sites, No water, Vault/pit toilet, Tent & RV camping: Free, Open all year, Reservations not accepted, Elevation: 5407ft/1648m, Telephone: 406-683-8000. Nearest town: Alder. GPS: 45.225556, -112.119413

43 • C2 | Toston Dam Lower

Total sites: 2, RV sites: 2, No water, Vault/pit toilet, Tent & RV camping: Free, Open all year, Reservations not accepted, Elevation: 3934ft/1199m, Telephone: 406-533-7600. Nearest town: Toston. GPS: 46.121894, -111.398164

44 • C2 | Toston Dam Upper

Total sites: 6, RV sites: 6, No water, Vault/pit toilet, Tent & RV camping: Free, Open all year, Reservations not accepted, Elevation: 3999ft/1219m, Telephone: 406-533-7600. Nearest town: Townsend. GPS: 46.121805, -111.409029

45 • C2 | Trapper Springs

Total sites: 15, RV sites: 15, Central water, Vault/pit toilet, No showers, No RV dump, Tent & RV camping: $12, Primarily for groups, Open all year, Reservations accepted, Elevation: 4480ft/1366m, Telephone: 406-683-8000. Nearest town: Norris. GPS: 45.605268, -111.570631

46 • C2 | West Madison

Total sites: 22, RV sites: 22, No water, Vault/pit toilet, Tent & RV camping: $4, Open all year, Reservations not accepted, Elevation: 5046ft/1538m, Telephone: 406-683-8000. Nearest town: Ennis. GPS: 45.298899, -111.755485

47 • C3 | Acton

Dispersed sites, No water, No toilets, Tent & RV camping: Free, Open all year, Reservations not accepted, Stay limit: 14 days, Elevation: 3949ft/1204m, Telephone: 406-896-5013. Nearest town: Billings. GPS: 46.044301, -108.663791

48 • C3 | Carbella

Total sites: 10, RV sites: 10, No water, Vault/pit toilet, Tent & RV camping: Free, Open all year, Reservations not accepted, Stay limit: 14 days, Elevation: 4987ft/1520m, Telephone: 406-533-7600. Nearest town: Gardiner. GPS: 45.212653, -110.900373

49 • C4 | Myers Bridge/Howrey Island

Total sites: 5, RV sites: 5, No water, Vault/pit toilet, No showers, No RV dump, Tent & RV camping: Free, Open all year, Reservations not accepted, Stay limit: 7 days, Elevation: 2658ft/810m, Telephone: 406-233-2800. Nearest town: Hysham. GPS: 46.254517, -107.342234

50 • C5 | Moorhead Recreation Site

Total sites: 8, RV sites: 8, No water, Vault/pit toilet, Tent & RV camping: Free, Reservations not accepted, Stay limit: 14

days, Elevation: 3362ft/1025m, Telephone: 406-233-2800. Nearest town: Broadus. GPS: 45.055143, -105.878317

51 • D2 | Big Sheep Creek Dispersed 1

Dispersed sites, No water, No toilets, Tent & RV camping: Free, Reservations not accepted, Stay limit: 14 days, Elevation: 6293ft/1918m. Nearest town: Dell. GPS: 44.668976, -112.755566

52 • D2 | Big Sheep Creek Dispersed 2

Dispersed sites, No water, No toilets, Tent & RV camping: Free, Reservations not accepted, Stay limit: 14 days, Elevation: 6369ft/1941m. Nearest town: Dell. GPS: 44.660439, -112.769189

53 • D2 | Big Sheep Creek Dispersed 3

Dispersed sites, No water, No toilets, Tents only: Free, Reservations not accepted, Stay limit: 14 days, Elevation: 6454ft/1967m. Nearest town: Dell. GPS: 44.636578, -112.794711

54 • D2 | Big Sheep Creek Dispersed 4

Dispersed sites, No water, No toilets, Tent & RV camping: Free, Reservations not accepted, Stay limit: 14 days, Elevation: 6515ft/1986m. Nearest town: Dell. GPS: 44.612042, -112.801989

55 • D2 | Deadwood Gulch

Total sites: 3, RV sites: 3, No water, Vault/pit toilet, Tent & RV camping: Free, Open May-Oct, Stay limit: 14 days, Elevation: 6312ft/1924m, Telephone: 406-683-8000. Nearest town: Dell. GPS: 44.663825, -112.761742

Nevada

UTAH

NEVADA

CALIFORNIA

ARIZONA

Reno

Winnemucca

Wells

Ely

Tonopah

Las Vegas

140

95

93

80

93

93

50

50

95

6

93

95

6

95

93

15

95

Nevada

Nevada State Office
1340 Financial Blvd
Reno NV 89502

Phone: 775-861-6500

Name	ID	Map	RVs	Tents	Free
Battle Mountain Dispersed 1	41	B3	✓	✓	✓
Big Den Creek	38	B2	✓	✓	✓
Big Rocks North	75	D4	✓	✓	✓
Black Rock Desert NCA	1	A1	✓	✓	✓
Black Rock Desert NCA – Black Rock Hot Springs	2	A1	✓	✓	✓
Black Rock Desert NCA – Cassidy Mine	3	A1	✓	✓	✓
Black Rock Desert NCA – Double Hot Springs	4	A1	✓	✓	✓
Black Rock Desert NCA – Hidden Spring	5	A1	✓	✓	✓
Black Rock Desert NCA – High Rock Canyon 1	6	A1		✓	✓
Black Rock Desert NCA – High Rock Canyon 2	7	A1		✓	✓
Black Rock Desert NCA – Jackson Creek	20	A2	✓	✓	✓
Black Rock Desert NCA – Pole Canyon	8	A1		✓	✓
Black Rock Desert NCA – Soldier Meadow	9	A1	✓	✓	✓
Black Rock Desert NCA – Soldier Meadow Cabin	10	A1	✓	✓	✓
Black Rock Desert NCA – Stevens Camp	11	A1	✓	✓	✓
Black Rock Desert NCA – Stevens Primitive 1	12	A1		✓	✓
Black Rock Desert NCA – Stevens Primitive 2	13	A1		✓	✓
Black Rock Desert NCA Dispersed	14	A1		✓	✓
Black Rock NCA – High Rock Canyon 3 (Yellow Rock Garage)	15	A1	✓	✓	✓
Black Rock NCA – Trego Hot Springs	16	A1	✓	✓	✓
Blue Mass Scenic Area Dispersed	47	B4	✓	✓	✓
Bombo's Pond	72	D3	✓	✓	✓
Bonnie Claire Lakebed	70	D2	✓		✓
Boulder Reservoir	17	A1	✓	✓	✓

Name	ID	Map	RVs	Tents	Free
Bull Frog	73	D3	✓	✓	✓
Carlin Canyon	29	A3	✓		✓
Cement Plant Dispersed	74	D3	✓		✓
Chief Mountain South	76	D4	✓	✓	✓
Chief Mountain West	77	D4	✓	✓	✓
Cleve Creek	60	C4	✓	✓	✓
Crescent Sand Dunes OHV	51	C2	✓	✓	✓
Divine Springs	18	A1	✓	✓	✓
Dry Lake	95	E4	✓		✓
Dry Valley OHV Area	36	B1	✓		✓
Elko Dispersed 1	30	A3	✓	✓	✓
Ely Elk Viewing Area	61	C4	✓		✓
Gap Mountain	62	C4	✓	✓	✓
Garnet Hill Dispersed	48	B4	✓	✓	✓
Gold Butte Wash Dispersed	78	D4	✓	✓	✓
Goshute Canyon	49	B4	✓	✓	✓
Hickison Petroglyph	42	B3	✓	✓	✓
Hwy 95 Tonopah	52	C2	✓	✓	✓
I-80 Dispersed	33	A4	✓	✓	✓
Illipah Reservoir	43	B3	✓	✓	✓
Jean/Roach Dry Lakes	96	E4	✓	✓	✓
Knob Hill	97	E4		✓	✓
Lahontan Cutthroat Natural Area	21	A2	✓	✓	✓
Lee Hot Springs	53	C2	✓	✓	✓
Logan Trail Dispersed 01	79	D4	✓	✓	✓
Logan Trail Dispersed 02	80	D4	✓	✓	✓
Logan Trail Dispersed 03 and 04	81	D4	✓	✓	✓
Logan Trail Dispersed 05	82	D4	✓	✓	✓
Logan Trail Dispersed 06	83	D4		✓	✓
Logan Trail Dispersed 07 (Bassett)	84	D4	✓	✓	✓
Logan Trail Dispersed 08	85	D4	✓	✓	✓
Logan Trail Dispersed 09	86	D4		✓	✓
Logan Trail Dispersed 10	87	D4		✓	✓
Logan Trail Dispersed 11	88	D4		✓	✓
Logan Trail Dispersed 12	89	D4		✓	✓
Lunar Crater NNL	58	C3	✓	✓	✓
Massacre Ranch	19	A1	✓	✓	✓
Mathews Canyon Dam	90	D4	✓	✓	✓
McKinney Tanks Dispersed	59	C3	✓	✓	✓
Meadow Valley East	63	C4	✓		✓
Meadow Valley West	64	C4	✓	✓	✓

Name	ID	Map	RVs	Tents	Free
Mill Creek	44	B3	✓	✓	✓
North Wildhorse Rec Area	31	A3	✓	✓	
Pahroc Wash	65	C4	✓	✓	✓
Patterson Pass	66	C4	✓	✓	✓
Pine Canyon Dam	91	D4	✓	✓	✓
Pine Forest RMA – Knott Creek 1	22	A2		✓	✓
Pine Forest RMA – Knott Creek 2	23	A2		✓	✓
Pine Forest RMA – Onion Reservoir	24	A2	✓	✓	✓
Porter Spring	39	B2	✓	✓	✓
Red Rock Canyon	94	E3	✓	✓	
Route 267	71	D2	✓	✓	✓
Sacramento Pass Rec Area – The Pond	67	C4	✓	✓	✓
Sacramento Pass Rec Area – Upper TH	68	C4	✓	✓	✓
Salmon Falls Creek Rec Area	34	A4	✓	✓	✓
Sand Mountain	40	B2	✓	✓	
Sonoma Canyon	25	A2	✓	✓	✓
Spencer Hot Springs	45	B3	✓	✓	✓
Stampede	69	C4	✓	✓	✓
Tabor Creek	35	A4	✓	✓	
The Mugwumps	37	B1	✓	✓	✓
Tonopah US-6 East	54	C2	✓		✓
Valley of Fire Hwy Dispersed	92	D4	✓	✓	✓
Walker Lake – Sportsmans Beach	55	C2	✓	✓	
Walker Lake – Tamarack	56	C2	✓	✓	✓
Walker Lake – Twenty Mile Beach	57	C2	✓	✓	
Water Canyon	26	A2	✓	✓	✓
Whitney Pocket	93	D4	✓	✓	✓
Wilson Canyon	50	C1	✓	✓	✓
Wilson Reservoir	32	A3	✓	✓	
Winnemucca Sand Dunes	27	A2	✓	✓	✓
Winnemucca Sand Dunes – Sand Pass	28	A2	✓	✓	✓
Zunino/Jiggs Reservoir	46	B3	✓	✓	

1 • A1 | Black Rock Desert NCA

Dispersed sites, Tent & RV camping: Free, Home of Burning Man, Reservations not accepted, Elevation: 3904ft/1190m, Telephone: 775-623-1500. Nearest town: Gerlach. GPS: 40.756479, -119.243193

2 • A1 | Black Rock Desert NCA – Black Rock Hot Springs

Dispersed sites, No water, No toilets, Tent & RV camping: Free, Reservations not accepted, Elevation: 3965ft/1209m, Telephone: 775-623-1500. Nearest town: Gerlach. GPS: 40.973479, -119.008026

3 • A1 | Black Rock Desert NCA – Cassidy Mine

Dispersed sites, No water, No toilets, Tent & RV camping: Free, Reservations not accepted, Elevation: 4146ft/1264m, Telephone: 775-623-1500. Nearest town: Gerlach. GPS: 40.830395, -119.232012

4 • A1 | Black Rock Desert NCA – Double Hot Springs

Dispersed sites, No water, No toilets, Tent & RV camping: Free, Reservations not accepted, Elevation: 3920ft/1195m, Telephone: 775-623-1500. Nearest town: Gerlach. GPS: 41.080119, -119.106001

5 • A1 | Black Rock Desert NCA – Hidden Spring

Dispersed sites, No water, No toilets, Tent & RV camping: Free, 4x4 high clearance vehicle required, Reservations not accepted, Elevation: 4537ft/1383m, Telephone: 530-279-6101. Nearest town: Gerlach. GPS: 41.351542, -119.223764

6 • A1 | Black Rock Desert NCA – High Rock Canyon 1

Dispersed sites, No water, No toilets, Tents only: Free, 4x4 required, Reservations not accepted, Elevation: 4938ft/1505m, Telephone: 775-623-1500. Nearest town: Gerlach. GPS: 41.314627, -119.319235

7 • A1 | Black Rock Desert NCA – High Rock Canyon 2

Dispersed sites, No water, No toilets, Tents only: Free, 4x4 required, Reservations not accepted, Elevation: 4997ft/1523m, Telephone: 775-623-1500. Nearest town: Gerlach. GPS: 41.342809, -119.356991

8 • A1 | Black Rock Desert NCA – Pole Canyon

Dispersed sites, No water, No toilets, Tents only: Free, 4x4 required, Reservations not accepted, Elevation: 5036ft/1535m, Telephone: 775-623-1500. Nearest town: Gerlach. GPS: 41.358704, -119.367806

9 • A1 | Black Rock Desert NCA – Soldier Meadow

Total sites: 7, RV sites: 7, No water, Vault/pit toilet, Tent & RV camping: Free, 4x4 high clearance vehicle recommended, Elevation: 4564ft/1391m, Telephone: 775-623-1500. Nearest town: Gerlach. GPS: 41.360607, -119.222902

10 • A1 | Black Rock Desert NCA – Soldier Meadow Cabin

Dispersed sites, No water, Vault/pit toilet, Tent & RV camping: Free, 4x4 high clearance vehicle recommended, Open all year, Reservations not accepted, Elevation: 4394ft/1339m, Telephone: 775-623-1500. Nearest town: Gerlach. GPS: 41.360476, -119.196633

11 • A1 | Black Rock Desert NCA – Stevens Camp

Total sites: 4, RV sites: 4, No water, Vault/pit toilet, Tent & RV camping: Free, Also cabins, Reservations not accepted, Elevation: 5766ft/1757m, Telephone: 530-279-6101. Nearest town: Cedarville. GPS: 41.490053, -119.491898

12 • A1 | Black Rock Desert NCA – Stevens Primitive 1

Dispersed sites, No water, No toilets, Tents only: Free, 4x4 high clearance vehicle required, Reservations not accepted, Elevation: 5710ft/1740m, Telephone: 530-279-6101. Nearest town: Cedarville. GPS: 41.487584, -119.495639

13 • A1 | Black Rock Desert NCA – Stevens Primitive 2

Dispersed sites, No water, No toilets, Tents only: Free, 4x4 high clearance vehicle required, Reservations not accepted, Elevation: 5701ft/1738m, Telephone: 530-279-6101. Nearest town: Cedarville. GPS: 41.486961, -119.494574

14 • A1 | Black Rock Desert NCA Dispersed

Dispersed sites, No water, Vault/pit toilet, Tents only: Free, Reservations not accepted, Elevation: 5852ft/1784m, Telephone: 775-623-1500. Nearest town: Gerlach. GPS: 41.456177, -119.565579

15 • A1 | Black Rock NCA – High Rock Canyon 3 (Yellow Rock Garage)

Dispersed sites, No water, No toilets, Tent & RV camping: Free, 4x4 required, Elevation: 5120ft/1561m, Telephone: 775-623-1500. Nearest town: Gerlach. GPS: 41.382051, -119.410947

16 • A1 | Black Rock NCA – Trego Hot Springs

Dispersed sites, No water, No toilets, Tent & RV camping: Free, Beside RR, Elevation: 3941ft/1201m, Telephone: 775-623-1500. Nearest town: Gerlach. GPS: 40.771217, -119.116607

17 • A1 | Boulder Reservoir

Total sites: 7, RV sites: 7, No water, No toilets, Tent & RV camping: Free, Reservations not accepted, Stay limit: 14 days, Elevation: 5768ft/1758m. Nearest town: Gerlach. GPS: 41.348359, -119.747428

18 • A1 | Divine Springs

Total sites: 5, RV sites: 5, No water, No toilets, Tent & RV camping: Free, Open all year, Reservations not accepted, Stay limit: 14 days, Elevation: 6040ft/1841m, Telephone: 530-233-4666. Nearest town: Gerlach. GPS: 41.349999, -119.862628

19 • A1 | Massacre Ranch

Total sites: 4, RV sites: 4, No water, Vault/pit toilet, Tent & RV camping: Free, Also cabins, Reservations not accepted, Stay limit: 14 days, Elevation: 5901ft/1799m, Telephone: 530-279-6101. Nearest town: Cedarville, CA. GPS: 41.561051, -119.587369

20 • A2 | Black Rock Desert NCA – Jackson Creek

Dispersed sites, No water, No toilets, Tent & RV camping: Free, Reservations not accepted, Elevation: 4345ft/1324m, Telephone: 775-623-1500. Nearest town: Gerlach. GPS: 41.321047, -118.532806

21 • A2 | Lahontan Cutthroat Natural Area

Dispersed sites, No toilets, Tent & RV camping: Free, Roads may be impassable in spring, Open Apr-Oct, Elevation: 6801ft/2073m, Telephone: 775-623-1503. Nearest town: Denio. GPS: 41.518882, -118.959338

22 • A2 | Pine Forest RMA – Knott Creek 1

Dispersed sites, No water, No toilets, Tents only: Free, Rough slippery roads - high-clearance 4x4 recommended, Stay limit: 14 days, Elevation: 6509ft/1984m. Nearest town: Winnemucca. GPS: 41.670011, -118.789005

23 • A2 | Pine Forest RMA – Knott Creek 2

Dispersed sites, No water, No toilets, Tents only: Free, Rough slippery roads - high-clearance 4x4 recommended, Open all year, Reservations not accepted, Stay limit: 14 days, Elevation: 6555ft/1998m. Nearest town: Winnemucca. GPS: 41.665176, -118.787162

24 • A2 | Pine Forest RMA – Onion Reservoir

Total sites: 6, RV sites: 6, No water, Vault/pit toilet, Tent & RV camping: Free, Nothing bigger than tent campers, Open Jun-Oct, Elevation: 7067ft/2154m, Telephone: 775-623-1500. Nearest town: Denio Junction. GPS: 41.690201, -118.745115

25 • A2 | Sonoma Canyon

Dispersed sites, No water, No toilets, Tent & RV camping: Free, Open all year, Elevation: 5079ft/1548m, Telephone: 775-623-1500. Nearest town: Winnemucca. GPS: 40.817678, -117.692705

26 • A2 | Water Canyon

Dispersed sites, No water, Vault/pit toilet, Tent & RV camping: Free, Open all year, Reservations not accepted, Elevation: 5453ft/1662m, Telephone: 775-623-1500. Nearest town: Winnemucca. GPS: 40.929559, -117.673613

27 • A2 | Winnemucca Sand Dunes

Dispersed sites, No water, No toilets, Tent & RV camping: Free, Reservations not accepted, Elevation: 4382ft/1336m, Telephone: 775-623-1500. Nearest town: Winnemucca. GPS: 41.084758, -117.707953

28 • A2 | Winnemucca Sand Dunes – Sand Pass

Dispersed sites, No water, No toilets, Tent & RV camping: Free, Reservations not accepted, Elevation: 4951ft/1509m, Telephone: 775-623-1500. Nearest town: Winnemucca. GPS: 41.120409, -117.748178

29 • A3 | Carlin Canyon

Dispersed sites, No water, No toilets, No tents/RVs: Free, Reservations not accepted, Elevation: 4965ft/1513m. Nearest town: Carlin. GPS: 40.726801, -116.009027

30 • A3 | Elko Dispersed 1

Dispersed sites, No water, No toilets, Tent & RV camping: Free, Other sites in this area, Reservations not accepted, Elevation: 5675ft/1730m. Nearest town: Elko. GPS: 40.846475, -115.849598

31 • A3 | North Wildhorse Rec Area

Total sites: 18, RV sites: 18, Central water, Vault/pit toilet, No showers, No RV dump, Tent & RV camping: $6, Open May-Nov, Reservations not accepted, Elevation: 6266ft/1910m, Telephone: 775-753-0200. Nearest town: Elko. GPS: 41.691102, -115.821188

32 • A3 | Wilson Reservoir

Total sites: 20, RV sites: 20, Central water, Vault/pit toilet, No showers, RV dump, Tent & RV camping: $4, Open Apr-Oct, Reservations not accepted, Elevation: 5312ft/1619m, Telephone: 775-753-0200. Nearest town: Elko. GPS: 41.672675, -116.340734

33 • A4 | I-80 Dispersed

Dispersed sites, No water, No toilets, Tent & RV camping: Free, Elevation: 6312ft/1924m. Nearest town: Wells. GPS: 41.064252, -114.521733

34 • A4 | Salmon Falls Creek Rec Area

Dispersed sites, No water, No toilets, Tent & RV camping: Free, 4x4/high-clearance vehicle recommended, Open all year, Reservations not accepted, Elevation: 5226ft/1593m, Telephone: 775-753-0200. Nearest town: Jackpot. GPS: 41.946451, -114.692868

35 • A4 | Tabor Creek

Total sites: 10, RV sites: 10, No water, Vault/pit toilet, Tent & RV camping: $2, Open Apr-Nov, Reservations not accepted, Stay limit: 14 days, Elevation: 6152ft/1875m, Telephone: 775-753-0200. Nearest town: Wells. GPS: 41.481576, -115.148808

36 • B1 | Dry Valley OHV Area

Dispersed sites, No water, Vault/pit toilet, No tents/RVs: Free, Reservations not accepted, Stay limit: 14 days, Elevation: 4258ft/1298m, Telephone: 530-257-0456. Nearest town: Reno. GPS: 40.237941, -119.855071

37 • B1 | The Mugwumps

Dispersed sites, No water, No toilets, Tent & RV camping: Free, Elevation: 3977ft/1212m. Nearest town: Fernley. GPS: 39.943436, -119.381019

38 • B2 | Big Den Creek

Dispersed sites, No water, No toilets, Tent & RV camping: Free, 4x4 required, Reservations not accepted, Elevation: 6632ft/2021m. Nearest town: Fallon. GPS: 39.318351, -117.788588

39 • B2 | Porter Spring

Total sites: 4, RV sites: 4, No water, Vault/pit toilet, No showers, No RV dump, Tent & RV camping: Free, Reservations not accepted, Elevation: 4451ft/1357m, Telephone: 775-623-1521. Nearest town: Lovelock. GPS: 40.415245, -118.866462

40 • B2 | Sand Mountain

Total sites: 100, RV sites: 100, No water, Vault/pit toilet, Tent & RV camping: $40, $40 for 1-7 days, Open Apr-Oct, Reservations not accepted, Stay limit: 14 days, Elevation: 4012ft/1223m, Telephone: 775-885-6000. Nearest town: Fallon. GPS: 39.294657, -118.404669

41 • B3 | Battle Mountain Dispersed 1

Dispersed sites, No water, No toilets, Tent & RV camping: Free, Reservations not accepted, Elevation: 4580ft/1396m. Nearest town: Battle Mountain. GPS: 40.611804, -116.987824

42 • B3 | Hickison Petroglyph

Total sites: 16, RV sites: 16, No water, Vault/pit toilet, Tent & RV camping: Free, Open all year, Reservations not accepted,

Elevation: 6581ft/2006m, Telephone: 775-635-4000. Nearest town: Austin. GPS: 39.448804, -116.751702

43 • B3 | Illipah Reservoir

Total sites: 14, RV sites: 14, No water, Vault/pit toilet, Tent & RV camping: Free, Open all year, Reservations not accepted, Elevation: 6837ft/2084m, Telephone: 775-289-1800. Nearest town: Ely. GPS: 39.334498, -115.389695

44 • B3 | Mill Creek

Total sites: 14, RV sites: 3, No water, Vault/pit toilet, Tent & RV camping: Free, Open all year, Reservations not accepted, Stay limit: 14 days, Elevation: 5243ft/1598m, Telephone: 775-635-4000. Nearest town: Battle Mountain. GPS: 40.356199, -116.993876

45 • B3 | Spencer Hot Springs

Dispersed sites, No water, No toilets, Tent & RV camping: Free, Be courteous and do not camp right on the springs, Elevation: 5685ft/1733m, Telephone: 775-635-4000. Nearest town: Austin. GPS: 39.326879, -116.857595

46 • B3 | Zunino/Jiggs Reservoir

Dispersed sites, No water, Vault/pit toilet, Tent & RV camping: $2, Open all year, Reservations not accepted, Elevation: 5584ft/1702m, Telephone: 775-753-0200. Nearest town: Elko. GPS: 40.459659, -115.655814

47 • B4 | Blue Mass Scenic Area Dispersed

Dispersed sites, No water, No toilets, Tent & RV camping: Free, Open all year, Reservations not accepted, Elevation: 5951ft/1814m, Telephone: 775-289-1800. Nearest town: Tippett. GPS: 39.762923, -114.284851

48 • B4 | Garnet Hill Dispersed

Dispersed sites, No water, Vault/pit toilet, Tent & RV camping: Free, Rockhound site, RVs and large trailers not recommended, Open all year, Reservations not accepted, Stay limit: 14 days, Elevation: 6867ft/2093m, Telephone: 775-289-1800. Nearest town: Ely. GPS: 39.262792, -114.927429

49 • B4 | Goshute Canyon

Total sites: 20, RV sites: 20, No water, No toilets, Tent & RV camping: Free, High-clearance vehicle needed, Open all year, Reservations not accepted, Elevation: 6230ft/1899m, Telephone: 775-289-1800. Nearest town: Ely. GPS: 40.048861, -114.797107

50 • C1 | Wilson Canyon

Dispersed sites, No water, Vault/pit toilet, Tent & RV camping: Free, Open all year, Reservations not accepted,

Elevation: 4710ft/1436m, Telephone: 775-885-6000. Nearest town: Yerington. GPS: 38.810376, -119.227669

51 • C2 | Crescent Sand Dunes OHV

Dispersed sites, No water, No toilets, Tent & RV camping: Free, Reservations not accepted, Stay limit: 14 days, Elevation: 5067ft/1544m, Telephone: 775-482-7800. Nearest town: Tonopah. GPS: 38.229141, -117.334046

52 • C2 | Hwy 95 Tonopah

Dispersed sites, No water, No toilets, Tent & RV camping: Free, Elevation: 6297ft/1919m. Nearest town: Tonopah. GPS: 38.049657, -117.218042

53 • C2 | Lee Hot Springs

Dispersed sites, No water, No toilets, Tent & RV camping: Free, VERY hot spring, Elevation: 4035ft/1230m. Nearest town: Fallon. GPS: 39.208828, -118.724601

54 • C2 | Tonopah US-6 East

Dispersed sites, No water, No toilets, No tents/RVs: Free, Parking lot, Open all year, Elevation: 5525ft/1684m. Nearest town: Tonopah. GPS: 38.071571, -117.126854

55 • C2 | Walker Lake – Sportsmans Beach

Total sites: 40, RV sites: 40, No water, Vault/pit toilet, Tent & RV camping: $6, Elevation: 4101ft/1250m, Telephone: 775-885-6000. Nearest town: Hawthorne. GPS: 38.691335, -118.770791

56 • C2 | Walker Lake – Tamarack

Total sites: 12, RV sites: 12, No water, Vault/pit toilet, Tent & RV camping: Free, Stay limit: 14 days, Elevation: 4042ft/1232m, Telephone: 775-885-6000. Nearest town: Hawthorne. GPS: 38.736558, -118.768079

57 • C2 | Walker Lake – Twenty Mile Beach

Dispersed sites, No water, Vault/pit toilet, Tent & RV camping: $4, Elevation: 4098ft/1249m, Telephone: 775-885-6000. Nearest town: Hawthorne. GPS: 38.752045, -118.765431

58 • C3 | Lunar Crater NNL

Dispersed sites, No water, No toilets, Tent & RV camping: Free, Elevation: 6008ft/1831m. Nearest town: Tonopah. GPS: 38.389013, -116.068358

59 • C3 | McKinney Tanks Dispersed

Dispersed sites, No water, No toilets, Tent & RV camping: Free, Don't camp near the tanks, Reservations not accepted, Elevation: 6268ft/1910m. GPS: 38.101925, -116.910456

60 • C4 | Cleve Creek

Total sites: 12, RV sites: 12, No water, Vault/pit toilet, Tent & RV camping: Free, Group site available, Open May-Sep, Reservations not accepted, Stay limit: 14 days, Elevation: 6278ft/1914m, Telephone: 775-289-1800. Nearest town: North Spring Valley. GPS: 39.213832, -114.543477

61 • C4 | Ely Elk Viewing Area

Dispersed sites, No water, Vault/pit toilet, No tents/RVs: Free, Reservations not accepted, Elevation: 6688ft/2039m. Nearest town: Ely. GPS: 39.102412, -114.760455

62 • C4 | Gap Mountain

Total sites: 6, RV sites: 6, No water, No toilets, Tent & RV camping: Free, Open all year, Reservations not accepted, Stay limit: 14 days, Elevation: 5482ft/1671m, Telephone: 775-289-1800. Nearest town: Ely. GPS: 38.328054, -115.050939

63 • C4 | Meadow Valley East

Dispersed sites, No water, No toilets, Tent & RV camping: Free, Reservations not accepted, Stay limit: 14 days, Elevation: 5728ft/1746m, Telephone: 775-289-1800. Nearest town: Pioche. GPS: 38.007412, -114.206104

64 • C4 | Meadow Valley West

Dispersed sites, No water, Vault/pit toilet, Tent & RV camping: Free, Reservations not accepted, Stay limit: 14 days, Elevation: 5745ft/1751m, Telephone: 775-289-1800. Nearest town: Pioche. GPS: 38.008223, -114.206913

65 • C4 | Pahroc Wash

Total sites: 1, RV sites: 1, No water, No toilets, Tent & RV camping: Free, Elevation: 4648ft/1417m, Telephone: 775-289-1800. Nearest town: Hiko. GPS: 37.783858, -115.059336

66 • C4 | Patterson Pass

Total sites: 10, RV sites: 10, No water, Vault/pit toilet, Tent & RV camping: Free, Reservations not accepted, Stay limit: 14 days, Elevation: 6175ft/1882m, Telephone: 775-289-1800. Nearest town: Pioche. GPS: 38.591928, -114.667508

67 • C4 | Sacramento Pass Rec Area – The Pond

Total sites: 6, RV sites: 6, No water, Vault/pit toilet, Tent & RV camping: Free, Reservations not accepted, Stay limit: 14 days, Elevation: 6728ft/2051m, Telephone: 775-289-1800. Nearest town: Baker. GPS: 39.121475, -114.304978

68 • C4 | Sacramento Pass Rec Area – Upper TH

Total sites: 4, RV sites: 4, No water, Vault/pit toilet, Tent & RV camping: Free, Reservations not accepted, Stay limit: 14 days, Elevation: 6867ft/2093m, Telephone: 775-289-1800. Nearest town: Baker. GPS: 39.114226, -114.303366

69 • C4 | Stampede

Total sites: 4, RV sites: 4, No water, Vault/pit toilet, Tent & RV camping: Free, Reservations not accepted, Elevation: 6187ft/1886m, Telephone: 775-289-1800. Nearest town: Pioche. GPS: 37.977477, -114.537203

70 • D2 | Bonnie Claire Lakebed

Dispersed sites, No water, No toilets, No tents/RVs: Free, Reservations not accepted, Elevation: 4019ft/1225m. Nearest town: Beatty. GPS: 37.171039, -117.152406

71 • D2 | Route 267

Dispersed sites, No water, No toilets, Tent & RV camping: Free, Elevation: 4144ft/1263m. Nearest town: Beatty. GPS: 37.075869, -117.267927

72 • D3 | Bombo's Pond

Dispersed sites, No water, No toilets, Tent & RV camping: Free, Good bird watching, Reservations not accepted, Elevation: 3194ft/974m. Nearest town: Beatty. GPS: 36.882328, -116.754357

73 • D3 | Bull Frog

Dispersed sites, No water, No toilets, Tent & RV camping: Free, Unconfirmed, Reservations not accepted, Elevation: 3627ft/1106m, Telephone: 775-482-7800. Nearest town: Beatty. GPS: 36.906879, -116.792472

74 • D3 | Cement Plant Dispersed

Dispersed sites, No water, No toilets, No tents/RVs: Free, Parking lot, Reservations not accepted, Elevation: 3108ft/947m. GPS: 36.819278, -116.717023

75 • D4 | Big Rocks North

Dispersed sites, No water, No toilets, Tent & RV camping: Free, Reservations not accepted, Stay limit: 14 days, Elevation: 5872ft/1790m. Nearest town: Crystal Springs. GPS: 37.717429, -114.950884

76 • D4 | Chief Mountain South

Total sites: 6, RV sites: 6, No water, Vault/pit toilet, Tent & RV camping: Free, Reservations not accepted, Stay limit: 14 days, Elevation: 6082ft/1854m, Telephone: 775-289-1800. Nearest town: Caliente. GPS: 37.604482, -114.659276

77 • D4 | Chief Mountain West

Total sites: 4, RV sites: 3, No water, Vault/pit toilet, Tent & RV camping: Free, Reservations not accepted, Stay limit: 14 days, Elevation: 4883ft/1488m, Telephone: 775-289-1800. Nearest town: Caliente. GPS: 37.66456, -114.754072

78 • D4 | Gold Butte Wash Dispersed

Dispersed sites, No water, No toilets, Tent & RV camping: Free, Reservations not accepted, Elevation: 1985ft/605m. GPS: 36.431053, -114.221322

79 • D4 | Logan Trail Dispersed 01

Dispersed sites, No water, No toilets, Tent & RV camping: Free, Reservations not accepted, Elevation: 1690ft/515m, Telephone: 702-515-5371. Nearest town: Logandale. GPS: 36.587679, -114.528121

80 • D4 | Logan Trail Dispersed 02

Dispersed sites, No water, No toilets, Tent & RV camping: Free, Reservations not accepted, Elevation: 1726ft/526m, Telephone: 702-515-5371. Nearest town: Logandale. GPS: 36.584563, -114.534615

81 • D4 | Logan Trail Dispersed 03 and 04

Dispersed sites, No water, No toilets, Tent & RV camping: Free, Reservations not accepted, Elevation: 1764ft/538m, Telephone: 702-515-5371. Nearest town: Logandale. GPS: 36.577214, -114.539489

82 • D4 | Logan Trail Dispersed 05

Dispersed sites, No water, No toilets, Tent & RV camping: Free, Reservations not accepted, Elevation: 1798ft/548m, Telephone: 702-515-5371. Nearest town: Logandale. GPS: 36.573604, -114.544418

83 • D4 | Logan Trail Dispersed 06

Dispersed sites, No water, No toilets, Tents only: Free, 4x4 required, Reservations not accepted, Elevation: 1842ft/561m, Telephone: 702-515-5371. Nearest town: Logandale. GPS: 36.563034, -114.547379

84 • D4 | Logan Trail Dispersed 07 (Bassett)

Dispersed sites, No water, Vault/pit toilet, Tent & RV camping: Free, Reservations not accepted, Elevation: 1869ft/570m, Telephone: 702-515-5371. Nearest town: Logandale. GPS: 36.559706, -114.550203

85 • D4 | Logan Trail Dispersed 08

Dispersed sites, No water, No toilets, Tent & RV camping: Free, Reservations not accepted, Elevation: 1919ft/585m, Telephone: 702-515-5371. Nearest town: Logandale. GPS: 36.549389, -114.550186

86 • D4 | Logan Trail Dispersed 09

Dispersed sites, No water, No toilets, Tents only: Free, Reservations not accepted, Elevation: 1997ft/609m, Telephone: 702-515-5372. Nearest town: Logandale. GPS: 36.534976, -114.552644

87 • D4 | Logan Trail Dispersed 10

Dispersed sites, No water, No toilets, Tents only: Free, Also walk-to sites, 4x4 required, Reservations not accepted, Elevation: 2035ft/620m, Telephone: 702-515-5373. Nearest town: Logandale. GPS: 36.529719, -114.554176

88 • D4 | Logan Trail Dispersed 11

Dispersed sites, No water, No toilets, Tents only: Free, Also hike-in sites, Reservations not accepted, Elevation: 1900ft/579m, Telephone: 702-515-5374. Nearest town: Logandale. GPS: 36.518984, -114.539317

89 • D4 | Logan Trail Dispersed 12

Dispersed sites, No water, No toilets, Tents only: Free, Also boat-in sites, 4x4 required, Reservations not accepted, Elevation: 1971ft/601m, Telephone: 702-515-5375. Nearest town: Logandale. GPS: 36.524897, -114.542503

90 • D4 | Mathews Canyon Dam

Total sites: 2, RV sites: 1, No water, No toilets, Tent & RV camping: Free, Nothing larger than truck camper, Reservations not accepted, Stay limit: 14 days, Elevation: 5462ft/1665m, Telephone: 775-726-8100. Nearest town: Caliente. GPS: 37.496477, -114.226259

91 • D4 | Pine Canyon Dam

Dispersed sites, No water, Vault/pit toilet, Tent & RV camping: Free, Reservations not accepted, Stay limit: 14 days, Elevation: 5686ft/1733m, Telephone: 775-726-8100. Nearest town: Caliente. GPS: 37.476707, -114.310578

92 • D4 | Valley of Fire Hwy Dispersed

Dispersed sites, No water, No toilets, Tent & RV camping: Free, Reservations not accepted, Elevation: 2280ft/695m. Nearest town: Las Vegas. GPS: 36.444389, -114.675385

93 • D4 | Whitney Pocket

Dispersed sites, No water, No toilets, Tent & RV camping: Free, Reservations not accepted, Elevation: 3018ft/920m. Nearest town: Mesquite. GPS: 36.522978, -114.140562

94 • E3 | Red Rock Canyon

Total sites: 53, RV sites: 45, Central water, Vault/pit toilet, No showers, No RV dump, Tents: $10-20/RVs: $20, Also walk-to/group sites, 7 reservable group sites - $60, Generator hours: 0600-2200, Open Sep-May, Reservations not accepted, Stay limit: 14 days, Elevation: 3398ft/1036m, Telephone: 702-515-5000. Nearest town: Las Vegas. GPS: 36.131724, -115.384344

95 • E4 | Dry Lake

Dispersed sites, No water, No toilets, No tents/RVs: Free, Elevation: 9562ft/2914m. Nearest town: Boulder City. GPS: 35.862536, -114.940344

96 • E4 | Jean/Roach Dry Lakes

Dispersed sites, No water, No toilets, Tent & RV camping: Free, Reservations not accepted, Elevation: 2809ft/856m, Telephone: 702-515-5000. Nearest town: Jean. GPS: 35.784779, -115.279298

97 • E4 | Knob Hill

Dispersed sites, No water, No toilets, Tents only: Free, Very rough road - high-clearance 4x4 required, Reservations not accepted, Elevation: 4173ft/1272m, Telephone: 702-515-5000. Nearest town: Nelson. GPS: 35.652256, -114.844691

New Mexico

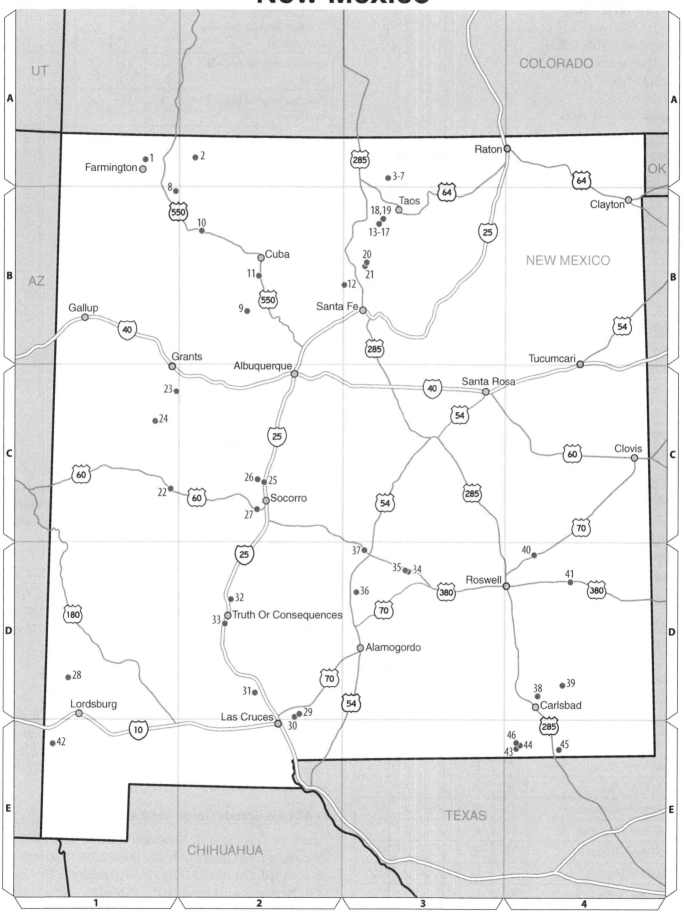

New Mexico

New Mexico State Office
310 Dinosaur Trail
Santa Fe NM 87508

Phone: 505-954-2000

Name	ID	Map	RVs	Tents	Free
Aguirre Spring	29	D2	✓	✓	
Alkali Lake OHV	38	D4	✓	✓	✓
Angel Peak	8	B1	✓	✓	✓
Baylor Canyon	30	D2	✓	✓	✓
Broad Canyon	31	D2		✓	✓
Brown Springs OHV Rec Area	1	A1	✓	✓	✓
Cabezon Peak Wilderness Study Area	9	B2		✓	✓
Chosa	43	E4	✓	✓	✓
CR 377 Dispersed 1	10	B2	✓	✓	✓
CR B90 Dispersed	25	C2	✓	✓	✓
Datil Well	22	C1	✓	✓	
Diablo Canyon Rec Area	12	B3	✓	✓	✓
El Malpais NCA – Joe Skeen	23	C1	✓	✓	✓
El Malpais Scenic ByWay	24	C1	✓	✓	✓
Fort Stanton NCA – Cave	34	D3	✓	✓	✓
Fort Stanton NCA – Rob Jaggers	35	D3	✓	✓	✓
Gila Lower Box Canyon – Nichol's Canyon	28	D1	✓	✓	✓
Granite Gap Dispersed	42	E1		✓	✓
Hackberry Lake OHV	39	D4	✓	✓	✓
Haystack Mountain OHV Area	40	D4	✓	✓	
Martin Ranch Road Dispersed	32	D2	✓		✓
Mescalero Sands North Dunes OHV Area	41	D4	✓	✓	
New Mexico Crags	11	B2	✓	✓	✓
Old Ladder Ranch Road	33	D2	✓	✓	✓
Orilla Verde – Arroyo Hondo	13	B3	✓	✓	
Orilla Verde – Lone Juniper	14	B3	✓	✓	
Orilla Verde – Petaca	15	B3	✓	✓	
Orilla Verde – Pilar	16	B3	✓	✓	
Orilla Verde – Rio Bravo	17	B3	✓	✓	
Orilla Verde – Rio Pueblo	18	B3	✓	✓	
Orilla Verde – Taos Jct	19	B3	✓	✓	
Parks Ranch Dispersed	44	E4	✓	✓	✓
Pecos River Corridor Rec Area	45	E4		✓	✓

Name	ID	Map	RVs	Tents	Free
Rio Grande Gorge Rec Area – Big Arsenic Springs	3	A3	✓	✓	
Rio Grande Gorge Rec Area – El Aguaje	4	A3	✓	✓	
Rio Grande Gorge Rec Area – La Junta Canyon	5	A3	✓	✓	
Rio Grande Gorge Rec Area – Little Arsenic Springs	6	A3	✓	✓	
Rio Grande Gorge Rec Area – Montoso	7	A3	✓	✓	
San Lorenzo Canyon Rec Area Dispersed	26	C2		✓	✓
Santa Cruz Lake Rec Area – North Lake	20	B3	✓	✓	
Santa Cruz Lake Rec Area – Overlook	21	B3	✓	✓	
Simon Canyon Rec Area Dispersed	2	A2		✓	✓
Sunset Reef	46	E4	✓	✓	✓
The Box	27	C2	✓	✓	✓
Three Rivers Petroglyph Site	36	D3	✓	✓	
Valley of Fires	37	D3	✓	✓	

1 • A1 | Brown Springs OHV Rec Area

Total sites: 10, RV sites: 10, No water, Vault/pit toilet, No showers, No RV dump, Tent & RV camping: Free, Permit required, Reservations not accepted, Elevation: 5725ft/1745m, Telephone: 505-564-7600. Nearest town: Farmington. GPS: 36.806269, -108.180906

2 • A2 | Simon Canyon Rec Area Dispersed

Dispersed sites, No water, No toilets, Tents only: Free, Dispersed camping beyond the parking lot, Elevation: 5725ft/1745m, Telephone: 505 599-8900. Nearest town: Farmington. GPS: 36.823354, -107.660314

3 • A3 | Rio Grande Gorge Rec Area – Big Arsenic Springs

Total sites: 6, RV sites: 6, No water, Vault/pit toilet, Tent & RV camping: $7, Generator hours: 0600-2200, Open all year, Reservations not accepted, Elevation: 7530ft/2295m, Telephone: 575-758-8851. Nearest town: Questa. GPS: 36.675042, -105.681069

4 • A3 | Rio Grande Gorge Rec Area – El Aguaje

Total sites: 7, RV sites: 7, No water, Vault/pit toilet, Tent & RV camping: $7, Generator hours: 0600-2200, Reservations not accepted, Elevation: 7333ft/2235m, Telephone: 575-758-8851. Nearest town: Questa. GPS: 36.666753, -105.671918

5 • A3 | Rio Grande Gorge Rec Area – La Junta Canyon

Total sites: 3, RV sites: 3, No water, Vault/pit toilet, Tent & RV camping: $7, Generator hours: 0600-2200, Reservations not accepted, Elevation: 7457ft/2273m, Telephone: 575-758-8851. Nearest town: Questa. GPS: 36.656744, -105.685583

6 • A3 | Rio Grande Gorge Rec Area – Little Arsenic Springs

Total sites: 6, RV sites: 6, Central water, Vault/pit toilet, Tent & RV camping: $7, Reservations not accepted, Elevation: 7507ft/2288m, Telephone: 575-758-8851. Nearest town: Questa. GPS: 36.667716, -105.680702

7 • A3 | Rio Grande Gorge Rec Area – Montoso

Total sites: 4, RV sites: 4, No water, Vault/pit toilet, Tent & RV camping: $7, Elevation: 7510ft/2289m, Telephone: 575-758-8851. Nearest town: Questa. GPS: 36.665605, -105.680792

8 • B1 | Angel Peak

Total sites: 9, RV sites: 4, No water, Vault/pit toilet, Tent & RV camping: Free, Open all year, Reservations not accepted, Elevation: 6697ft/2041m, Telephone: 505-564-7600. Nearest town: Bloomfield. GPS: 36.548202, -107.860305

9 • B2 | Cabezon Peak Wilderness Study Area

Dispersed sites, No water, No toilets, Tents only: Free, High clearance vehicles only, Open all year, Elevation: 6443ft/1964m, Telephone: 505-761-8700. Nearest town: San Ysidro. GPS: 35.596932, -107.105271

10 • B2 | CR 377 Dispersed 1

Dispersed sites, No water, No toilets, Tent & RV camping: Free, Several locations in this area, Reservations not accepted, Elevation: 7166ft/2184m. Nearest town: Cuba. GPS: 36.235711, -107.584146

11 • B2 | New Mexico Crags

Dispersed sites, No water, No toilets, Tent & RV camping: Free, Elevation: 6689ft/2039m. Nearest town: Cuba. GPS: 35.877045, -106.994828

12 • B3 | Diablo Canyon Rec Area

Total sites: 8, RV sites: 4, No water, No toilets, Tent & RV camping: Free, No large RVs, Reservations not accepted, Elevation: 5852ft/1784m, Telephone: 575-758-8851. Nearest town: White Rock. GPS: 35.804312, -106.135861

13 • B3 | Orilla Verde – Arroyo Hondo

Total sites: 5, RV sites: 5, Central water, Vault/pit toilet, No showers, No RV dump, Tent & RV camping: $7, Generator hours: 0600-2200, Open all year, Reservations not accepted, Elevation: 6073ft/1851m, Telephone: 575-758-8851. Nearest town: Pilar. GPS: 36.297111, -105.773311

14 • B3 | Orilla Verde – Lone Juniper

Total sites: 4, RV sites: 4, Central water, Vault/pit toilet, No showers, No RV dump, Tent & RV camping: $7, Generator hours: 0600-2200, Open all year, Reservations not accepted, Elevation: 6056ft/1846m, Telephone: 575-758-8851. Nearest town: Pilar. GPS: 36.300507, -105.771833

15 • B3 | Orilla Verde – Petaca

Total sites: 6, RV sites: 4, Central water, Vault/pit toilet, No showers, No RV dump, Tent & RV camping: $7, CG closed UFN - construction, Generator hours: 0600-2200, Open all year, Reservations not accepted, Elevation: 6109ft/1862m, Telephone: 575-758-8851. Nearest town: Pilar. GPS: 36.307573, -105.766747

16 • B3 | Orilla Verde – Pilar

Total sites: 12, RV sites: 9, Electric sites: 9, Water at site, Flush toilet, No showers, No RV dump, Tents: $7/RVs: $15, Generator hours: 0600-2200, Open all year, Reservations not accepted, Elevation: 6066ft/1849m, Telephone: 575-758-8851. Nearest town: Pilar. GPS: 36.285621, -105.786404

17 • B3 | Orilla Verde – Rio Bravo

Total sites: 12, RV sites: 4, Electric sites: 4, Water at site, Flush toilet, Pay showers, No RV dump, Tents: $7/RVs: $15, Generator hours: 0600-2200, Open all year, Reservations not accepted, Elevation: 6043ft/1842m, Telephone: 575-758-8851. Nearest town: Pilar. GPS: 36.292001, -105.781732

18 • B3 | Orilla Verde – Rio Pueblo

Total sites: 6, RV sites: 3, Vault/pit toilet, Tent & RV camping: $5, Generator hours: 0600-2200, Open all year, Reservations not accepted, Elevation: 6120ft/1865m, Telephone: 575-758-8851. Nearest town: Taos. GPS: 36.336423, -105.731342

19 • B3 | Orilla Verde – Taos Jct

Total sites: 4, RV sites: 3, Central water, Vault/pit toilet, No showers, No RV dump, Tent & RV camping: $7, Generator hours: 0600-2200, Reservations not accepted, Elevation: 6174ft/1882m, Telephone: 575-758-8851. Nearest town: Carson. GPS: 36.335619, -105.736437

20 • B3 | Santa Cruz Lake Rec Area – North Lake

Total sites: 12, RV sites: 6, Central water, Vault/pit toilet, No showers, No RV dump, Tent & RV camping: $7, No water in winter, Open all year, Elevation: 6358ft/1938m, Telephone: 505-758-8851. Nearest town: Chimayo. GPS: 35.980247, -105.913079

21 • B3 | Santa Cruz Lake Rec Area – Overlook

Total sites: 14, RV sites: 14, No water, Vault/pit toilet, Tent & RV camping: $7, Open May-Oct, Elevation: 6657ft/2029m, Telephone: 505-758-8851. Nearest town: Chimayo. GPS: 35.964009, -105.918055

22 • C1 | Datil Well

Total sites: 22, RV sites: 22, Electric sites: 3, Central water, Vault/pit toilet, No showers, No RV dump, Tent & RV camping: $5, No water in winter, Open all year, Reservations not accepted, Elevation: 7424ft/2263m, Telephone: 575-835-0412. Nearest town: Datil. GPS: 34.153692, -107.857804

23 • C1 | El Malpais NCA – Joe Skeen

Total sites: 11, RV sites: 10, No water, Vault/pit toilet, Tent & RV camping: Free, Open all year, Reservations not accepted, Elevation: 6959ft/2121m, Telephone: 505-240-0300. Nearest town: Grants. GPS: 34.943585, -107.820616

24 • C1 | El Malpais Scenic ByWay

Dispersed sites, No water, No toilets, Tent & RV camping: Free, Elevation: 7097ft/2163m. Nearest town: Pie Town. GPS: 34.705727, -108.028635

25 • C2 | CR B90 Dispersed

Dispersed sites, No water, No toilets, Tent & RV camping: Free, Narrow tunnel under highway, Reservations not accepted, Elevation: 4743ft/1446m. GPS: 34.222971, -106.923076

26 • C2 | San Lorenzo Canyon Rec Area Dispersed

Dispersed sites, No water, No toilets, Tents only: Free, Soft sand - 4x4 high-clearance vehicles recommended, Elevation: 5134ft/1565m, Telephone: 505-835-0412. Nearest town: Lemitar. GPS: 34.242941, -106.985649

27 • C2 | The Box

Dispersed sites, No water, Vault/pit toilet, Tent & RV camping: Free, Open all year, Reservations not accepted, Elevation: 5464ft/1665m, Telephone: 505-835-0412. Nearest town: Socorro. GPS: 34.001755, -106.992534

28 • D1 | Gila Lower Box Canyon – Nichol's Canyon

Dispersed sites, No water, No toilets, Tent & RV camping: Free, 4x4 high-clearance vehicle required, Open all year, Reservations not accepted, Stay limit: 14 days, Elevation: 4200ft/1280m, Telephone: 505-525-4300. Nearest town: Lordsburg. GPS: 32.632224, -108.826635

29 • D2 | Aguirre Spring

Total sites: 57, RV sites: 57, Central water, Vault/pit toilet, Tent & RV camping: $7, 2 reservable group sites: $50, Drinking water 3 miles before the entrance at the camp host site, Entrance gate locked at night, Open all year, Reservations not accepted, Stay limit: 14 days, Elevation: 5597ft/1706m, Telephone: 575-525-4300. Nearest town: Las Cruces. GPS: 32.370458, -106.560915

30 • D2 | Baylor Canyon

Dispersed sites, No water, No toilets, Tent & RV camping: Free, Elevation: 5183ft/1580m. Nearest town: Las Cruces. GPS: 32.346346, -106.609177

31 • D2 | Broad Canyon

Dispersed sites, No water, No toilets, Tents only: Free, Trailers not recommended, Elevation: 4005ft/1221m. Nearest town: Las Cruces. GPS: 32.534222, -106.989956

32 • D2 | Martin Ranch Road Dispersed

Dispersed sites, No toilets, No tents/RVs: Free, Elevation: 4777ft/1456m. Nearest town: Truth or Consequences. GPS: 33.284633, -107.24445

33 • D2 | Old Ladder Ranch Road

Dispersed sites, No water, No toilets, Tent & RV camping: Free, Reservations not accepted, Elevation: 4227ft/1288m. Nearest town: Williamsburg. GPS: 33.100689, -107.285217

34 • D3 | Fort Stanton NCA – Cave

Total sites: 5, RV sites: 5, No water, Vault/pit toilet, Tents: Free/RVs: $8, Dump fee - $15, Open all year, Reservations not accepted, Elevation: 6198ft/1889m, Telephone: 575-627-0220. Nearest town: Lincoln. GPS: 33.506302, -105.492426

35 • D3 | Fort Stanton NCA – Rob Jaggers

Total sites: 16, RV sites: 16, Electric sites: 8, Central water, Vault/pit toilet, No showers, RV dump, Tents: Free/RVs: $5-10, Dump fee - $15, Dispersed free camping sites, Open all year, Elevation: 6220ft/1896m, Telephone: 575-627-0220. Nearest town: Lincoln. GPS: 33.514451, -105.510863

36 • D3 | Three Rivers Petroglyph Site

Total sites: 10, RV sites: 7, Electric sites: 2, Water at site, Flush toilet, No showers, No RV dump, Tents: $7/RVs: $7-18, Open all year, Reservations not accepted, Elevation: 5001ft/1524m, Telephone: 575-525-4300. Nearest town: Tularosa. GPS: 33.344642, -106.008569

37 • D3 | Valley of Fires

Total sites: 25, RV sites: 25, Electric sites: 13, Water at site, Flush toilet, Free showers, RV dump, Tents: $7/RVs: $12-18, Generator hours: 0700-2200, Open all year, Reservations not accepted, Stay limit: 14 days, Elevation: 5259ft/1603m, Telephone: 575-648-2241. Nearest town: Carrizozo. GPS: 33.681119, -105.924216

38 • D4 | Alkali Lake OHV

Dispersed sites, No water, No toilets, Tent & RV camping: Free, Open all year, Elevation: 3281ft/1000m. Nearest town: Carlsbad. GPS: 32.498919, -104.211436

39 • D4 | Hackberry Lake OHV

Dispersed sites, No water, No toilets, Tent & RV camping: Free, Open all year, Reservations not accepted, Elevation: 3196ft/974m, Telephone: 575-234-5972. Nearest town: Carlsbad. GPS: 32.570251, -103.968716

40 • D4 | Haystack Mountain OHV Area

Dispersed sites, No water, Vault/pit toilet, Tent & RV camping: $5, Open all year, Reservations not accepted, Stay limit: 14 days, Elevation: 4048ft/1234m, Telephone: 575-627-0272. Nearest town: Roswell. GPS: 33.637816, -104.226917

41 • D4 | Mescalero Sands North Dunes OHV Area

Dispersed sites, No water, Vault/pit toilet, Tent & RV camping: $5, Reservations not accepted, Elevation: 4102ft/1250m, Telephone: 505-627-0272. Nearest town: Roswell. GPS: 33.402592, -103.861683

42 • E1 | Granite Gap Dispersed

Dispersed sites, No water, No toilets, Tents only: Free, 4x4 needed, Elevation: 4496ft/1370m. Nearest town: Lordsburg. GPS: 32.095282, -108.970462

43 • E4 | Chosa

Dispersed sites, No water, No toilets, Tent & RV camping: Free, Room for 25 RVs, Reservations not accepted, Stay limit: 14 days, Elevation: 3744ft/1141m. Nearest town: Whites City. GPS: 32.088528, -104.432161

44 • E4 | Parks Ranch Dispersed

Dispersed sites, No water, No toilets, Tent & RV camping: Free, Reservations not accepted, Elevation: 3567ft/1087m, Telephone: 575-234-5927. Nearest town: Whites City. GPS: 32.110525, -104.406711

45 • E4 | Pecos River Corridor Rec Area

Dispersed sites, No water, No toilets, Tents only: Free, Open all year, Elevation: 2874ft/876m, Telephone: 575-234-5972. Nearest town: Loving. GPS: 32.065404, -104.010155

46 • E4 | Sunset Reef

Total sites: 11, RV sites: 5, No water, Vault/pit toilet, Tent & RV camping: Free, Reservations not accepted, Stay limit: 5 days, Elevation: 3602ft/1098m, Telephone: 575-234-5927. Nearest town: Whites City. GPS: 32.119464, -104.424408

North Dakota

North Dakota

Montana/Dakotas State Office
5001 Southgate Dr
Billings MT 59101

Phone: 406-896-5004

Name	ID	Map	RVs	Tents	Free
Schnell Recreation Area	1	C2	✓	✓	

1 • C2 | Schnell Recreation Area

Total sites: 6, RV sites: 6, Central water, Vault/pit toilet, No showers, No RV dump, Tent & RV camping: $5, Open May-Oct, Reservations not accepted, Stay limit: 14 days, Elevation: 2316ft/706m, Telephone: 701-225-9148. Nearest town: Richardton. GPS: 46.885054, -102.257659

Oregon

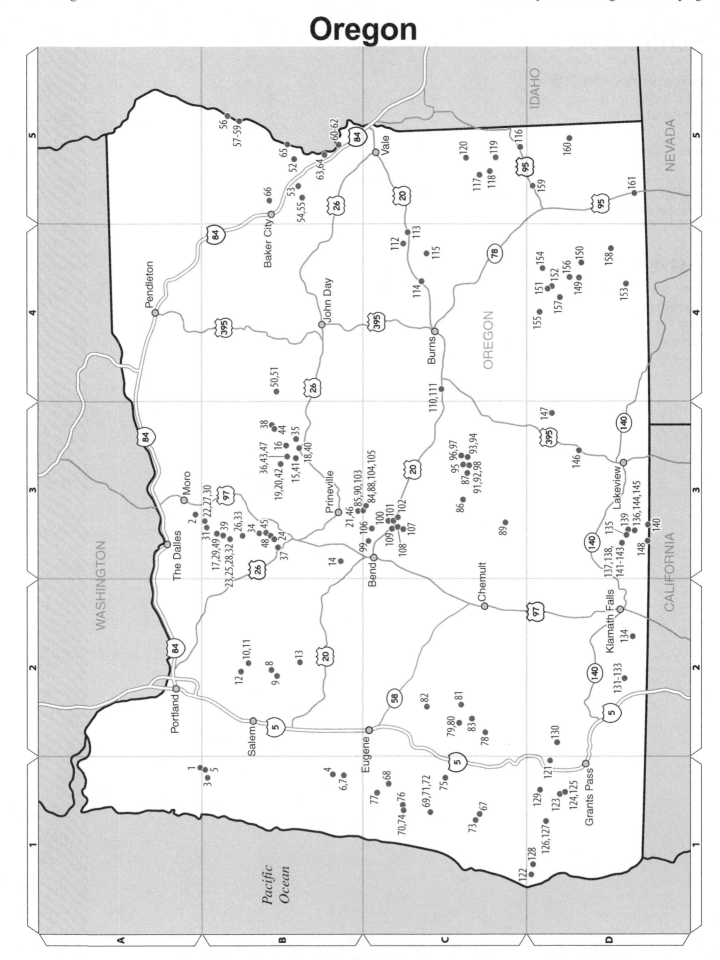

Oregon

Oregon/Washington State Office
1220 SW 3rd Ave
Portland OR 97204

Phone: 503-808-6001

Name	ID	Map	RVs	Tents	Free
Alder Glen	3	B1	✓	✓	
Alsea Falls	4	B1	✓	✓	
Alvord Desert	149	D4	✓	✓	✓
Antelope Reservoir	116	C5	✓	✓	✓
Barr Road North OHV	14	B3	✓	✓	✓
Basser Diggins	52	B5		✓	
Bear Creek Road Dispersed	15	B3	✓	✓	✓
Big Bend	50	B4	✓	✓	
Big Bend (Crooked River)	84	C3	✓	✓	
Big Sand Gap	150	D4	✓	✓	✓
Birch Creek Historic Ranch	117	C5	✓	✓	✓
Black Canyon TH	16	B3		✓	✓
Blue Hole	17	B3	✓	✓	
Bridge Creek	18	B3	✓	✓	✓
Burma Pond	121	D1	✓	✓	✓
Burnt Mountain (Skeeter Camp)	67	C1		✓	✓
Burnt Ranch	19	B3	✓	✓	✓
Burnt Ranch Dispersed	20	B3	✓	✓	✓
Burnt River Canyon #1 Dispersed	53	B5	✓	✓	✓
Burnt River Canyon #2 Dispersed	54	B5	✓	✓	✓
Burnt River Canyon #3 Dispersed	55	B5	✓	✓	✓
Castle Rock	21	B3	✓	✓	
Cavitt Creek Falls	78	C2	✓	✓	
Chickahominy Recreation Site	110	C4	✓	✓	
Chickahominy Reservoir	111	C4	✓	✓	
Chimney Rock	85	C3	✓	✓	
Christmas Valley Sand Dunes – Green Mountain	86	C3	✓	✓	✓
Christmas Valley Sand Dunes – Junipers	87	C3	✓	✓	✓
Chukar Park	112	C4	✓	✓	
Clay Creek	68	C1	✓	✓	
Cobble Rock	88	C3	✓	✓	
Coffee Pot Crater	118	C5	✓	✓	✓
Copper Creek	56	B5	✓	✓	✓

Name	ID	Map	RVs	Tents	Free
Cow Lakes	119	C5	✓	✓	✓
Deschutes River – Beavertail	22	B3	✓	✓	
Deschutes River – Devils Canyon	23	B3	✓	✓	
Deschutes River – Frog Springs	24	B3	✓	✓	✓
Deschutes River – Harpham Flat	25	B3	✓	✓	
Deschutes River – Hole in Wall	26	B3		✓	
Deschutes River – Jones Canyon	27	B3	✓	✓	
Deschutes River – Long Bend	28	B3	✓	✓	
Deschutes River – Macks Canyon	2	A3	✓	✓	
Deschutes River – Oak Springs	29	B3	✓	✓	
Deschutes River – Rattlesnake Canyon	30	B3	✓	✓	
Deschutes River – Twin Springs	31	B3	✓	✓	
Deschutes River – Wapinitia	32	B3	✓	✓	
Deschutes River – Windy Flat	33	B3		✓	
Deschutes River – Wingdam	34	B3	✓	✓	
Dovre	1	A1	✓	✓	
Duncan Reservoir	89	C3	✓	✓	✓
East Shore	69	C1	✓	✓	✓
Edson Creek	122	D1	✓	✓	
Elderberry Flats	130	D2	✓	✓	✓
Elkhorn Valley	8	B2	✓	✓	
Fan Creek	5	B1	✓	✓	
Fawn Creek	70	C1	✓	✓	✓
Fish Lake	151	D4	✓	✓	
Fishermen's Bend	9	B2	✓	✓	
Gerber Rec Area – Barnes Valley	135	D3	✓	✓	✓
Gerber Rec Area – Basin	136	D3	✓	✓	✓
Gerber Rec Area – Miller Creek	137	D3	✓	✓	✓
Gerber Rec Area – North	138	D3	✓	✓	
Gerber Rec Area – Pitch Log Creek	139	D3	✓	✓	✓
Gerber Rec Area – Rock Creek	140	D3	✓	✓	✓
Gerber Rec Area – South	141	D3	✓	✓	
Gerber Rec Area – Stan H Spring	142	D3	✓	✓	✓
Gerber Rec Area – The Potholes	143	D3	✓	✓	✓
Gerber Rec Area – Upper Midway	144	D3	✓	✓	✓
Gerber Rec Area – Wildhorse	145	D3	✓	✓	✓
Hells Canyon Reservoir – Airstrip	57	B5	✓	✓	✓
Hells Canyon Reservoir – Bob's Creek	58	B5	✓	✓	✓
Hells Canyon Reservoir – Westfall	59	B5	✓	✓	✓
Hidden Springs	35	B3	✓	✓	✓

Name	ID	Map	RVs	Tents	Free
Hult Pond	6	B1	✓	✓	✓
Hyatt Lake	131	D2	✓	✓	
Hyatt Lake – Wildcat	132	D2	✓	✓	
Hyatt Lake Horse Camp	133	D2	✓	✓	
Jackman Park	152	D4	✓	✓	
Juntura Hot Springs	113	C4	✓	✓	✓
Lake Abert	146	D3	✓		✓
Little Cottonwood Creek Canyon	153	D4	✓	✓	✓
Lone Pine (Crooked River)	90	C3	✓	✓	
Lone Pine (North Fork John Day)	51	B4	✓	✓	
Loon Lake	71	C1	✓	✓	
Loon Lake East Shore	72	C1		✓	✓
Lost Forest RNA – North Dunes 1	91	C3	✓	✓	✓
Lost Forest RNA – North Dunes 2	92	C3	✓	✓	✓
Lost Forest RNA – Road 6121	93	C3	✓	✓	✓
Lost Forest RNA – Road 6121	94	C3	✓	✓	✓
Lost Forest RNA – Road 6141	95	C3	✓	✓	✓
Lost Forest RNA – Road 6141A	96	C3	✓	✓	✓
Lost Forest RNA – Road 6151 East	97	C3	✓	✓	✓
Lost Forest RNA – Road 6151 West	98	C3	✓	✓	✓
Mann Lake Rec Area	154	D4	✓	✓	✓
Manning Pasture	36	B3	✓	✓	✓
Mayfield Pond	99	C3	✓	✓	✓
Mecca Flat	37	B3	✓	✓	
Millpond	79	C2	✓	✓	
Molalla River Rec Area – Red Dog	10	B2	✓	✓	✓
Molalla River Rec Area – Shadow View	11	B2	✓	✓	✓
Molalla River Rec Area – Three Bears	12	B2		✓	
Muleshoe	38	B3	✓	✓	
North Millican OHV – Cinder Pit	100	C3	✓	✓	✓
North Millican OHV – North Horse Camp	101	C3	✓	✓	✓
North Millican OHV – ODOT Pit	102	C3	✓	✓	✓
Oasis	39	B3	✓	✓	
Old Logging Road	40	B3	✓	✓	✓
Owyhee River – Rome Launch	159	D5	✓	✓	✓
Page Springs	155	D4	✓	✓	
Painted Hills NM – Red Hill	41	B3		✓	✓
Palisades	103	C3	✓	✓	
Park Creek Recreation Site	73	C1	✓	✓	✓

Name	ID	Map	RVs	Tents	Free
Pike Creek Canyon	156	D4		✓	
Poison Butte	104	C3	✓	✓	
Post Pile	105	C3	✓	✓	
Priest Hole	42	B3	✓	✓	✓
Reynolds Pond	106	C3	✓	✓	✓
Rock Creek	80	C2	✓	✓	
Rocky Road	43	B3	✓	✓	✓
Rogue River – Argo Landing	123	D1	✓	✓	✓
Rogue River – Chair Riffle	124	D1		✓	
Rogue River – Rand Landing	125	D1	✓	✓	
Rogue River – Tucker Flat	126	D1		✓	✓
Rogue River Ranch NHS	127	D1		✓	✓
Scaredman Rec Site	81	C2	✓	✓	✓
Service Creek	44	B3	✓	✓	
Sharps Creek	82	C2	✓	✓	
Sixes River	128	D1	✓	✓	
Skull Creek	129	D1	✓	✓	✓
Slocum Creek (Leslie Gulch)	120	C5	✓	✓	✓
Smith River Falls	74	C1	✓	✓	✓
Snake River Dispersed 1	60	B5	✓	✓	✓
Snake River Dispersed 2	61	B5	✓	✓	✓
Snake River Dispersed 3	62	B5	✓	✓	✓
Snake River Road Dispersed	63	B5	✓	✓	✓
South Junction	45	B3	✓	✓	
South Millican OHV – Evan Wells	107	C3	✓	✓	✓
South Millican OHV – Ford Road	108	C3	✓	✓	✓
South Millican OHV – South Horse Camp	109	C3	✓	✓	✓
South Steens	157	D4	✓	✓	
Spring Rec Site	64	B5	✓	✓	
Stillwater	46	B3	✓	✓	
Stinkingwater Pass Dispersed	114	C4	✓	✓	✓
Stovepipe Springs	47	B3	✓	✓	✓
Sunstone Collection Area	147	D3	✓	✓	✓
Susan Creek	83	C2	✓	✓	
Swedes Landing	65	B5	✓	✓	✓
Three Forks	160	D5		✓	✓
Topsy	134	D2	✓	✓	
Trout Creek	48	B3	✓	✓	
Tyee	75	C1	✓	✓	
Upper Lake Creek	7	B1	✓	✓	✓

Name	ID	Map	RVs	Tents	Free
US 95 Dispersed	161	D5	✓	✓	✓
Vincent Creek	76	C1	✓	✓	✓
Virtue Flat OHV Area	66	B5	✓	✓	✓
Warm Springs	115	C4	✓	✓	✓
White River	49	B3	✓	✓	
Whittaker Creek	77	C1	✓	✓	
Willow Creek Hot Springs	158	D4	✓	✓	✓
Willow Valley Reservoir	148	D3	✓	✓	✓
Yellowbottom	13	B2		✓	

1 • A1 | Dovre

Total sites: 9, RV sites: 9, Central water, Vault/pit toilet, No showers, No RV dump, Tent & RV camping: $10, Open Apr-Oct, Reservations not accepted, Elevation: 1496ft/456m, Telephone: 503-375-5646. Nearest town: McMinnville. GPS: 45.316222, -123.478444

2 • A3 | Deschutes River – Macks Canyon

Total sites: 17, RV sites: 17, No water, Vault/pit toilet, Tent & RV camping: $8-12, 3 group sites: $25-$35, Stay limit: 14 days, Elevation: 456ft/139m, Telephone: 541-416-6700. Nearest town: Maupin. GPS: 45.391203, -120.877934

3 • B1 | Alder Glen

Total sites: 10, RV sites: 10, Central water, Vault/pit toilet, No showers, No RV dump, Tent & RV camping: $10, Open May-Nov, Reservations not accepted, Stay limit: 14 days, Elevation: 866ft/264m, Telephone: 503-375-5646. Nearest town: Corvallis. GPS: 45.265834, -123.579099

4 • B1 | Alsea Falls

Total sites: 21, RV sites: 21, Central water, Vault/pit toilet, No showers, No RV dump, Tent & RV camping: $12, Group site: $20, Open May-Sep, Reservations accepted, Elevation: 918ft/280m, Telephone: 503-375-5646. Nearest town: Alsea. GPS: 44.320753, -123.487344

5 • B1 | Fan Creek

Total sites: 11, RV sites: 11, Central water, Vault/pit toilet, No showers, No RV dump, Tent & RV camping: $10, Open May-Sep, Reservations not accepted, Elevation: 1306ft/398m, Telephone: 541-574-3100. Nearest town: McMinnville. GPS: 45.290839, -123.493558

6 • B1 | Hult Pond

Dispersed sites, Vault/pit toilet, Tent & RV camping: Free, Reservations not accepted, Stay limit: 14 days, Elevation: 820ft/250m, Telephone: 541-683-6600. Nearest town: Eugene. GPS: 44.240359, -123.495455

7 • B1 | Upper Lake Creek

Dispersed sites, No water, Vault/pit toilet, Tent & RV camping: Free, Open all year, Reservations not accepted, Elevation: 793ft/242m, Telephone: 541-683-6600. Nearest town: Horton. GPS: 44.237569, -123.499515

8 • B2 | Elkhorn Valley

Total sites: 23, RV sites: 23, Central water, Vault/pit toilet, No showers, No RV dump, Tent & RV camping: $14, Non-potable water available, Open May-Sep, Reservations not accepted, Stay limit: 14 days, Elevation: 983ft/300m, Telephone: 503-375-5646. Nearest town: Salem. GPS: 44.799605, -122.453921

9 • B2 | Fishermen's Bend

Total sites: 40, RV sites: 40, Electric sites: 40, Water at site, Flush toilet, Free showers, RV dump, Tents: $22/RVs: $22-28, Some FHU, Group sites $85-$105, Open May-Oct, Reservations required, Stay limit: 14 days, Elevation: 814ft/248m, Telephone: 503-897-2406. Nearest town: Mill City. GPS: 44.755859, -122.512207

10 • B2 | Molalla River Rec Area – Red Dog

Dispersed sites, No water, No toilets, Tent & RV camping: Free, Elevation: 1604ft/489m, Telephone: 503-375-5646. Nearest town: Salem. GPS: 44.980721, -122.387494

11 • B2 | Molalla River Rec Area – Shadow View

Dispersed sites, No water, No toilets, Tent & RV camping: Free, Elevation: 1545ft/471m, Telephone: 503-375-5646. Nearest town: Salem. GPS: 44.978639, -122.390582

12 • B2 | Molalla River Rec Area – Three Bears

Total sites: 15, RV sites: 0, Central water, Vault/pit toilet, No showers, No RV dump, Tents only: $10, Open May-Sep, Reservations not accepted, Elevation: 809ft/247m, Telephone: 503-315-5935. Nearest town: Molalla. GPS: 45.033403, -122.485533

13 • B2 | Yellowbottom

Total sites: 22, RV sites: 0, Central water, Vault/pit toilet, No showers, No RV dump, Tents only: $12, Trailers not advised - tight turns, Open May-Sep, Reservations not accepted, Elevation: 1432ft/436m, Telephone: 503-375-5646. Nearest town: Sweet Home. GPS: 44.589151, -122.373033

14 • B3 | Barr Road North OHV

Dispersed sites, No water, Vault/pit toilet, Tent & RV camping: Free, Open all year, Reservations not accepted,

Stay limit: 14 days, Elevation: 3046ft/928m, Telephone: 541-416-6700. Nearest town: Redmond. GPS: 44.288496, -121.335717

15 • B3 | Bear Creek Road Dispersed

Dispersed sites, No water, No toilets, Tent & RV camping: Free, Elevation: 2363ft/720m. Nearest town: Mitchell. GPS: 44.629654, -120.307737

16 • B3 | Black Canyon TH

Dispersed sites, No water, No toilets, Tents only: Free, Elevation: 2014ft/614m, Telephone: 208-678-0439. Nearest town: Mitchell. GPS: 44.708087, -120.171594

17 • B3 | Blue Hole

Total sites: 1, RV sites: 1, No water, Vault/pit toilet, Tent & RV camping: $8-12, Elevation: 955ft/291m, Telephone: 541-416-6700. Nearest town: Maupin. GPS: 45.213238, -121.073056

18 • B3 | Bridge Creek

Dispersed sites, No water, No toilets, Tent & RV camping: Free, No large RVs, Elevation: 3576ft/1090m. Nearest town: Mitchell. GPS: 44.612901, -120.210477

19 • B3 | Burnt Ranch

Dispersed sites, No water, Vault/pit toilet, Tent & RV camping: Free, Elevation: 1499ft/457m, Telephone: 541-416-6700. Nearest town: Mitchell. GPS: 44.746191, -120.364384

20 • B3 | Burnt Ranch Dispersed

Dispersed sites, No water, No toilets, Tent & RV camping: Free, Elevation: 1459ft/445m, Telephone: 541-416-6700. Nearest town: Mitchell. GPS: 44.742745, -120.361204

21 • B3 | Castle Rock

Total sites: 6, RV sites: 6, No water, Vault/pit toilet, Tent & RV camping: $8, Elevation: 3012ft/918m, Telephone: 541-416-6700. Nearest town: Prineville. GPS: 44.157727, -120.834338

22 • B3 | Deschutes River – Beavertail

Total sites: 15, RV sites: 15, Central water, Vault/pit toilet, No showers, No RV dump, Tent & RV camping: $8-12, Reservations not accepted, Elevation: 594ft/181m, Telephone: 541-416-6700. Nearest town: Maupin. GPS: 45.33667, -120.94873

23 • B3 | Deschutes River – Devils Canyon

Total sites: 4, RV sites: 4, No water, Vault/pit toilet, Tent & RV camping: $8-12, Elevation: 927ft/283m, Telephone: 541-416-6700. GPS: 45.117987, -121.130059

24 • B3 | Deschutes River – Frog Springs

Dispersed sites, No water, Vault/pit toilet, Tent & RV camping: Free, Also boat-in sites, Reservations not accepted, Elevation: 1337ft/408m, Telephone: 541-416-6700. Nearest town: Madras. GPS: 44.794962, -121.123623

25 • B3 | Deschutes River – Harpham Flat

Total sites: 9, RV sites: 9, No water, Vault/pit toilet, Tent & RV camping: $8-12, Elevation: 909ft/277m, Telephone: 541-416-6700. Nearest town: Maupin. GPS: 45.135723, -121.121149

26 • B3 | Deschutes River – Hole in Wall

Dispersed sites, No water, Vault/pit toilet, Tents only: Fee unk, Also boat-in sites, Elevation: 1029ft/314m, Telephone: 541-416-6700. GPS: 45.036396, -121.080191

27 • B3 | Deschutes River – Jones Canyon

Total sites: 8, RV sites: 8, No water, Vault/pit toilet, Tent & RV camping: $8-12, Also boat-in and group sites, Group sites: $25-$35, Open all year, Reservations not accepted, Elevation: 725ft/221m, Telephone: 541-416-6700. Nearest town: Maupin. GPS: 45.308164, -120.957302

28 • B3 | Deschutes River – Long Bend

Total sites: 4, RV sites: 4, No water, Vault/pit toilet, Tent & RV camping: $8-12, Elevation: 965ft/294m, Telephone: 541-416-6700. Nearest town: Maupin. GPS: 45.126919, -121.128946

29 • B3 | Deschutes River – Oak Springs

Total sites: 6, RV sites: 6, No water, Vault/pit toilet, Tent & RV camping: $8-12, Also boat-in and group sites, Group site: $35-$35, Elevation: 776ft/237m, Telephone: 541-416-6700. Nearest town: Maupin. GPS: 45.219056, -121.074855

30 • B3 | Deschutes River – Rattlesnake Canyon

Dispersed sites, No water, Vault/pit toilet, Tent & RV camping: $8-12, Group Site: $25-$35, Elevation: 547ft/167m, Telephone: 541-416-6700. Nearest town: Maupin. GPS: 45.336424, -120.931266

31 • B3 | Deschutes River – Twin Springs

Total sites: 7, RV sites: 7, No water, Vault/pit toilet, Tent & RV camping: $8-12, Also boat-in sites, Open all year, Reservations not accepted, Elevation: 632ft/193m,

Telephone: 541-416-6700. Nearest town: Maupin. GPS: 45.308966, -121.005112

32 • B3 | Deschutes River – Wapinitia

Total sites: 6, RV sites: 6, No water, Vault/pit toilet, Tent & RV camping: $8-12, Reservations not accepted, Elevation: 882ft/269m, Telephone: 541-416-6700. Nearest town: Maupin. GPS: 45.144593, -121.125319

33 • B3 | Deschutes River – Windy Flat

Dispersed sites, No water, Vault/pit toilet, Tents only: Fee unk, Also boat-in sites, Reservations not accepted, Elevation: 1018ft/310m, Telephone: 541-416-6700. GPS: 45.038669, -121.096958

34 • B3 | Deschutes River – Wingdam

Dispersed sites, No water, No toilets, Tent & RV camping: Fee unk, Reservations not accepted, Elevation: 1224ft/373m, Telephone: 541-416-6700. Nearest town: Warm Springs. GPS: 44.901781, -121.068593

35 • B3 | Hidden Springs

Dispersed sites, No water, No toilets, Tent & RV camping: Free, High-clearance 4x4 vehicle recommended, Elevation: 3625ft/1105m, Telephone: 208-678-0439. Nearest town: Mitchell. GPS: 44.630544, -120.103385

36 • B3 | Manning Pasture

Dispersed sites, No water, No toilets, Tent & RV camping: Free, Reservations not accepted, Elevation: 1749ft/533m. Nearest town: Mitchell. GPS: 44.696335, -120.284758

37 • B3 | Mecca Flat

Total sites: 10, RV sites: 10, No water, Vault/pit toilet, Tent & RV camping: $8-12, Group site $25-$35, Reservations not accepted, Stay limit: 14 days, Elevation: 1421ft/433m, Telephone: 541-416-6700. Nearest town: Warm Springs. GPS: 44.770377, -121.207693

38 • B3 | Muleshoe

Total sites: 13, RV sites: 6, No water, Vault/pit toilet, Tent & RV camping: $5, Open all year, Reservations not accepted, Elevation: 1713ft/522m, Telephone: 541-416-6700. Nearest town: Spray. GPS: 44.807404, -119.967098

39 • B3 | Oasis

Total sites: 10, RV sites: 10, No water, Vault/pit toilet, Tent & RV camping: $8-12, Reservations not accepted, Elevation: 850ft/259m, Telephone: 541-416-6700. Nearest town: Maupin. GPS: 45.183507, -121.083511

40 • B3 | Old Logging Road

Dispersed sites, No water, No toilets, Tent & RV camping: Free, Reservations not accepted, Elevation: 2907ft/886m, Telephone: 208-678-0439. Nearest town: Mitchell. GPS: 44.606215, -120.185941

41 • B3 | Painted Hills NM – Red Hill

Dispersed sites, No water, No toilets, Tents only: Free, Reservations not accepted, Elevation: 2230ft/680m, Telephone: 541-416-6700. Nearest town: Mitchell. GPS: 44.635594, -120.292826

42 • B3 | Priest Hole

Dispersed sites, No water, Vault/pit toilet, Tent & RV camping: Free, Winter access difficult, Open all year, Reservations not accepted, Stay limit: 14 days, Elevation: 1480ft/451m, Telephone: 541-416-6700. Nearest town: Prineville. GPS: 44.741664, -120.354182

43 • B3 | Rocky Road

Dispersed sites, No water, No toilets, Tent & RV camping: Free, Reservations not accepted, Elevation: 1760ft/536m. Nearest town: Mitchell. GPS: 44.691157, -120.281767

44 • B3 | Service Creek

Total sites: 6, RV sites: 6, No water, Vault/pit toilet, Tent & RV camping: $5, Reservations not accepted, Elevation: 1654ft/504m, Telephone: 541-416-6700. Nearest town: Spray. GPS: 44.793195, -120.001292

45 • B3 | South Junction

Total sites: 11, RV sites: 11, No water, Vault/pit toilet, Tent & RV camping: $8-12, Reservations not accepted, Elevation: 1263ft/385m, Telephone: 541-416-6700. Nearest town: Shaniko Jct. GPS: 44.856322, -121.061452

46 • B3 | Stillwater

Total sites: 10, RV sites: 10, No water, Vault/pit toilet, Tent & RV camping: $8, Reservations not accepted, Stay limit: 14 days, Elevation: 2999ft/914m, Telephone: 541-416-6700. Nearest town: Prineville. GPS: 44.145196, -120.829289

47 • B3 | Stovepipe Springs

Dispersed sites, No water, No toilets, Tent & RV camping: Free, Reservations not accepted, Elevation: 1950ft/594m. Nearest town: Mitchell. GPS: 44.708267, -120.271621

48 • B3 | Trout Creek

Total sites: 21, RV sites: 21, No water, Vault/pit toilet, Tent & RV camping: $8-12, 3 group sites: $25-$35, Reservations not accepted, Elevation: 1299ft/396m, Telephone: 541-416-6700. Nearest town: Madras. GPS: 44.816111, -121.093899

49 • B3 | White River

Total sites: 3, RV sites: 3, No water, Vault/pit toilet, Tent & RV camping: $8-12, 3 group sites: $25-$35, Reservations not accepted, Elevation: 794ft/242m, Telephone: 541-416-6700. Nearest town: Maupin. GPS: 45.232308, -121.067142

50 • B4 | Big Bend

Total sites: 4, RV sites: 4, No water, Vault/pit toilet, Tent & RV camping: $5, Reservations not accepted, Elevation: 1873ft/571m. Nearest town: Kimberly. GPS: 44.780905, -119.610867

51 • B4 | Lone Pine (North Fork John Day)

Total sites: 5, RV sites: 5, No water, Vault/pit toilet, Tent & RV camping: $5, Reservations not accepted, Elevation: 1906ft/581m, Telephone: 541-416-6700. Nearest town: Kimberly. GPS: 44.777669, -119.623754

52 • B5 | Basser Diggins

Total sites: 3, RV sites: 0, No water, Vault/pit toilet, Tents only: Fee unk, Open Jun-Oct, Reservations not accepted, Stay limit: 14 days, Elevation: 5937ft/1810m, Telephone: 541-523-1256. Nearest town: Durkee. GPS: 44.597434, -117.260002

53 • B5 | Burnt River Canyon #1 Dispersed

Dispersed sites, No water, No toilets, Tent & RV camping: Free, Elevation: 2793ft/851m. Nearest town: Durkee. GPS: 44.575676, -117.539316

54 • B5 | Burnt River Canyon #2 Dispersed

Dispersed sites, No water, No toilets, Tent & RV camping: Free, Elevation: 3153ft/961m. Nearest town: Durkee. GPS: 44.549977, -117.646749

55 • B5 | Burnt River Canyon #3 Dispersed

Dispersed sites, No water, No toilets, Tent & RV camping: Free, Elevation: 3189ft/972m. Nearest town: Durkee. GPS: 44.551231, -117.662511

56 • B5 | Copper Creek

Total sites: 8, RV sites: 2, No water, Vault/pit toilet, Tent & RV camping: Free, Also boat-in sites, Reservations not accepted, Elevation: 1718ft/524m, Telephone: 541-523-1256. Nearest town: Copperfield. GPS: 45.079317, -116.785996

57 • B5 | Hells Canyon Reservoir – Airstrip

Total sites: 12, RV sites: 12, No water, Vault/pit toilet, Tent & RV camping: Free, Reservations not accepted, Elevation: 1705ft/520m, Telephone: 541-473-3144. Nearest town: Copperfield. GPS: 45.010676, -116.849156

58 • B5 | Hells Canyon Reservoir – Bob's Creek

Total sites: 13, RV sites: 13, No water, Vault/pit toilet, Tent & RV camping: Free, Reservations not accepted, Elevation: 1706ft/520m, Telephone: 541-473-3144. Nearest town: Copperfield. GPS: 44.998042, -116.849666

59 • B5 | Hells Canyon Reservoir – Westfall

Total sites: 15, RV sites: 15, No water, Vault/pit toilet, Tent & RV camping: Free, Reservations not accepted, Elevation: 1718ft/524m, Telephone: 541-473-3144. Nearest town: Copperfield. GPS: 44.990557, -116.854616

60 • B5 | Snake River Dispersed 1

Dispersed sites, No water, Vault/pit toilet, Tent & RV camping: Free, Reservations not accepted, Elevation: 2087ft/636m. Nearest town: Ontario. GPS: 44.262869, -117.127494

61 • B5 | Snake River Dispersed 2

Dispersed sites, No water, No toilets, Tent & RV camping: Free, Reservations not accepted, Elevation: 2089ft/637m. Nearest town: Ontario. GPS: 44.256776, -117.138609

62 • B5 | Snake River Dispersed 3

Dispersed sites, No water, No toilets, Tent & RV camping: Free, Reservations not accepted, Elevation: 2093ft/638m. Nearest town: Ontario. GPS: 44.257497, -117.166672

63 • B5 | Snake River Road Dispersed

Dispersed sites, No water, No toilets, Tent & RV camping: Free, Near RR, Reservations not accepted, Elevation: 2083ft/635m. Nearest town: Huntington. GPS: 44.364799, -117.228376

64 • B5 | Spring Rec Site

Total sites: 35, RV sites: 35, Central water, Vault/pit toilet, No showers, No RV dump, Tent & RV camping: $5, Reservations not accepted, Elevation: 2070ft/631m, Telephone: 541-523-1256. Nearest town: Huntington. GPS: 44.376805, -117.238436

65 • B5 | Swedes Landing

Total sites: 3, RV sites: 3, No water, Vault/pit toilet, Tent & RV camping: Free, Stay limit: 14 days, Elevation: 2076ft/633m, Telephone: 541-473-3144. Nearest town: Richland. GPS: 44.640762, -117.106561

66 • B5 | Virtue Flat OHV Area

Dispersed sites, No water, Vault/pit toilet, Tent & RV camping: Free, Reservations not accepted, Stay limit: 14 days, Elevation: 3344ft/1019m, Telephone: 541-523-1256. Nearest town: Baker City. GPS: 44.797479, -117.673282

67 • C1 | Burnt Mountain (Skeeter Camp)

Total sites: 4, RV sites: 0, No water, Vault/pit toilet, Tents only: Free, Elevation: 2087ft/636m, Telephone: 541-756-0100. Nearest town: Coquille. GPS: 43.220577, -123.833076

68 • C1 | Clay Creek

Total sites: 21, RV sites: 21, Central water, Vault/pit toilet, No showers, No RV dump, Tent & RV camping: $10, Generator hours: 0600-2200, Open May-Nov, Reservations not accepted, Elevation: 558ft/170m, Telephone: 541-683-6600. Nearest town: Florence. GPS: 43.905029, -123.568359

69 • C1 | East Shore

Total sites: 6, RV sites: 6, No water, Vault/pit toilet, Tent & RV camping: Free, Open all year, Reservations not accepted, Elevation: 508ft/155m, Telephone: 541-756-0100. Nearest town: Reedsport. GPS: 43.577356, -123.818879

70 • C1 | Fawn Creek

Dispersed sites, No water, Vault/pit toilet, Tent & RV camping: Free, Open Jun-Sep, Reservations not accepted, Elevation: 64ft/20m, Telephone: 541-756-0100. Nearest town: Reedsport. GPS: 43.784104, -123.829722

71 • C1 | Loon Lake

Total sites: 43, RV sites: 43, Central water, Flush toilet, Free showers, RV dump, Tent & RV camping: $18, CG closed 2020 season - storm damage, Open May-Sep, Reservations accepted, Elevation: 472ft/144m, Telephone: 541-756-0100. Nearest town: Reedsport. GPS: 43.598389, -123.847168

72 • C1 | Loon Lake East Shore

Total sites: 6, No water, Vault/pit toilet, Tents only: Free, Reservations not accepted, Elevation: 474ft/144m, Telephone: 541-756-0100. Nearest town: Reedsport. GPS: 43.59216, -123.83504

73 • C1 | Park Creek Recreation Site

Total sites: 15, RV sites: 15, No water, Vault/pit toilet, Tent & RV camping: Free, Open Jun-Sep, Reservations not accepted, Stay limit: 14 days, Elevation: 732ft/223m, Telephone: 541-756-0100. Nearest town: Coquille. GPS: 43.245609, -123.895221

74 • C1 | Smith River Falls

Total sites: 10, RV sites: 10, No water, Vault/pit toilet, Tent & RV camping: Free, Open May-Sep, Reservations not accepted, Stay limit: 14 days, Elevation: 89ft/27m, Telephone: 541-756-0100. Nearest town: Reedsport. GPS: 43.784532, -123.814232

75 • C1 | Tyee

Total sites: 15, RV sites: 15, Central water, Vault/pit toilet, No showers, No RV dump, Tent & RV camping: $14, Reservations not accepted, Stay limit: 14 days, Elevation: 203ft/62m, Telephone: 541-440-4930. Nearest town: Sutherlin. GPS: 43.484859, -123.484358

76 • C1 | Vincent Creek

Total sites: 5, RV sites: 5, No water, Vault/pit toilet, Tent & RV camping: Free, Open May-Sep, Reservations not accepted, Stay limit: 14 days, Elevation: 213ft/65m, Telephone: 541-756-0100. Nearest town: Gardiner. GPS: 43.79275, -123.77734

77 • C1 | Whittaker Creek

Total sites: 31, RV sites: 15, Central water, Vault/pit toilet, No showers, No RV dump, Tent & RV camping: $10, Open May-Sep, Reservations not accepted, Elevation: 384ft/117m, Telephone: 541-683-6600. Nearest town: Mapleton. GPS: 43.985733, -123.665568

78 • C2 | Cavitt Creek Falls

Total sites: 10, RV sites: 10, Central water, Vault/pit toilet, No showers, No RV dump, Tent & RV camping: $14, Small RVs, Open May-Sep, Reservations not accepted, Stay limit: 14 days, Elevation: 1152ft/351m, Telephone: 541-440-4930. Nearest town: Roseburg. GPS: 43.199491, -123.023511

79 • C2 | Millpond

Total sites: 12, RV sites: 12, Central water, Vault/pit toilet, No showers, No RV dump, Tent & RV camping: $14, Open May-Sep, Reservations not accepted, Stay limit: 14 days, Elevation: 1057ft/322m, Telephone: 541-440-4930. Nearest town: Sutherlin. GPS: 43.380354, -122.949907

80 • C2 | Rock Creek

Total sites: 17, RV sites: 17, Central water, Vault/pit toilet, No showers, No RV dump, Tent & RV camping: $14, Open May-Sep, Reservations not accepted, Stay limit: 14 days, Elevation: 1220ft/372m, Telephone: 541-440-4930. Nearest town: Roseburg. GPS: 43.397922, -122.929964

81 • C2 | Scaredman Rec Site

Total sites: 9, RV sites: 9, Central water, Vault/pit toilet, No showers, No RV dump, Tent & RV camping: Free, Reservations not accepted, Stay limit: 14 days, Elevation: 1552ft/473m, Telephone: 541-464-3291. Nearest town: Roseburg. GPS: 43.380398, -122.760446

82 • C2 | Sharps Creek

Total sites: 11, RV sites: 11, Central water, Vault/pit toilet, No showers, No RV dump, Tent & RV camping: $8, Open May-Sep, Reservations not accepted, Elevation: 1368ft/417m, Telephone: 541-683-6600. Nearest town: Cottage Grove. GPS: 43.632322, -122.779103

83 • C2 | Susan Creek

Total sites: 29, RV sites: 29, Central water, Flush toilet, Free showers, No RV dump, Tent & RV camping: $20, Open May-Sep, Reservations accepted, Elevation: 1037ft/316m, Telephone: 541-440-4930. Nearest town: Glide. GPS: 43.296858, -122.891005

84 • C3 | Big Bend (Crooked River)

Total sites: 13, RV sites: 13, Central water, Vault/pit toilet, Tent & RV camping: $8, Group fee: $16, Reservations not accepted, Stay limit: 14 days, Elevation: 3110ft/948m, Telephone: 541-416-6700. Nearest town: Prineville. GPS: 44.112186, -120.794519

85 • C3 | Chimney Rock

Total sites: 16, RV sites: 8, Central water, Vault/pit toilet, No showers, No RV dump, Tent & RV camping: $8, Open all year, Reservations not accepted, Stay limit: 14 days, Elevation: 3176ft/968m, Telephone: 541-416-6700. Nearest town: Prineville. GPS: 44.137133, -120.815438

86 • C3 | Christmas Valley Sand Dunes – Green Mountain

Dispersed sites, No water, No toilets, Tent & RV camping: Free, 4x4 recommended, Stay limit: 14 days, Elevation: 5148ft/1569m, Telephone: 541-947-2177. Nearest town: Christmas Valley. GPS: 43.386162, -120.723501

87 • C3 | Christmas Valley Sand Dunes – Junipers

Dispersed sites, No water, No toilets, Tent & RV camping: Free, Elevation: 4301ft/1311m, Telephone: 541-947-2177. Nearest town: Christmas Valley. GPS: 43.352751, -120.45185

88 • C3 | Cobble Rock

Total sites: 15, RV sites: 15, No water, Vault/pit toilet, Tent & RV camping: $8, Reservations not accepted, Stay limit: 14 days, Elevation: 3087ft/941m, Telephone: 541-416-6700. Nearest town: Prineville. GPS: 44.128344, -120.809851

89 • C3 | Duncan Reservoir

Total sites: 4, RV sites: 4, No water, Vault/pit toilet, Tent & RV camping: Free, Group site, Reservations not accepted, Stay limit: 14 days, Elevation: 4850ft/1478m, Telephone: 541-947-2177. Nearest town: Silver Lake. GPS: 43.071274, -120.945024

90 • C3 | Lone Pine (Crooked River)

Total sites: 6, RV sites: 6, No water, Vault/pit toilet, Tent & RV camping: $8, Group site $16, Reservations not accepted, Elevation: 3074ft/937m, Telephone: 541-416-6700. Nearest town: Prineville. GPS: 44.130376, -120.838202

91 • C3 | Lost Forest RNA – North Dunes 1

Dispersed sites, No water, Tent & RV camping: Free, Elevation: 4304ft/1312m, Telephone: 541-947-2177. Nearest town: Silver Lake. GPS: 43.345923, -120.367678

92 • C3 | Lost Forest RNA – North Dunes 2

Dispersed sites, No water, Tent & RV camping: Free, Elevation: 4301ft/1311m, Telephone: 541-947-2177. Nearest town: Silver Lake. GPS: 43.354543, -120.385034

93 • C3 | Lost Forest RNA – Road 6121

Dispersed sites, No water, Tent & RV camping: Free, Elevation: 4498ft/1371m, Telephone: 541-947-2177. Nearest town: Silver Lake. GPS: 43.342445, -120.308821

94 • C3 | Lost Forest RNA – Road 6121

Dispersed sites, No water, Tent & RV camping: Free, Elevation: 4603ft/1403m, Telephone: 541-947-2177. Nearest town: Silver Lake. GPS: 43.394291, -120.260598

95 • C3 | Lost Forest RNA – Road 6141

Dispersed sites, No water, Tent & RV camping: Free, Elevation: 4478ft/1365m, Telephone: 541-947-2177. Nearest town: Silver Lake. GPS: 43.380766, -120.363897

96 • C3 | Lost Forest RNA – Road 6141A

Dispersed sites, No water, Tent & RV camping: Free, Elevation: 4560ft/1390m, Telephone: 541-947-2177. Nearest town: Silver Lake. GPS: 43.393516, -120.305474

97 • C3 | Lost Forest RNA – Road 6151 East

Dispersed sites, No water, Tent & RV camping: Free, Elevation: 4626ft/1410m, Telephone: 541-947-2177. Nearest town: Silver Lake. GPS: 43.363108, -120.281817

98 • C3 | Lost Forest RNA – Road 6151 West

Dispersed sites, No water, Tent & RV camping: Free, Elevation: 4321ft/1317m, Telephone: 541-947-2177. Nearest town: Silver Lake. GPS: 43.359873, -120.370591

99 • C3 | Mayfield Pond

Dispersed sites, No water, No toilets, Tent & RV camping: Free, Lots of shooting here, Reservations not accepted, Elevation: 3304ft/1007m, Telephone: 541-416-6700. Nearest town: Bend. GPS: 44.083311, -121.130578

100 • C3 | North Millican OHV – Cinder Pit

Dispersed sites, No water, No toilets, Tent & RV camping: Free, Open all year, Reservations not accepted, Elevation: 4220ft/1286m, Telephone: 541-416-6700. Nearest town: Bend. GPS: 43.931147, -120.934254

101 • C3 | North Millican OHV – North Horse Camp

Dispersed sites, No water, No toilets, Tent & RV camping: Free, Open all year, Reservations not accepted, Elevation: 4427ft/1349m, Telephone: 541-416-6700. Nearest town: Bend. GPS: 43.899473, -120.928866

102 • C3 | North Millican OHV – ODOT Pit

Dispersed sites, No water, No toilets, Tent & RV camping: Free, Open all year, Reservations not accepted, Elevation: 4406ft/1343m, Telephone: 541-416-6700. Nearest town: Bend. GPS: 43.876213, -120.895928

103 • C3 | Palisades

Total sites: 14, RV sites: 14, No water, Vault/pit toilet, Tent & RV camping: $8, Open May-Sep, Reservations not accepted, Stay limit: 14 days, Elevation: 3031ft/924m, Telephone: 541-416-6700. Nearest town: Prineville. GPS: 44.131133, -120.821148

104 • C3 | Poison Butte

Total sites: 5, RV sites: 5, No water, Vault/pit toilet, Tent & RV camping: $8, Reservations not accepted, Elevation: 3072ft/936m, Telephone: 541-416-6879. Nearest town: Prineville. GPS: 44.119722, -120.797486

105 • C3 | Post Pile

Total sites: 7, RV sites: 7, No water, Vault/pit toilet, Tent & RV camping: $8, Reservations not accepted, Stay limit: 14 days, Elevation: 3057ft/932m, Telephone: 541-416-6700. Nearest town: Prineville. GPS: 44.128881, -120.801331

106 • C3 | Reynolds Pond

Dispersed sites, No water, No toilets, Tent & RV camping: Free, Open all year, Reservations not accepted, Stay limit: 14 days, Elevation: 3378ft/1030m, Telephone: 541-416-6700. Nearest town: Bend. GPS: 44.059379, -121.015983

107 • C3 | South Millican OHV – Evan Wells

Dispersed sites, No water, No toilets, Tent & RV camping: Free, Open all year, Elevation: 4357ft/1328m, Telephone: 541-416-6700. Nearest town: Bend. GPS: 43.832128, -121.016717

108 • C3 | South Millican OHV – Ford Road

Dispersed sites, No water, No toilets, Tent & RV camping: Free, Open all year, Elevation: 4229ft/1289m, Telephone: 541-416-6700. Nearest town: Bend. GPS: 43.874044, -120.987088

109 • C3 | South Millican OHV – South Horse Camp

Dispersed sites, No water, No toilets, Tent & RV camping: Free, Open all year, Reservations not accepted, Elevation: 4358ft/1328m, Telephone: 541-416-6700. Nearest town: Bend. GPS: 43.905068, -121.011998

110 • C4 | Chickahominy Recreation Site

Total sites: 28, RV sites: 28, Central water, Vault/pit toilet, No showers, No RV dump, Tent & RV camping: $8, Reservations not accepted, Stay limit: 14 days, Elevation: 4301ft/1311m, Telephone: 541-573-4400. Nearest town: Juntura. GPS: 43.545977, -119.612532

111 • C4 | Chickahominy Reservoir

Total sites: 28, RV sites: 28, Central water, Vault/pit toilet, No showers, No RV dump, Tent & RV camping: $8, Open all year, Reservations not accepted, Stay limit: 14 days, Elevation: 4295ft/1309m, Telephone: 541-573-4400. Nearest town: Riley. GPS: 43.547272, -119.612565

112 • C4 | Chukar Park

Total sites: 18, RV sites: 18, Central water, Vault/pit toilet, No showers, No RV dump, Tent & RV camping: $5, Open all year, Reservations not accepted, Elevation: 3120ft/951m, Telephone: 541-473-3144. Nearest town: Juntura. GPS: 43.803306, -118.155344

113 • C4 | Juntura Hot Springs

Dispersed sites, No water, No toilets, Tent & RV camping: Free, Rough road, Reservations not accepted, Elevation: 2914ft/888m, Telephone: 541-473-3144. Nearest town: Juntura. GPS: 43.775482, -118.048699

114 • C4 | Stinkingwater Pass Dispersed

Dispersed sites, No water, No toilets, Tent & RV camping: Free, Rough road, Reservations not accepted, Elevation:

4824ft/1470m. Nearest town: Burns. GPS: 43.679544, -118.535566

115 • C4 | Warm Springs

Dispersed sites, No water, Vault/pit toilet, Tent & RV camping: Free, Open all year, Elevation: 3432ft/1046m, Telephone: 406 821-3201. Nearest town: Juntura. GPS: 43.638843, -118.256317

116 • C5 | Antelope Reservoir

Total sites: 4, RV sites: 4, No water, Vault/pit toilet, Tent & RV camping: Free, Elevation: 4339ft/1323m, Telephone: 541-473-3144. Nearest town: Jordan Valley. GPS: 42.908492, -117.236901

117 • C5 | Birch Creek Historic Ranch

Total sites: 5, RV sites: 5, No water, Vault/pit toilet, Tent & RV camping: Free, Also boat-in sites, Rough road - high clearance 4x4 recommended, Open Mar-Oct, Reservations not accepted, Stay limit: 14 days, Elevation: 2737ft/834m, Telephone: 541-473-3144. Nearest town: Jordan Valley. GPS: 43.226118, -117.495357

118 • C5 | Coffee Pot Crater

Dispersed sites, No water, No toilets, Tent & RV camping: Free, Reservations not accepted, Stay limit: 14 days, Elevation: 4638ft/1414m, Telephone: 541-473-3144. Nearest town: Jordan Valley. GPS: 43.146211, -117.461179

119 • C5 | Cow Lakes

Total sites: 10, RV sites: 10, No water, Vault/pit toilet, Tent & RV camping: Free, Open all year, Elevation: 4362ft/1330m, Telephone: 541-473-3144. Nearest town: Jordan Valley. GPS: 43.096335, -117.328217

120 • C5 | Slocum Creek (Leslie Gulch)

Total sites: 12, RV sites: 12, No water, Vault/pit toilet, Tent & RV camping: Free, Large RVs not recommended, Roads may be impassable when wet, Open Mar-Nov, Elevation: 2831ft/863m, Telephone: 541-473-3144. Nearest town: Rockville. GPS: 43.322755, -117.322659

121 • D1 | Burma Pond

Dispersed sites, No water, No toilets, Tent & RV camping: Free, 4x4 recommended, Elevation: 2887ft/880m, Telephone: 541-618-2200. Nearest town: Wolf Creek. GPS: 42.703913, -123.274292

122 • D1 | Edson Creek

Total sites: 27, RV sites: 27, Central water, Vault/pit toilet, No showers, No RV dump, Tent & RV camping: $8, 5 reservable group sites, Open May-Sep, Reservations not accepted, Elevation: 74ft/23m, Telephone: 541-756-0100. Nearest town: Port Orford. GPS: 42.815189, -124.411047

123 • D1 | Rogue River – Argo Landing

Dispersed sites, No water, Vault/pit toilet, Tent & RV camping: Free, Also boat-in sites, Use of fire pans mandatory, Elevation: 625ft/191m, Telephone: 541-479-3735. Nearest town: Galice. GPS: 42.625185, -123.597193

124 • D1 | Rogue River – Chair Riffle

Dispersed sites, No water, Vault/pit toilet, Tents only: $10, Also boat-in sites, Permit required - $10/person/trip, 4x4 required, Use of fire pans mandatory, Elevation: 673ft/205m, Telephone: 541-479-3735. Nearest town: Galice. GPS: 42.591254, -123.584646

125 • D1 | Rogue River – Rand Landing

Dispersed sites, No water, Vault/pit toilet, Tent & RV camping: $10, Also boat-in sites, Permit required - $10/person/trip, Use of fire pans mandatory, Elevation: 667ft/203m, Telephone: 541-479-3735. Nearest town: Galice. GPS: 42.593335, -123.581906

126 • D1 | Rogue River – Tucker Flat

Total sites: 6, No water, Vault/pit toilet, Tents only: Free, Permit required - $10/person/trip, Use of fire pans mandatory, Open May-Oct, Elevation: 528ft/161m, Telephone: 541-479-3735. Nearest town: Galice. GPS: 42.721769, -123.881799

127 • D1 | Rogue River Ranch NHS

Dispersed sites, Central water, Vault/pit toilet, Tents only: Free, Check with caretaker before camping, Reservations not accepted, Elevation: 484ft/148m, Telephone: 541-618-2200. Nearest town: Galice. GPS: 42.719165, -123.881483

128 • D1 | Sixes River

Total sites: 19, RV sites: 19, Central water, Vault/pit toilet, No showers, No RV dump, Tent & RV camping: $8, Open Jun-Sep, Reservations not accepted, Elevation: 205ft/62m, Telephone: 541-756-0100. Nearest town: Port Orford. GPS: 42.804456, -124.308044

129 • D1 | Skull Creek

Total sites: 5, No water, Vault/pit toilet, No showers, No RV dump, Tent & RV camping: Free, Bear-proof trash receptacles, Reservations not accepted, Elevation: 1198ft/365m, Telephone: 541-618-2200. Nearest town: Glendale. GPS: 42.771925, -123.570627

130 • D2 | Elderberry Flats

Total sites: 11, RV sites: 11, No water, Vault/pit toilet, Tent & RV camping: Free, Open May-Sep, Reservations not accepted, Stay limit: 14 days, Elevation: 2103ft/641m, Telephone: 541-618-2200. Nearest town: Rogue River. GPS: 42.662449, -123.098957

131 • D2 | Hyatt Lake

Total sites: 56, RV sites: 56, Central water, Flush toilet, Free showers, RV dump, Tent & RV camping: $12-15, Open Apr-Sep, Reservations required, Stay limit: 14 days, Elevation: 5069ft/1545m, Telephone: 541-482-2031. Nearest town: Ashland. GPS: 42.168421, -122.463215

132 • D2 | Hyatt Lake – Wildcat

Total sites: 12, RV sites: 12, Central water, Vault/pit toilet, No showers, No RV dump, Tent & RV camping: $7, Showers, Dump at Hyatt Main CG, Reservations required, Stay limit: 14 days, Elevation: 5027ft/1532m, Telephone: 541-482-2031. Nearest town: Ashland. GPS: 42.183478, -122.449189

133 • D2 | Hyatt Lake Horse Camp

Total sites: 5, RV sites: 5, No water, Vault/pit toilet, Tent & RV camping: $10, Must have horse, Open May-Sep, Stay limit: 14 days, Elevation: 5043ft/1537m, Telephone: 541-482-2031. Nearest town: Ashland. GPS: 42.180825, -122.452958

134 • D2 | Topsy

Total sites: 15, RV sites: 15, Central water, Vault/pit toilet, No showers, RV dump, Tent & RV camping: $7, Open May-Oct, Reservations not accepted, Elevation: 3829ft/1167m, Telephone: 541-947-2177. Nearest town: Keno. GPS: 42.123533, -122.042112

135 • D3 | Gerber Rec Area – Barnes Valley

Dispersed sites, No water, Vault/pit toilet, Tent & RV camping: Free, Reservations not accepted, Elevation: 4851ft/1479m, Telephone: 541-947-2177. Nearest town: Bonanza. GPS: 42.176164, -121.060695

136 • D3 | Gerber Rec Area – Basin

Dispersed sites, No water, Vault/pit toilet, Tent & RV camping: Free, Reservations not accepted, Elevation: 5258ft/1603m, Telephone: 541-947-2177. Nearest town: Bonanza. GPS: 42.119429, -121.007431

137 • D3 | Gerber Rec Area – Miller Creek

Dispersed sites, No water, Vault/pit toilet, Tent & RV camping: Free, Reservations not accepted, Elevation:

4844ft/1476m, Telephone: 541-947-2177. Nearest town: Bonanza. GPS: 42.184356, -121.130149

138 • D3 | Gerber Rec Area – North

Total sites: 12, RV sites: 12, No water, Vault/pit toilet, Tent & RV camping: $7, Free in winter, Reservations not accepted, Elevation: 4850ft/1478m, Telephone: 541-947-2177. Nearest town: Bonanza. GPS: 42.218467, -121.134301

139 • D3 | Gerber Rec Area – Pitch Log Creek

Dispersed sites, No water, No toilets, Tent & RV camping: Free, Reservations not accepted, Elevation: 5138ft/1566m, Telephone: 541-947-2177. Nearest town: Bonanza. GPS: 42.159267, -121.007028

140 • D3 | Gerber Rec Area – Rock Creek

Dispersed sites, No water, Vault/pit toilet, Tent & RV camping: Free, Reservations not accepted, Elevation: 4939ft/1505m, Telephone: 541-947-2177. Nearest town: Bonanza. GPS: 42.009966, -120.962246

141 • D3 | Gerber Rec Area – South

Total sites: 15, RV sites: 15, Central water, Vault/pit toilet, No showers, RV dump, Tent & RV camping: $7, Free in winter, Reservations not accepted, Elevation: 4856ft/1480m, Telephone: 541-947-2177. Nearest town: Bonanza. GPS: 42.203376, -121.129497

142 • D3 | Gerber Rec Area – Stan H Spring

Dispersed sites, No water, Vault/pit toilet, Tent & RV camping: Free, Reservations not accepted, Elevation: 4855ft/1480m, Telephone: 541-947-2177. Nearest town: Bonanza. GPS: 42.229975, -121.139046

143 • D3 | Gerber Rec Area – The Potholes

Dispersed sites, No water, Vault/pit toilet, Tent & RV camping: Free, Reservations not accepted, Elevation: 4942ft/1506m, Telephone: 541-947-2177. Nearest town: Bonanza. GPS: 42.218683, -121.150489

144 • D3 | Gerber Rec Area – Upper Midway

Dispersed sites, No water, Vault/pit toilet, Tent & RV camping: Free, Reservations not accepted, Elevation: 5194ft/1583m, Telephone: 541-947-2177. Nearest town: Bonanza. GPS: 42.113348, -121.024898

145 • D3 | Gerber Rec Area – Wildhorse

Dispersed sites, No water, Vault/pit toilet, Tent & RV camping: Free, Reservations not accepted, Elevation: 5214ft/1589m, Telephone: 541-947-2177. Nearest town: Bonanza. GPS: 42.125849, -121.012685

146 • D3 | Lake Abert

Dispersed sites, No water, No toilets, No tents/RVs: Free, Reservations not accepted, Elevation: 4281ft/1305m. Nearest town: Lakeview. GPS: 42.529484, -120.233293

147 • D3 | Sunstone Collection Area

Dispersed sites, No water, Vault/pit toilet, Tent & RV camping: Free, Impassable in wet weather, Reservations not accepted, Elevation: 4632ft/1412m, Telephone: 541-947-2177. Nearest town: Plush. GPS: 42.723815, -119.860471

148 • D3 | Willow Valley Reservoir

Dispersed sites, No water, Vault/pit toilet, Tent & RV camping: Free, Reservations not accepted, Elevation: 4537ft/1383m, Telephone: 541-883-6916. Nearest town: Malin. GPS: 42.008756, -121.116621

149 • D4 | Alvord Desert

Dispersed sites, No water, No toilets, Tent & RV camping: Free, Reservations not accepted, Elevation: 4044ft/1233m, Telephone: 541-573-4400. Nearest town: Fields. GPS: 42.508042, -118.532443

150 • D4 | Big Sand Gap

Dispersed sites, No water, No toilets, Tent & RV camping: Free, Impossible to cross Playa when wet, Elevation: 4106ft/1252m, Telephone: 541-573-4400. Nearest town: Fields. GPS: 42.489535, -118.388323

151 • D4 | Fish Lake

Total sites: 23, RV sites: 23, Central water, Vault/pit toilet, No showers, No RV dump, Tent & RV camping: $8, Open Jun-Oct, Reservations not accepted, Stay limit: 14 days, Elevation: 7418ft/2261m, Telephone: 541-573-4400. Nearest town: Fields. GPS: 42.738281, -118.643555

152 • D4 | Jackman Park

Total sites: 6, RV sites: 6, No water, Vault/pit toilet, Tent & RV camping: $6, Open Jun-Oct, Reservations not accepted, Stay limit: 14 days, Elevation: 7726ft/2355m, Telephone: 541-416-6700. Nearest town: Fields. GPS: 42.718883, -118.623699

153 • D4 | Little Cottonwood Creek Canyon

Total sites: 8, No water, No toilets, Tent & RV camping: Free, Dispersed sites along road, Reservations not accepted, Elevation: 4314ft/1315m. Nearest town: Fields. GPS: 42.161832, -118.609509

154 • D4 | Mann Lake Rec Area

Dispersed sites, No water, Vault/pit toilet, Tent & RV camping: Free, Reservations not accepted, Stay limit: 14 days, Elevation: 4206ft/1282m, Telephone: 541-573-4400. Nearest town: Fields. GPS: 42.777916, -118.438809

155 • D4 | Page Springs

Total sites: 17, RV sites: 17, Central water, Vault/pit toilet, No showers, No RV dump, Tent & RV camping: $8, Open all year, Reservations not accepted, Elevation: 4275ft/1303m, Telephone: 541-573-4400. Nearest town: Frenchglen. GPS: 42.803153, -118.866856

156 • D4 | Pike Creek Canyon

Dispersed sites, No water, No toilets, Tents only: $5, 4x4 required, Reservations not accepted, Elevation: 4389ft/1338m, Telephone: 541-573-4400. Nearest town: Fields. GPS: 42.578066, -118.533484

157 • D4 | South Steens

Total sites: 51, RV sites: 51, Central water, Vault/pit toilet, No showers, No RV dump, Tent & RV camping: $6, 15 equestrian sites, Open May-Oct, Reservations not accepted, Stay limit: 14 days, Elevation: 5331ft/1625m, Telephone: 541-573-4400. Nearest town: Fields . GPS: 42.656191, -118.728025

158 • D4 | Willow Creek Hot Springs

Total sites: 4, RV sites: 4, No water, Vault/pit toilet, Tent & RV camping: Free, Clothing optional, Reservations not accepted, Elevation: 4544ft/1385m, Telephone: 541-473-3144. Nearest town: Fields. GPS: 42.275257, -118.265472

159 • D5 | Owyhee River – Rome Launch

Total sites: 5, RV sites: 5, Central water, Vault/pit toilet, Tent & RV camping: Free, Open Mar-Nov, Reservations not accepted, Elevation: 3387ft/1032m, Telephone: 541-473-3144. Nearest town: Rome. GPS: 42.835951, -117.620959

160 • D5 | Three Forks

Total sites: 5, RV sites: 0, No water, Vault/pit toilet, Tents only: Free, 4x4 high clearance vehicle recommended, Reservations not accepted, Stay limit: 14 days, Elevation: 3983ft/1214m, Telephone: 541-473-3144. Nearest town: Jordan Valley. GPS: 42.545174, -117.167141

161 • D5 | US 95 Dispersed

Dispersed sites, No water, No toilets, Tent & RV camping: Free, Reservations not accepted, Elevation: 4658ft/1420m. Nearest town: McDermitt. GPS: 42.076278, -117.733884

South Dakota

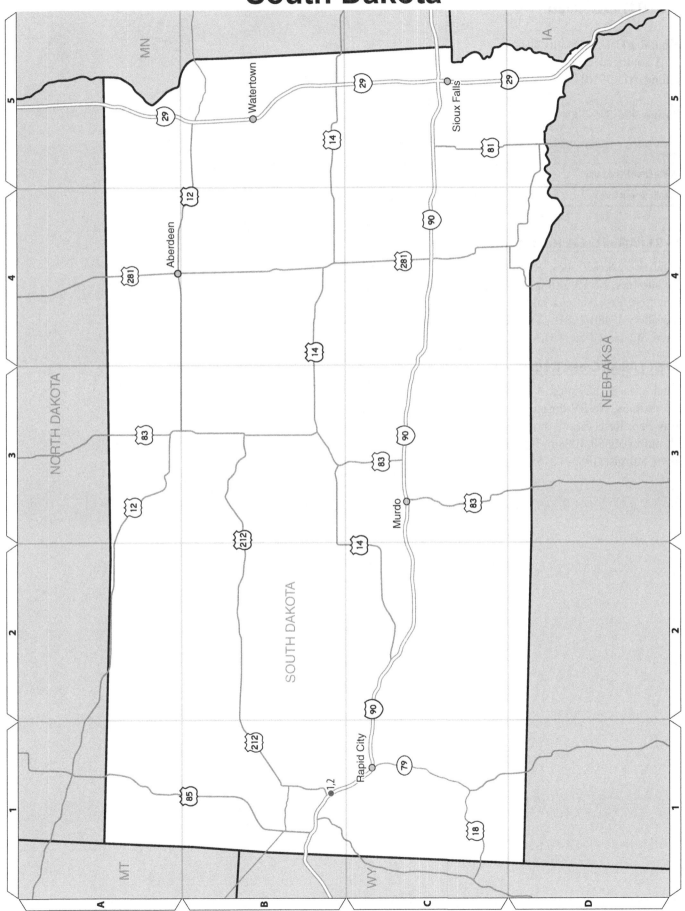

South Dakota

Montana/Dakotas State Office
5001 Southgate Dr
Billings MT 59101

Phone: 406-896-5004

Name	ID	Map	RVs	Tents	Free
Alkali Creek Horse Camp	1	B1	✓	✓	
Alkali Creek TH Camp	2	B1	✓	✓	

1 • B1 | Alkali Creek Horse Camp

Total sites: 6, RV sites: 6, Central water, Vault/pit toilet, No showers, No RV dump, Tent & RV camping: $8, Open May-Sep, Reservations not accepted, Stay limit: 14 days, Elevation: 3548ft/1081m, Telephone: 605-892-7000. Nearest town: Sturgis. GPS: 44.37706, -103.465762

2 • B1 | Alkali Creek TH Camp

Total sites: 5, RV sites: 3, Central water, Vault/pit toilet, No showers, No RV dump, Tent & RV camping: $8, Open May-Sep, Reservations not accepted, Stay limit: 14 days, Elevation: 3555ft/1084m, Telephone: 605-892-7000. Nearest town: Sturgis. GPS: 44.375508, -103.467551

Utah

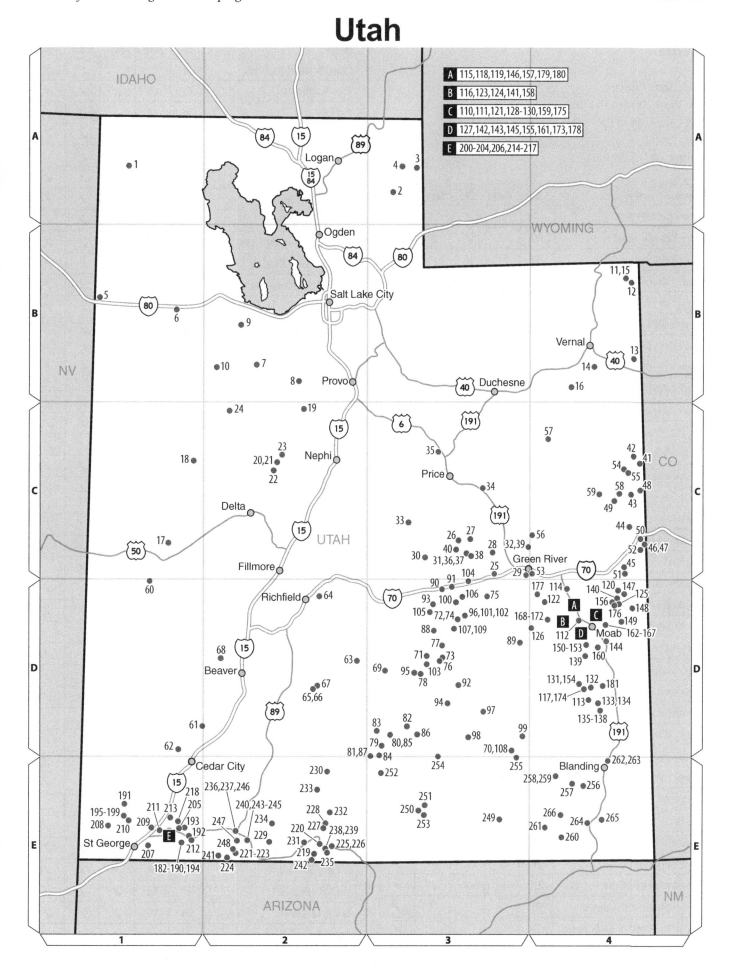

Map legend:

A 115,118,119,146,157,179,180
B 116,123,124,141,158
C 110,111,121,128-130,159,175
D 127,142,143,145,155,161,173,178
E 200-204,206,214-217

Utah

Utah State Office
440 West 200 South Suite 500
Salt Lake City UT 84101

Phone: 801-539-4001

Name	ID	Map	RVs	Tents	Free
Amasa Basin ATV Area	17	C1	✓	✓	✓
Apple Valley Dispersed 1	182	E1	✓	✓	✓
Apple Valley Dispersed 2	183	E1	✓	✓	✓
Apple Valley Dispersed 3	184	E1	✓	✓	✓
Apple Valley Dispersed 4	185	E1		✓	✓
Apple Valley Dispersed 5	186	E1	✓	✓	✓
Apple Valley Dispersed 6	187	E1	✓	✓	✓
Apple Valley Dispersed 7	188	E1	✓	✓	✓
Apple Valley Dispersed 8	189	E1	✓	✓	✓
Apple Valley Dispersed 9	190	E1	✓	✓	✓
Arch Canyon/Comb Wash	256	E4	✓	✓	✓
Atchee Ridge 1	41	C4	✓	✓	✓
Atchee Ridge 2	42	C4	✓	✓	✓
Bailey S Lower Rd	257	E4	✓	✓	✓
Baker Dam	191	E1	✓	✓	
Bea's Lewis Flat	69	D3	✓	✓	✓
Big Bend	110	D4	✓	✓	
Big Bend Creek	111	D4		✓	✓
Big Rocks SRMA	63	D2	✓	✓	✓
Birch Creek	2	A3	✓		✓
Bismarck Peak Dispersed	19	C2	✓	✓	✓
Black Dragon Canyon Dispersed	25	C3	✓	✓	✓
Blue Notch Road	70	D3	✓	✓	✓
Bonneville Salt Flats	5	B1	✓	✓	✓
Book Cliffs Ridge	43	C4	✓	✓	✓
Bride Canyon	112	D4	✓	✓	✓
Bridge Hollow	11	B4	✓	✓	
Bridgeport	12	B4	✓	✓	✓
Bridger Jack Mesa	113	D4	✓	✓	✓
Bryson Canyon Dispersed	44	C4	✓		✓
Buckhorn Dispersed	26	C3	✓	✓	✓
Buckskin Gulch Trailhead	219	E2	✓	✓	✓
Cainville Wash Road Dispersed	71	D3		✓	✓
Cedar Mountain Overlook Dispersed	27	C3		✓	✓

Name	ID	Map	RVs	Tents	Free
Chute Canyon TH Dispersed	72	D3		✓	✓
Cisco Boat Ramp	45	C4	✓	✓	✓
Clay Hills	249	E3	✓	✓	✓
Cliff Ridge	13	B4	✓	✓	✓
Clover Springs	7	B2	✓	✓	
Coal Mine Wash	73	D3	✓	✓	✓
Coal Pits Wash Dispersed	192	E1		✓	✓
Cockscomb Dispersed	220	E2	✓	✓	✓
Colorado River – Grand Camp	46	C4		✓	✓
Colorado River – Stateline	47	C4		✓	✓
Copper Ridge Dinosaur Tracksite	114	D4	✓	✓	✓
Coral Pink Sand Dunes – Meadows	221	E2	✓	✓	✓
Coral Pink Sand Dunes – Ponderosa Grove	222	E2	✓	✓	
Coral Pink Sand Dunes – Sand Spring	223	E2	✓	✓	✓
Coral Pink Sand Dunes Dispersed	224	E2	✓	✓	✓
Cottonwood Canyon Dispersed 1	225	E2	✓	✓	✓
Cottonwood Canyon Dispersed 2	226	E2	✓	✓	✓
Cottonwood Canyon Dispersed 3	227	E2	✓	✓	✓
Cottonwood Canyon Hoodoo TH Dispersed	228	E2	✓	✓	✓
Cottonwood Wash TH	28	C3		✓	✓
Courthouse Rock	115	D4	✓	✓	
Cowboy Camp	116	D4		✓	
Crack Canyon TH Dispersed	74	D3		✓	✓
Crawford Dispersed	3	A3	✓	✓	✓
Creek Pasture	117	D4	✓	✓	
Crocodile Staging Area	229	E2	✓		✓
Crystal Geyser Dispersed	29	C3	✓	✓	✓
Dalton Well Road Dispersed	118	D4	✓	✓	✓
Dalton Well Road Dispersed	119	D4	✓	✓	✓
Dewey Bridge	120	D4	✓	✓	
Dick Canyon	48	C4	✓	✓	✓
Divide Ridge	49	C4	✓	✓	✓
Drinks Canyon	121	D4	✓	✓	
Dripping Spring	122	D4		✓	✓
Dubinky Well Road #1	123	D4	✓	✓	✓
Dubinky Well Road #2	124	D4	✓	✓	✓
Dutch Flat Dispersed	30	C3	✓	✓	✓
Eardley Canyon TH	75	D3	✓	✓	
Equestrian	31	C3	✓	✓	✓

Name	ID	Map	RVs	Tents	Free
Factory Butte – Swing Arm City OHV Area	76	D3	✓	✓	✓
Factory Butte Dispersed	77	D3	✓	✓	✓
Fisher Towers	125	D4		✓	
Fivehole Arch TH	126	D4		✓	✓
Fivemile Pass Rec Area	8	B2	✓	✓	✓
Fossil Mountain Dispersed	60	D1	✓	✓	✓
Fremont River	78	D3	✓	✓	✓
Gaucamole TH	193	E1	✓	✓	✓
Glenwood Open OHV Area	64	D2	✓	✓	✓
Gold Bar	127	D4	✓	✓	
Goose Island	128	D4	✓	✓	
Gooseberry Mesa Dispersed	194	E1	✓	✓	✓
Grand Gulch	258	E4		✓	✓
Grand Staircase Escalante NM – Calf Creek	79	D3	✓	✓	
Grand Staircase Escalante NM – Dance Hall Rock	250	E3	✓	✓	✓
Grand Staircase Escalante NM – Deer Creek	80	D3	✓	✓	
Grand Staircase Escalante NM – Forty Mile Spring	251	E3	✓	✓	✓
Grand Staircase Escalante NM – Harris Wash	252	E3	✓	✓	✓
Grand Staircase Escalante NM – Henrieville Creek	230	E2	✓	✓	✓
Grand Staircase Escalante NM – Hole in the Rock	81	D3	✓	✓	✓
Grand Staircase Escalante NM – Horse Canyon	82	D3	✓	✓	✓
Grand Staircase Escalante NM – Kitchen Corral Wash	231	E2	✓	✓	✓
Grand Staircase Escalante NM – North New Home Bench	83	D3	✓	✓	✓
Grand Staircase Escalante NM – Pump Canyon Springs	232	E2	✓	✓	✓
Grand Staircase Escalante NM – Rock Springs Bench	233	E2	✓	✓	✓
Grand Staircase Escalante NM – Skutumpah Terrace	234	E2	✓	✓	✓
Grand Staircase Escalante NM – Sooner Rocks	253	E3	✓	✓	✓
Grand Staircase Escalante NM – Spencer Flat	84	D3	✓	✓	✓
Grand Staircase Escalante NM – Steep Creek Bench	85	D3	✓	✓	✓

Name	ID	Map	RVs	Tents	Free
Grand Staircase Escalante NM – Stud Horse Peaks	86	D3	✓	✓	✓
Grand Staircase Escalante NM – Tin Can Flat	87	D3	✓	✓	✓
Grand Staircase Escalante NM – White House	235	E2	✓	✓	
Grandstaff	129	D4		✓	
Green River Bridge	14	B4	✓	✓	✓
Hal Canyon	130	D4		✓	
Halls Creek	254	E3		✓	✓
Hamburger Rock	131	D4	✓	✓	
Hart Point Dispersed	132	D4	✓	✓	✓
Hart Point Road Dispersed	133	D4	✓	✓	✓
Hart Point Road Dispersed	134	D4	✓	✓	✓
Hart Point Road Dispersed	135	D4	✓	✓	✓
Hart Point Road Dispersed	136	D4	✓	✓	✓
Hart Point Road Dispersed	137	D4	✓	✓	✓
Hart Point Road Dispersed	138	D4	✓	✓	✓
Hastings Road Dispersed	32	C3	✓	✓	✓
Hatch Point	139	D4	✓	✓	
Hidden Splendor TH	88	D3	✓	✓	✓
Hittle Bottom	140	D4	✓	✓	
Horseman Park Rd Dispersed	195	E1	✓	✓	✓
Horseman Park Rd Dispersed	196	E1	✓	✓	✓
Horseman Park Rd Dispersed	197	E1	✓	✓	✓
Horseman Park Rd Dispersed	198	E1	✓	✓	✓
Horseman Park Rd Dispersed	199	E1	✓	✓	✓
Horseshoe Canyon	89	D3		✓	✓
Horseshoe Knolls	9	B2	✓	✓	✓
Horsethief	141	D4	✓	✓	
Hunter Canyon	142	D4		✓	
Hurricane Cliffs RA	200	E1	✓	✓	✓
Hurricane Cliffs RA	201	E1	✓	✓	✓
Hurricane Cliffs RA	202	E1	✓	✓	✓
Hurricane Cliffs RA	203	E1		✓	✓
Hurricane Cliffs RA	204	E1	✓	✓	✓
Indian Crossing	15	B4	✓	✓	
Ingham Pass Dispersed	1	A1		✓	✓
Jacob's Chair	255	E3	✓		✓
Jct 95-261	259	E4	✓	✓	✓
Joe's Valley Bouldering Area	33	C3	✓	✓	✓
Justesen Flats ATV	90	D3	✓	✓	✓

Name	ID	Map	RVs	Tents	Free
Kane Creek Dispersed	143	D4	✓	✓	
Ken's Lake	144	D4	✓	✓	
King's Bottom	145	D4	✓	✓	
Klondike Bluffs Dispersed	146	D4	✓	✓	✓
Knolls OHV SRMA	6	B1	✓	✓	
Kokopelli's Trail – Bitter Creek Overlook	50	C4		✓	
Kokopelli's Trail – Cowskin	147	D4		✓	
Kokopelli's Trail – Fish Ford	51	C4	✓	✓	✓
Kokopelli's Trail – Hideout Canyon	148	D4		✓	
Kokopelli's Trail – Rock Castle	149	D4	✓	✓	
Kokopelli's Trail – Westwater	52	C4		✓	
Kolob Creekside	205	E1	✓	✓	✓
La Verkin Overlook Rd	206	E1	✓	✓	✓
Ledge A	150	D4	✓	✓	
Ledge B	151	D4	✓	✓	
Ledge C	152	D4		✓	
Ledge D	153	D4		✓	
Little Creek	4	A3	✓	✓	
Little Sahara RA – Jericho	20	C2	✓	✓	✓
Little Sahara RA – Oasis	21	C2	✓	✓	✓
Little Sahara RA – Sand Mountain	22	C2	✓	✓	✓
Little Sahara RA – White Sands	23	C2	✓	✓	✓
Little Valley Road Dispersed	53	C4	✓	✓	✓
Lockhart Rd South	154	D4	✓	✓	✓
Lone Warrior Dispersed	91	D3		✓	✓
Lonesome Beaver	92	D3		✓	
Long Canyon Dispersed	155	D4	✓	✓	✓
Long Valley Recreation Area	207	E1	✓	✓	✓
Lower Onion Creek	156	D4	✓	✓	
Lucky Strike Mine Dispersed	93	D3		✓	✓
Manganese Wash Dispersed	208	E1	✓	✓	✓
McCook Ridge 1	54	C4	✓	✓	✓
McCook Ridge 2	55	C4	✓	✓	✓
McMillan Spring	94	D3	✓	✓	
Mexican Hat Dispersed	260	E4	✓	✓	✓
Mill Canyon	157	D4	✓	✓	✓
Mineral Point Road	158	D4	✓	✓	✓
Mount Carmel	236	E2	✓	✓	✓
Mount Carmel Jct ATV	237	E2	✓	✓	✓
Mud Springs Plateau	34	C3	✓	✓	✓

Name	ID	Map	RVs	Tents	Free
Muley Point	261	E4	✓	✓	✓
Nefertiti Rapids	56	C4	✓	✓	✓
Notom Rd	95	D3	✓	✓	✓
Oak Grove	159	D4		✓	
Otter Creek Reservoir – Fisherman's Beach	65	D2	✓	✓	✓
Otter Creek Reservoir – South Point	66	D2	✓	✓	✓
Otter Creek Reservoir East Side Dispersed 1	67	D2	✓	✓	✓
Paria Contact Station	238	E2	✓		✓
Paria Contact Station	239	E2	✓		✓
Parowan Gap	61	D1	✓	✓	✓
Peek-A-Boo ATV Area	240	E2	✓	✓	✓
Pelican Lake	16	B4	✓	✓	
Picture Frame Arch	160	D4		✓	✓
Pine Spring Kiosk	241	E2	✓	✓	✓
Price Canyon	35	C3	✓	✓	
Pucker Pass Dispersed	161	D4		✓	✓
Recapture Reservoir East Side	262	E4	✓	✓	✓
Recapture Reservoir West Side	263	E4	✓	✓	✓
Red Cliffs	209	E1	✓	✓	
Road 033 Dispersed	210	E1	✓	✓	✓
Rock Corral	68	D2	✓	✓	✓
Rocky Peak	62	D1	✓	✓	
San Juan River – Sand Island	264	E4	✓	✓	
San Juan River – Swinging Bridge	265	E4		✓	✓
San Rafael Bridge North	36	C3	✓	✓	
San Rafael Bridge South	37	C3	✓	✓	
San Rafael River Dispersed	38	C3	✓	✓	✓
San Rafael Swell Dispersed	96	D3	✓	✓	✓
Sand Cove Primitive	211	E1	✓	✓	✓
Sand Flat Rec Area – Juniper	162	D4	✓	✓	
Sand Flats – Area A	163	D4	✓	✓	
Sand Flats – Area B	164	D4		✓	
Sand Flats – Area C/D	165	D4		✓	
Sand Flats – Area E	166	D4	✓	✓	
Sand Flats – Area F/G/H	167	D4		✓	
Sand Wash Rec Area	57	C4		✓	✓
Sandthrax Dispersed	97	D3	✓	✓	✓
Seep Ridge	58	C4	✓	✓	✓
Simpson Springs	24	C2	✓	✓	

Name	ID	Map	RVs	Tents	Free
Smithsonian Butte Dispersed	212	E1	✓	✓	✓
Spring Canyon Road – Site 1	168	D4	✓	✓	✓
Spring Canyon Road – Site 2	169	D4	✓	✓	✓
Spring Canyon Road – Site 3	170	D4	✓	✓	✓
Spring Canyon Road – Site 4	171	D4	✓	✓	✓
Spring Canyon Road – Site 5	172	D4	✓	✓	✓
Spring Site	173	D4		✓	
Starr Springs	98	D3	✓	✓	
Stateline	242	E2	✓	✓	✓
Sundance	99	D3		✓	✓
Superbowl	174	D4	✓	✓	
Swasey's Beach	39	C3	✓	✓	
Taylor Flat Dispersed	100	D3	✓	✓	✓
Temple Mountain East	101	D3	✓	✓	✓
Temple Mountain West Dispersed	102	D3	✓	✓	✓
The Arch site 1	243	E2	✓	✓	✓
The Arch site 2	244	E2	✓	✓	✓
The Arch site 3	245	E2	✓	✓	✓
The Mix Pad	103	D3	✓	✓	✓
The Wedge	40	C3	✓	✓	✓
The Wickiup Dispersed	104	D3	✓	✓	✓
Tomsich Butte TH	105	D3	✓	✓	✓
Topaz Mountain Rockhound Area	18	C1	✓	✓	✓
Toquerville Falls	213	E1	✓	✓	✓
Twin Hollows Canyon Dispersed	246	E2	✓	✓	✓
Twin Knolls Dispersed	106	D3	✓	✓	✓
Upper Big Bend	175	D4		✓	
Upper Onion Creek	176	D4	✓	✓	
Valley of the Gods	266	E4	✓	✓	✓
Virgin Dam Dispersed	214	E1	✓	✓	✓
Virgin Dam Dispersed	215	E1	✓	✓	✓
Virgin Dam Dispersed	216	E1		✓	✓
Virgin Dam Dispersed	217	E1	✓	✓	✓
White Rock Dispersed	10	B2	✓	✓	✓
White Wash Sand Dunes	177	D4	✓	✓	✓
Wild Horse Dispersed	107	D3	✓	✓	✓
William's Bottom	178	D4	✓	✓	
Willow Springs Trail Dispersed 1	179	D4	✓	✓	✓
Willow Springs Trail Dispersed 2	180	D4	✓	✓	✓
Windwhistle	181	D4	✓	✓	
Wingate Dispersed 1	108	D3	✓		✓

Name	ID	Map	RVs	Tents	Free
Winter Ridge	59	C4	✓	✓	✓
Wld Horse Road Dispersed	109	D3	✓	✓	✓
Yellowjacket Canyon Dispersed	247	E2	✓	✓	✓
Yellowjacket Spring Dispersed	248	E2	✓	✓	✓
Zion View	218	E1	✓	✓	✓

1 • A1 | Ingham Pass Dispersed

Dispersed sites, No water, No toilets, Tents only: Free, High-clearance vehicle recommended, Elevation: 7571ft/2308m, Telephone: 801-977-4300. GPS: 41.661937, -113.741883

2 • A3 | Birch Creek

Dispersed sites, No water, Vault/pit toilet, Tent & RV camping: Free, Walk-to sites, RV camping permitted in parking lot, Open May-Oct, Reservations not accepted, Stay limit: 14 days, Elevation: 6929ft/2112m, Telephone: 801-977-4300. Nearest town: Woodruff. GPS: 41.505868, -111.317264

3 • A3 | Crawford Dispersed

Dispersed sites, No water, No toilets, Tent & RV camping: Free, Elevation: 7608ft/2319m. Nearest town: Randolph. GPS: 41.660204, -111.095804

4 • A3 | Little Creek

Total sites: 10, RV sites: 10, Central water, Vault/pit toilet, Tent & RV camping: $12, Water availability seasonal, Reservable group site $65, Reservations not accepted, Elevation: 6398ft/1950m, Telephone: 801-977-4300. Nearest town: Randolph. GPS: 41.677759, -111.226079

5 • B1 | Bonneville Salt Flats

Dispersed sites, No water, No toilets, Tent & RV camping: Free, Elevation: 4285ft/1306m. Nearest town: Wendover. GPS: 40.771949, -113.981459

6 • B1 | Knolls OHV SRMA

Dispersed sites, No water, Vault/pit toilet, Tent & RV camping: $10, Open all year, Reservations not accepted, Elevation: 4265ft/1300m, Telephone: 801-977-4300. Nearest town: Wendover. GPS: 40.710347, -113.284765

7 • B2 | Clover Springs

Total sites: 10, RV sites: 10, No water, Vault/pit toilet, Tent & RV camping: $12, Group site: $45, 2 equestrian sites, Open May-Oct, Reservations not accepted, Elevation: 6063ft/1848m, Telephone: 801-977-4300. Nearest town: Tooele. GPS: 40.347131, -112.550598

8 • B2 | Fivemile Pass Rec Area

Dispersed sites, No water, Vault/pit toilet, Tent & RV camping: Free, Reservations not accepted, Stay limit: 14 days, Elevation: 5259ft/1603m, Telephone: 801-977-4300. Nearest town: Fairfield. GPS: 40.237158, -112.162782

9 • B2 | Horseshoe Knolls

Dispersed sites, No water, No toilets, Tent & RV camping: Free, Reservations not accepted, Stay limit: 14 days, Elevation: 4455ft/1358m, Telephone: 801-977-4300. Nearest town: Grantsville. GPS: 40.612882, -112.698021

10 • B2 | White Rock Dispersed

Dispersed sites, No water, No toilets, Tent & RV camping: Free, Reservations not accepted, Elevation: 5346ft/1629m, Telephone: 801-977-4300. Nearest town: Tooele. GPS: 40.322602, -112.905177

11 • B4 | Bridge Hollow

Total sites: 13, RV sites: 13, Vault/pit toilet, Tent & RV camping: $5, 1 group site, Open all year, Reservations not accepted, Elevation: 5408ft/1648m, Telephone: 435-781-4400. Nearest town: Vernal. GPS: 40.898667, -109.170169

12 • B4 | Bridgeport

Dispersed sites, No water, No toilets, Tent & RV camping: Free, Reservations not accepted, Elevation: 5433ft/1656m, Telephone: 435-781-4400. Nearest town: Vernal. GPS: 40.879303, -109.135604

13 • B4 | Cliff Ridge

Dispersed sites, No water, No toilets, Tent & RV camping: Free, Hang-gliding area, Stay limit: 14 days, Elevation: 8123ft/2476m, Telephone: 435-781-4400. Nearest town: Vernal. GPS: 40.367685, -109.119664

14 • B4 | Green River Bridge

Dispersed sites, No water, No toilets, Tent & RV camping: Free, Elevation: 4721ft/1439m, Telephone: 435-636-3600. Nearest town: Vernal. GPS: 40.313971, -109.482154

15 • B4 | Indian Crossing

Total sites: 22, RV sites: 22, Vault/pit toilet, RV dump, Tent & RV camping: $5, Open May-Oct, Stay limit: 14 days, Elevation: 5495ft/1675m, Telephone: 435-781-4400. Nearest town: Vernal. GPS: 40.898, -109.183

16 • B4 | Pelican Lake

Total sites: 13, RV sites: 13, No water, Vault/pit toilet, Tent & RV camping: Free, 6 defined sites, several dispersed sites, Open May-Oct, Reservations not accepted, Stay limit: 14 days, Elevation: 4817ft/1468m, Telephone: 435-781-4400. Nearest town: Vernal. GPS: 40.181905, -109.692984

17 • C1 | Amasa Basin ATV Area

Dispersed sites, No water, Vault/pit toilet, Tent & RV camping: Free, Elevation: 6027ft/1837m, Telephone: 435-743-3123. Nearest town: Delta. GPS: 39.141673, -113.307273

18 • C1 | Topaz Mountain Rockhound Area

Dispersed sites, No water, No toilets, Tent & RV camping: Free, Reservations not accepted, Elevation: 5766ft/1757m, Telephone: 435-743-3100. Nearest town: Delta. GPS: 39.696368, -113.098419

19 • C2 | Bismarck Peak Dispersed

Dispersed sites, No water, No toilets, Tent & RV camping: Free, Reservations not accepted, Elevation: 5744ft/1751m. Nearest town: Eureka. GPS: 40.051927, -112.120545

20 • C2 | Little Sahara RA – Jericho

Total sites: 40, RV sites: 40, No toilets, Tent & RV camping: Free, Open all year, Reservations not accepted, Elevation: 5030ft/1533m, Telephone: 435-743-3100. Nearest town: Nephi. GPS: 39.686812, -112.367833

21 • C2 | Little Sahara RA – Oasis

Total sites: 115, RV sites: 115, Central water, No toilets, No showers, RV dump, Tent & RV camping: Free, Open all year, Reservations not accepted, Elevation: 5019ft/1530m, Telephone: 435-743-3100. Nearest town: Nephi. GPS: 39.689381, -112.353918

22 • C2 | Little Sahara RA – Sand Mountain

Dispersed sites, Central water, No toilets, Tent & RV camping: Free, Open all year, Reservations not accepted, Elevation: 4928ft/1502m, Telephone: 435-743-3100. Nearest town: Nephi. GPS: 39.639164, -112.389114

23 • C2 | Little Sahara RA – White Sands

Total sites: 100, Central water, Vault/pit toilet, No showers, No RV dump, Tent & RV camping: Free, No water in winter, Open all year, Reservations not accepted, Elevation: 5338ft/1627m, Telephone: 435-743-3100. Nearest town: Nephi. GPS: 39.740705, -112.314718

24 • C2 | Simpson Springs

Total sites: 20, RV sites: 20, Central water, Vault/pit toilet, Tent & RV camping: $15, Open all year, Reservations not accepted, Stay limit: 14 days, Elevation: 5115ft/1559m, Telephone: 801-977-4300. Nearest town: Lehi. GPS: 40.034791, -112.782234

25 • C3 | Black Dragon Canyon Dispersed

Dispersed sites, No water, No toilets, Tent & RV camping: Free, Elevation: 4323ft/1318m. Nearest town: Green River. GPS: 38.937449, -110.419039

26 • C3 | Buckhorn Dispersed

Dispersed sites, No water, No toilets, Tent & RV camping: Free, Reservations not accepted, Stay limit: 14 days, Elevation: 5568ft/1697m, Telephone: 435-636-3600. GPS: 39.166901, -110.737517

27 • C3 | Cedar Mountain Overlook Dispersed

Dispersed sites, No water, No toilets, Tents only: Free, Elevation: 7556ft/2303m. Nearest town: Green River. GPS: 39.176759, -110.630995

28 • C3 | Cottonwood Wash TH

Dispersed sites, No water, No toilets, Tents only: Free, Reservations not accepted, Elevation: 4848ft/1478m, Telephone: 435-636-3600. Nearest town: Green River. GPS: 39.080932, -110.436123

29 • C3 | Crystal Geyser Dispersed

Dispersed sites, No water, No toilets, Tent & RV camping: Free, Elevation: 4058ft/1237m. Nearest town: Green River. GPS: 38.937007, -110.134721

30 • C3 | Dutch Flat Dispersed

Dispersed sites, No water, No toilets, Tent & RV camping: Free, Elevation: 6079ft/1853m. Nearest town: Ferron. GPS: 39.058163, -111.040176

31 • C3 | Equestrian

Total sites: 6, RV sites: 6, No water, No toilets, Tent & RV camping: Free, Reservations not accepted, Stay limit: 14 days, Elevation: 5104ft/1556m, Telephone: 435-636-3600. GPS: 39.080745, -110.662402

32 • C3 | Hastings Road Dispersed

Dispersed sites, No water, No toilets, Tent & RV camping: Free, Elevation: 4128ft/1258m. Nearest town: Green River. GPS: 39.122974, -110.113897

33 • C3 | Joe's Valley Bouldering Area

Dispersed sites, No water, No toilets, Tent & RV camping: Free, Reservations not accepted, Stay limit: 14 days, Elevation: 6579ft/2005m, Telephone: 435-636-3600. Nearest town: Orangeville. GPS: 39.290121, -111.178235

34 • C3 | Mud Springs Plateau

Dispersed sites, No water, No toilets, Tent & RV camping: Free, Elevation: 5699ft/1737m. Nearest town: Wellington. GPS: 39.513338, -110.518894

35 • C3 | Price Canyon

Total sites: 12, RV sites: 7, No water, Vault/pit toilet, Tent & RV camping: $8, Narrow steep access with switchbacks, Open May-Oct, Reservations not accepted, Elevation: 7818ft/2383m, Telephone: 435-636-3600. Nearest town: Price. GPS: 39.76001, -110.91748

36 • C3 | San Rafael Bridge North

Total sites: 6, RV sites: 6, No water, Vault/pit toilet, Tent & RV camping: $8, Reservations not accepted, Stay limit: 14 days, Elevation: 5104ft/1556m, Telephone: 435-636-3600. Nearest town: Cleveland. GPS: 39.080876, -110.664043

37 • C3 | San Rafael Bridge South

Total sites: 11, RV sites: 11, No water, Vault/pit toilet, Tent & RV camping: $6, Stay limit: 14 days, Elevation: 5118ft/1560m, Telephone: 435-636-3600. Nearest town: Cleveland. GPS: 39.079382, -110.665914

38 • C3 | San Rafael River Dispersed

Dispersed sites, No water, No toilets, Tent & RV camping: Free, Elevation: 5118ft/1560m. Nearest town: Green River. GPS: 39.058956, -110.631925

39 • C3 | Swasey's Beach

Total sites: 12, RV sites: 7, No water, Vault/pit toilet, Tent & RV camping: $15, Group site: $75-$100, Reservations not accepted, Stay limit: 14 days, Elevation: 4137ft/1261m, Telephone: 435-636-3600. Nearest town: Green River. GPS: 39.112121, -110.108914

40 • C3 | The Wedge

Dispersed sites, No water, Vault/pit toilet, Tent & RV camping: Free, No camping on rim, Elevation: 6120ft/1865m, Telephone: 435-636-3600. Nearest town: Green River. GPS: 39.106799, -110.763913

41 • C4 | Atchee Ridge 1

Dispersed sites, No water, No toilets, Tent & RV camping: Free, Elevation: 7748ft/2362m. Nearest town: Dinosaur (CO). GPS: 39.660605, -109.096294

42 • C4 | Atchee Ridge 2

Dispersed sites, No water, No toilets, Tent & RV camping: Free, Elevation: 7243ft/2208m. Nearest town: Dinosaur (CO). GPS: 39.706875, -109.143266

43 • C4 | Book Cliffs Ridge

Dispersed sites, No water, No toilets, Tent & RV camping: Free, Numerous dispersed sites along road, Elevation: 8417ft/2566m. GPS: 39.451047, -109.180469

44 • C4 | Bryson Canyon Dispersed

Dispersed sites, No water, No toilets, No tents/RVs: Free, Reservations not accepted, Elevation: 5042ft/1537m. Nearest town: Cisco. GPS: 39.237879, -109.202382

45 • C4 | Cisco Boat Ramp

Dispersed sites, No water, No toilets, Tent & RV camping: Free, Reservations not accepted, Elevation: 4163ft/1269m. Nearest town: Cisco. GPS: 38.969865, -109.251941

46 • C4 | Colorado River – Grand Camp

Dispersed sites, No water, Tents only: Free, Also boat-in sites, No open fires, Elevation: 4333ft/1321m. Nearest town: Fruita, CO. GPS: 39.121814, -109.065428

47 • C4 | Colorado River – Stateline

Dispersed sites, No water, Tents only: Free, Also boat-in sites, No open fires, Elevation: 4333ft/1321m. Nearest town: Fruita, CO. GPS: 39.118068, -109.051685

48 • C4 | Dick Canyon

Dispersed sites, No water, No toilets, Tent & RV camping: Free, Elevation: 8217ft/2505m. Nearest town: Thompson. GPS: 39.483769, -109.090487

49 • C4 | Divide Ridge

Dispersed sites, No water, No toilets, Tent & RV camping: Free, Elevation: 8240ft/2512m. Nearest town: Thompson. GPS: 39.416928, -109.332891

50 • C4 | Kokopelli's Trail – Bitter Creek Overlook

Total sites: 5, RV sites: 0, No water, No toilets, Tents only: $20, Reservations not accepted, Elevation: 5060ft/1542m, Telephone: 435-259-2100. GPS: 39.157014, -109.108319

51 • C4 | Kokopelli's Trail – Fish Ford

Total sites: 10, RV sites: 10, No water, Vault/pit toilet, No showers, No RV dump, Tent & RV camping: Free, Reservations not accepted, Stay limit: 14 days, Elevation: 4157ft/1267m, Telephone: 435-259-2100. Nearest town: Moab. GPS: 38.923652, -109.247883

52 • C4 | Kokopelli's Trail – Westwater

Total sites: 15, RV sites: 0, No water, Vault/pit toilet, No showers, No RV dump, Tents only: $20, Also boat-in and group sites, Group site: $100, Reservations not accepted, Stay limit: 14 days, Elevation: 4335ft/1321m, Telephone: 435-259-2100. Nearest town: Fruita, CO. GPS: 39.087471, -109.101798

53 • C4 | Little Valley Road Dispersed

Dispersed sites, No water, No toilets, Tent & RV camping: Free, Elevation: 4311ft/1314m. Nearest town: Green River. GPS: 38.948153, -110.095078

54 • C4 | McCook Ridge 1

Dispersed sites, No water, No toilets, Tent & RV camping: Free, Elevation: 7101ft/2164m. Nearest town: Thompson. GPS: 39.622204, -109.230632

55 • C4 | McCook Ridge 2

Dispersed sites, No water, No toilets, Tent & RV camping: Free, Elevation: 7306ft/2227m. Nearest town: Thompson. GPS: 39.601343, -109.204659

56 • C4 | Nefertiti Rapids

Dispersed sites, No water, Vault/pit toilet, Tent & RV camping: Free, Elevation: 4163ft/1269m, Telephone: 435-636-3600. Nearest town: Green River. GPS: 39.195279, -110.077249

57 • C4 | Sand Wash Rec Area

Dispersed sites, No water, Vault/pit toilet, Tents only: Free, For those who plan to put in to Desolation and Gray Canyons of the Green River the next day, Reservations not accepted, Elevation: 4638ft/1414m, Telephone: 434-636-3600. Nearest town: Myton. GPS: 39.839579, -109.913639

58 • C4 | Seep Ridge

Dispersed sites, No water, No toilets, Tent & RV camping: Free, Numerous dispersed sites along road, Elevation: 8043ft/2452m. Nearest town: Loma (CO). GPS: 39.462642, -109.283744

59 • C4 | Winter Ridge

Dispersed sites, No water, No toilets, Tent & RV camping: Free, Nothing larger than van/TC, Elevation: 7544ft/2299m. GPS: 39.460987, -109.460495

60 • D1 | Fossil Mountain Dispersed

Dispersed sites, No water, No toilets, Tent & RV camping: Free, Nothing larger than TC, Reservations not accepted, Elevation: 5619ft/1713m, Telephone: 435-743-3100. Nearest town: Delta. GPS: 38.881279, -113.468213

61 • D1 | Parowan Gap

Dispersed sites, No water, No toilets, Tent & RV camping: Free, Near Parowan Gap Petroglyph Site, Open all year,

Reservations not accepted, Elevation: 5644ft/1720m. Nearest town: Parowan. GPS: 37.912233, -112.980007

62 • D1 | Rocky Peak

Total sites: 18, RV sites: 18, No water, Vault/pit toilet, Tent & RV camping: $5, Reservations not accepted, Stay limit: 14 days, Elevation: 5950ft/1814m, Telephone: 435-865-3000. Nearest town: Cedar City. GPS: 37.760197, -113.185846

63 • D2 | Big Rocks SRMA

Dispersed sites, No water, No toilets, Tent & RV camping: Free, Small rigs, Reservations not accepted, Elevation: 7101ft/2164m, Telephone: 435-896-1500. Nearest town: Loa. GPS: 38.360632, -111.635449

64 • D2 | Glenwood Open OHV Area

Dispersed sites, No water, No toilets, Tent & RV camping: Free, Reservations not accepted, Stay limit: 14 days, Elevation: 5441ft/1658m, Telephone: 435-896-1500. Nearest town: Glenwood. GPS: 38.796833, -111.973966

65 • D2 | Otter Creek Reservoir – Fisherman's Beach

Dispersed sites, No water, No toilets, Tent & RV camping: Free, Stay limit: 14 days, Elevation: 6417ft/1956m, Telephone: 435-896-1500. Nearest town: Antimony. GPS: 38.180109, -112.012049

66 • D2 | Otter Creek Reservoir – South Point

Dispersed sites, No water, No toilets, Tent & RV camping: Free, Reservations not accepted, Stay limit: 14 days, Elevation: 6387ft/1947m, Telephone: 435-896-1500. Nearest town: Antimony. GPS: 38.173026, -112.014363

67 • D2 | Otter Creek Reservoir East Side Dispersed 1

Dispersed sites, No water, No toilets, Tent & RV camping: Free, Numerous sites along lakeshore, Reservations not accepted, Stay limit: 14 days, Elevation: 6395ft/1949m, Telephone: 435-896-1500. Nearest town: Antimony. GPS: 38.196095, -111.987703

68 • D2 | Rock Corral

Dispersed sites, No water, Vault/pit toilet, Tent & RV camping: Free, Open May-Nov, Elevation: 7093ft/2162m, Telephone: 435-586-2401. Nearest town: Milford. GPS: 38.372466, -112.834018

69 • D3 | Bea's Lewis Flat

Dispersed sites, No water, No toilets, Tent & RV camping: Free, Elevation: 6744ft/2056m. Nearest town: Torrey. GPS: 38.297556, -111.388149

70 • D3 | Blue Notch Road

Dispersed sites, No water, No toilets, Tent & RV camping: Free, Elevation: 4831ft/1472m. Nearest town: Bluff. GPS: 37.763527, -110.293623

71 • D3 | Cainville Wash Road Dispersed

Dispersed sites, No water, No toilets, Tents only: Free, 4x4 recommended, Elevation: 5050ft/1539m. Nearest town: Hanksville. GPS: 38.391212, -111.026977

72 • D3 | Chute Canyon TH Dispersed

Dispersed sites, No water, No toilets, Tents only: Free, Reservations not accepted, Stay limit: 14 days, Elevation: 5177ft/1578m. Nearest town: Green River. GPS: 38.629154, -110.763255

73 • D3 | Coal Mine Wash

Dispersed sites, No water, Vault/pit toilet, Tent & RV camping: Free, Elevation: 4662ft/1421m. Nearest town: Hanksville. GPS: 38.378011, -110.899811

74 • D3 | Crack Canyon TH Dispersed

Dispersed sites, No water, No toilets, Tents only: Free, Elevation: 5541ft/1689m. Nearest town: Green River. GPS: 38.643072, -110.745229

75 • D3 | Eardley Canyon TH

Dispersed sites, No water, No toilets, Tent & RV camping: Free, Reservations not accepted, Elevation: 4437ft/1352m, Telephone: 435-636-3600. Nearest town: Green River. GPS: 38.785751, -110.488572

76 • D3 | Factory Butte – Swing Arm City OHV Area

Dispersed sites, No water, No toilets, Tent & RV camping: Free, Reservations not accepted, Elevation: 4504ft/1373m, Telephone: 435-896-1500. Nearest town: Hanksville. GPS: 38.365783, -110.912165

77 • D3 | Factory Butte Dispersed

Dispersed sites, No water, No toilets, Tent & RV camping: Free, Reservations not accepted, Elevation: 4786ft/1459m. Nearest town: Hanksville. GPS: 38.460529, -110.888207

78 • D3 | Fremont River

Dispersed sites, No water, No toilets, Tent & RV camping: Free, Elevation: 4827ft/1471m. Nearest town: Hanksville. GPS: 38.275295, -111.081531

79 • D3 | Grand Staircase Escalante NM – Calf Creek

Total sites: 13, RV sites: 13, Water available, Flush toilet, No showers, No RV dump, Tent & RV camping: $15,

Reservations not accepted, Stay limit: 14 days, Elevation: 5410ft/1649m, Telephone: 435-644-1200. Nearest town: Escalante. GPS: 37.794563, -111.413507

80 • D3 | Grand Staircase Escalante NM – Deer Creek

Total sites: 7, RV sites: 7, No water, Vault/pit toilet, No showers, No RV dump, Tent & RV camping: $10, No trailers - may have to back out, Reservations not accepted, Stay limit: 14 days, Elevation: 5735ft/1748m, Telephone: 435-644-1200. Nearest town: Boulder. GPS: 37.855989, -111.355417

81 • D3 | Grand Staircase Escalante NM – Hole in the Rock

Dispersed sites, No water, No toilets, Tent & RV camping: Free, Free permit required, Elevation: 5738ft/1749m, Telephone: 435-644-1200. Nearest town: Henrieville. GPS: 37.722533, -111.527442

82 • D3 | Grand Staircase Escalante NM – Horse Canyon

Dispersed sites, No water, No toilets, Tent & RV camping: Free, Free permit required, Elevation: 5968ft/1819m, Telephone: 435-644-1200. Nearest town: Escalante. GPS: 37.922027, -111.204368

83 • D3 | Grand Staircase Escalante NM – North New Home Bench

Dispersed sites, No water, No toilets, Tent & RV camping: Free, Free permit required, Elevation: 6809ft/2075m, Telephone: 435-644-1200. Nearest town: Boulder. GPS: 37.889317, -111.460758

84 • D3 | Grand Staircase Escalante NM – Spencer Flat

Dispersed sites, No water, No toilets, Tent & RV camping: Free, Free permit required, Elevation: 5958ft/1816m, Telephone: 435-644-1200. Nearest town: Escalante. GPS: 37.726621, -111.443822

85 • D3 | Grand Staircase Escalante NM – Steep Creek Bench

Dispersed sites, No water, No toilets, Tent & RV camping: Free, Free permit required, Elevation: 5928ft/1807m, Telephone: 435-644-1200. Nearest town: Boulder. GPS: 37.870443, -111.337437

86 • D3 | Grand Staircase Escalante NM – Stud Horse Peaks

Dispersed sites, No water, No toilets, Tent & RV camping: Free, Free permit required, Elevation: 6782ft/2067m, Telephone: 435-644-1200. Nearest town: Boulder. GPS: 37.868192, -111.111702

87 • D3 | Grand Staircase Escalante NM – Tin Can Flat

Dispersed sites, No water, No toilets, Tent & RV camping: Free, Free permit required, Elevation: 5683ft/1732m, Telephone: 435-644-1200. Nearest town: Escalante. GPS: 37.714589, -111.514899

88 • D3 | Hidden Splendor TH

Dispersed sites, No water, No toilets, Tent & RV camping: Free, Reservations not accepted, Stay limit: 14 days, Elevation: 4798ft/1462m, Telephone: 435-636-3600. Nearest town: Green River. GPS: 38.566717, -110.959271

89 • D3 | Horseshoe Canyon

Dispersed sites, No water, Vault/pit toilet, Tents only: Free, 4x4 recommended, Elevation: 5343ft/1629m, Telephone: 435-259-2652. GPS: 38.474033, -110.200291

90 • D3 | Justesen Flats ATV

Dispersed sites, No water, No toilets, Tent & RV camping: Free, Elevation: 7116ft/2169m. Nearest town: Green River. GPS: 38.842505, -110.884172

91 • D3 | Lone Warrior Dispersed

Dispersed sites, No water, No toilets, Tents only: Free, Elevation: 7103ft/2165m. Nearest town: Green River. GPS: 38.852684, -110.800735

92 • D3 | Lonesome Beaver

Total sites: 5, RV sites: 0, No water, Vault/pit toilet, Tents only: Donation, Rough road - high clearance vehicles with 4x4 recommended, Open May-Oct, Stay limit: 14 days, Elevation: 5489ft/1673m, Telephone: 435-542-3461. Nearest town: Hanksville. GPS: 38.197021, -110.747314

93 • D3 | Lucky Strike Mine Dispersed

Dispersed sites, No water, No toilets, Tents only: Free, Elevation: 5650ft/1722m. Nearest town: Green River. GPS: 38.736217, -110.965392

94 • D3 | McMillan Spring

Total sites: 10, RV sites: 10, Central water, Vault/pit toilet, No showers, No RV dump, Tent & RV camping: Donation, Reservations not accepted, Stay limit: 14 days, Elevation: 8412ft/2564m, Telephone: 435-542-3461. Nearest town: Hanksville. GPS: 38.072626, -110.848074

95 • D3 | Notom Rd

Dispersed sites, No water, No toilets, Tent & RV camping: Free, Steep road, Elevation: 5178ft/1578m. Nearest town: Hanksville. GPS: 38.278062, -111.130572

96 • D3 | San Rafael Swell Dispersed

Dispersed sites, No water, No toilets, Tent & RV camping: Free, Elevation: 5600ft/1707m. Nearest town: Green River. GPS: 38.656072, -110.710213

97 • D3 | Sandthrax Dispersed

Total sites: 17, RV sites: 7, No water, No toilets, Tent & RV camping: Free, Beware of deep sand, Elevation: 4450ft/1356m, Telephone: 435-542-3461. Nearest town: Hanksville. GPS: 38.016308, -110.532063

98 • D3 | Starr Springs

Total sites: 12, RV sites: 12, Central water, Vault/pit toilet, Tent & RV camping: $10, Group site: $20, Open Apr-Nov, Reservations not accepted, Stay limit: 14 days, Elevation: 6220ft/1896m, Telephone: 435-542-3461. Nearest town: Hanksville. GPS: 37.849886, -110.662685

99 • D3 | Sundance

Dispersed sites, No water, No toilets, Tents only: Free, Elevation: 5623ft/1714m. Nearest town: Hite. GPS: 37.847602, -110.190984

100 • D3 | Taylor Flat Dispersed

Dispersed sites, No water, No toilets, Tent & RV camping: Free, Elevation: 6709ft/2045m. Nearest town: Green River. GPS: 38.753533, -110.763605

101 • D3 | Temple Mountain East

Dispersed sites, No water, Vault/pit toilet, Tent & RV camping: Free, Jeep and ATV area, Stay limit: 14 days, Elevation: 5318ft/1621m, Telephone: 435-636-3600. Nearest town: Hanksville. GPS: 38.656662, -110.661364

102 • D3 | Temple Mountain West Dispersed

Dispersed sites, No water, Vault/pit toilet, Tent & RV camping: Free, Stay limit: 14 days, Elevation: 5453ft/1662m, Telephone: 435-636-3600. Nearest town: Green River. GPS: 38.667704, -110.684824

103 • D3 | The Mix Pad

Dispersed sites, No water, No toilets, Tent & RV camping: Free, Dispersed camping along road, Subject to flooding, Elevation: 4665ft/1422m. Nearest town: Hanksville. GPS: 38.339493, -111.030876

104 • D3 | The Wickiup Dispersed

Dispersed sites, No water, No toilets, Tent & RV camping: Free, Elevation: 6700ft/2042m. Nearest town: Green River. GPS: 38.893472, -110.652176

105 • D3 | Tomsich Butte TH

Dispersed sites, No water, No toilets, Tent & RV camping: Free, Reservations not accepted, Stay limit: 14 days, Elevation: 5070ft/1545m, Telephone: 435-636-3600. Nearest town: Green River. GPS: 38.684886, -111.000075

106 • D3 | Twin Knolls Dispersed

Dispersed sites, No water, No toilets, Tent & RV camping: Free, Elevation: 6696ft/2041m. Nearest town: Green River. GPS: 38.788848, -110.709829

107 • D3 | Wild Horse Dispersed

Dispersed sites, No water, No toilets, Tent & RV camping: Free, Nothing larger than van/TC, Elevation: 5101ft/1555m. Nearest town: Green River. GPS: 38.575297, -110.797697

108 • D3 | Wingate Dispersed 1

Dispersed sites, No water, No toilets, No tents/RVs: Free, Open all year, Reservations not accepted, Elevation: 4636ft/1413m. Nearest town: Bluff. GPS: 37.742743, -110.281077

109 • D3 | Wld Horse Road Dispersed

Dispersed sites, No water, No toilets, Tent & RV camping: Free, Numerous spots, Elevation: 4879ft/1487m. Nearest town: Hanksville. GPS: 38.577351, -110.772861

110 • D4 | Big Bend

Total sites: 23, RV sites: 23, No water, Vault/pit toilet, Tent & RV camping: $20, 3 group sites - $100-$175, Open all year, Reservations not accepted, Stay limit: 14 days, Elevation: 4014ft/1223m, Telephone: 435-259-2100. Nearest town: Moab. GPS: 38.648707, -109.479982

111 • D4 | Big Bend Creek

Dispersed sites, No water, Vault/pit toilet, Tents only: Free, Reservations not accepted, Elevation: 4078ft/1243m. Nearest town: Moab. GPS: 38.651913, -109.477491

112 • D4 | Bride Canyon

Total sites: 6, RV sites: 6, No water, No toilets, Tent & RV camping: Free, Reservations not accepted, Elevation: 4874ft/1486m, Telephone: 435-259-2100. Nearest town: Moab. GPS: 38.612017, -109.666318

113 • D4 | Bridger Jack Mesa

Dispersed sites, No water, No toilets, Tent & RV camping: Free, Open all year, Reservations not accepted, Elevation: 5287ft/1611m, Telephone: 435-587-1500. Nearest town: Monticello. GPS: 38.086116, -109.594379

114 • D4 | Copper Ridge Dinosaur Tracksite

Dispersed sites, No water, Vault/pit toilet, Tent & RV camping: Free, Many sites along road, Avoid No Camping spots and No Vehicle signs, No shade, Verizon/ATT both OK, Reservations not accepted, Stay limit: 14 days, Elevation: 4695ft/1431m, Telephone: 435-259-2100. Nearest town: Moab. GPS: 38.829819, -109.765039

115 • D4 | Courthouse Rock

Total sites: 20, RV sites: 20, No water, Vault/pit toilet, No showers, No RV dump, Tent & RV camping: $20, Generator hours: 0800-2000, Reservations not accepted, Stay limit: 14 days, Elevation: 4531ft/1381m, Telephone: 435-259-2100. Nearest town: Moab. GPS: 38.720285, -109.734087

116 • D4 | Cowboy Camp

Total sites: 7, No water, Vault/pit toilet, Tents only: $20, Reservations not accepted, Stay limit: 14 days, Elevation: 6146ft/1873m, Telephone: 435-259-2100. Nearest town: Moab. GPS: 38.561861, -109.796468

117 • D4 | Creek Pasture

Total sites: 32, RV sites: 32, No water, Vault/pit toilet, Tent & RV camping: $15, Group fee: $65, Open all year, Reservations not accepted, Elevation: 4867ft/1483m, Telephone: 435-587-1500. Nearest town: Monticello. GPS: 38.166514, -109.631814

118 • D4 | Dalton Well Road Dispersed

Dispersed sites, No water, No toilets, Tent & RV camping: Free, Elevation: 4403ft/1342m. Nearest town: Moab. GPS: 38.716143, -109.691953

119 • D4 | Dalton Well Road Dispersed

Dispersed sites, No water, No toilets, Tent & RV camping: Free, Open all year, Reservations not accepted, Elevation: 4414ft/1345m. Nearest town: Moab. GPS: 38.722837, -109.690397

120 • D4 | Dewey Bridge

Total sites: 7, RV sites: 7, No water, Vault/pit toilet, Tent & RV camping: $20, 2 group sites $75, Not for large RVs, Open all year, Reservations not accepted, Stay limit: 14 days, Elevation: 4114ft/1254m, Telephone: 435-259-2100. Nearest town: Moab. GPS: 38.810694, -109.307838

121 • D4 | Drinks Canyon

Total sites: 17, RV sites: 13, No water, Vault/pit toilet, Tent & RV camping: $20, Only small RVs, Open all year, Reservations not accepted, Stay limit: 14 days, Elevation: 3986ft/1215m, Telephone: 435-259-2100. Nearest town: Moab. GPS: 38.633007, -109.486419

122 • D4 | Dripping Spring

Dispersed sites, No water, No toilets, Tents only: Free, Elevation: 4355ft/1327m, Telephone: 435-259-2100. Nearest town: Moab. GPS: 38.746016, -109.966119

123 • D4 | Dubinky Well Road #1

Dispersed sites, No water, No toilets, Tent & RV camping: Free, Elevation: 5298ft/1615m, Telephone: 435-259-2100. Nearest town: Moab. GPS: 38.643814, -109.819371

124 • D4 | Dubinky Well Road #2

Dispersed sites, No water, No toilets, Tent & RV camping: Free, Elevation: 5187ft/1581m, Telephone: 435-259-2100. Nearest town: Moab. GPS: 38.656348, -109.827185

125 • D4 | Fisher Towers

Total sites: 5, RV sites: 0, No water, Vault/pit toilet, Tents only: $20, Reservations not accepted, Stay limit: 14 days, Elevation: 4711ft/1436m, Telephone: 435-259-2100. Nearest town: Moab. GPS: 38.725313, -109.309127

126 • D4 | Fivehole Arch TH

Dispersed sites, No water, No toilets, Tents only: Free, 4x4 required, Reservations not accepted, Elevation: 5160ft/1573m, Telephone: 435-636-3600. Nearest town: Moab. GPS: 38.574185, -110.090755

127 • D4 | Gold Bar

Total sites: 9, RV sites: 9, No water, Vault/pit toilet, Tent & RV camping: $20, 4 reservable group sites: $75, Open all year, Reservations not accepted, Stay limit: 14 days, Elevation: 4029ft/1228m, Telephone: 435-259-2102. Nearest town: Moab. GPS: 38.575335, -109.633553

128 • D4 | Goose Island

Total sites: 19, RV sites: 19, No water, Vault/pit toilet, Tent & RV camping: $20, 2 reservable group sites: $75, Open all year, Reservations not accepted, Stay limit: 14 days, Elevation: 3986ft/1215m, Telephone: 435-259-2100. Nearest town: Moab. GPS: 38.610936, -109.558037

129 • D4 | Grandstaff

Total sites: 16, RV sites: 0, No water, Vault/pit toilet, Tents only: $20, No generators, Reservations not accepted, Stay limit: 14 days, Elevation: 3981ft/1213m, Telephone: 435-259-2100. Nearest town: Moab. GPS: 38.611726, -109.532977

130 • D4 | Hal Canyon

Total sites: 11, No water, Vault/pit toilet, Tents only: $20, Also walk-to sites, Open all year, Reservations not accepted, Stay limit: 14 days, Elevation: 4019ft/1225m, Telephone: 435-259-2100. Nearest town: Moab. GPS: 38.641179, -109.477566

131 • D4 | Hamburger Rock

Total sites: 10, RV sites: 10, No water, Vault/pit toilet, Tent & RV camping: $15, Open all year, Reservations not accepted, Elevation: 4887ft/1490m, Telephone: 435-259-2102. Nearest town: Moab. GPS: 38.192048, -109.669626

132 • D4 | Hart Point Dispersed

Dispersed sites, No water, No toilets, Tent & RV camping: Free, No large RVs, Elevation: 6392ft/1948m. Nearest town: Monticello. GPS: 38.162275, -109.574864

133 • D4 | Hart Point Road Dispersed

Dispersed sites, No water, No toilets, Tent & RV camping: Free, Elevation: 6631ft/2021m. Nearest town: Monticello. GPS: 38.069763, -109.514162

134 • D4 | Hart Point Road Dispersed

Dispersed sites, No water, No toilets, Tent & RV camping: Free, Elevation: 6637ft/2023m. Nearest town: Monticello. GPS: 38.064989, -109.516922

135 • D4 | Hart Point Road Dispersed

Dispersed sites, No water, No toilets, Tent & RV camping: Free, Elevation: 6652ft/2028m. Nearest town: Monticello. GPS: 38.018738, -109.495227

136 • D4 | Hart Point Road Dispersed

Dispersed sites, No water, No toilets, Tent & RV camping: Free, Elevation: 6701ft/2042m. Nearest town: Monticello. GPS: 38.034225, -109.499171

137 • D4 | Hart Point Road Dispersed

Dispersed sites, No water, No toilets, Tent & RV camping: Free, Elevation: 6738ft/2054m. Nearest town: Monticello. GPS: 38.048863, -109.504119

138 • D4 | Hart Point Road Dispersed

Dispersed sites, No water, No toilets, Tent & RV camping: Free, Elevation: 6765ft/2062m. Nearest town: Monticello. GPS: 38.011034, -109.490983

139 • D4 | Hatch Point

Total sites: 10, RV sites: 10, No water, Vault/pit toilet, Tent & RV camping: $20, Open all year, Reservations not accepted, Elevation: 5830ft/1777m, Telephone: 435-259-2100. Nearest town: Moab. GPS: 38.380395, -109.616857

140 • D4 | Hittle Bottom

Total sites: 15, RV sites: 15, No water, Vault/pit toilet, Tent & RV camping: $20, Also group site, Only small RVs, Open all year, Reservations not accepted, Stay limit: 14 days, Elevation: 4104ft/1251m, Telephone: 435-259-2102. Nearest town: Moab. GPS: 38.760552, -109.323556

141 • D4 | Horsethief

Total sites: 60, RV sites: 60, No water, Vault/pit toilet, Tent & RV camping: $20, Group site: $100, Open all year, Reservations not accepted, Stay limit: 14 days, Elevation: 5845ft/1782m, Telephone: 435-259-2100. Nearest town: Moab. GPS: 38.584079, -109.814005

142 • D4 | Hunter Canyon

Total sites: 10, No water, Vault/pit toilet, Tents only: $20, Open all year, Reservations not accepted, Stay limit: 14 days, Elevation: 4295ft/1309m, Telephone: 435-259-2100. Nearest town: Moab. GPS: 38.510154, -109.597016

143 • D4 | Kane Creek Dispersed

Dispersed sites, No water, Vault/pit toilet, Tent & RV camping: $15, Open all year, Reservations not accepted, Elevation: 4165ft/1269m. Nearest town: Moab. GPS: 38.497764, -109.618488

144 • D4 | Ken's Lake

Total sites: 31, RV sites: 31, No water, Vault/pit toilet, Tent & RV camping: $20, Group sites: $125-$150, Open all year, Reservations accepted, Stay limit: 14 days, Elevation: 5085ft/1550m, Telephone: 435-259-2102. Nearest town: Moab. GPS: 38.477904, -109.422975

145 • D4 | King's Bottom

Total sites: 21, RV sites: 21, No water, Vault/pit toilet, Tent & RV camping: $20, Only small RVs, Open all year, Reservations not accepted, Stay limit: 14 days, Elevation: 4003ft/1220m, Telephone: 435-259-2100. Nearest town: Moab. GPS: 38.557407, -109.584527

146 • D4 | Klondike Bluffs Dispersed

Dispersed sites, No water, No toilets, Tent & RV camping: Free, 4x4 recommended, Elevation: 4648ft/1417m. Nearest town: Moab. GPS: 38.758029, -109.725517

147 • D4 | Kokopelli's Trail – Cowskin

Total sites: 5, No water, No toilets, No showers, No RV dump, Tents only: $20, Reservations not accepted, Elevation:

4733ft/1443m, Telephone: 435-259-2100. Nearest town: Moab. GPS: 38.785115, -109.263282

148 • D4 | Kokopelli's Trail – Hideout Canyon

Dispersed sites, No water, No toilets, Tents only: $20, 4x4 high-clearance required, Reservations not accepted, Elevation: 5566ft/1697m, Telephone: 435-259-2100. Nearest town: Moab. GPS: 38.691031, -109.190672

149 • D4 | Kokopelli's Trail – Rock Castle

Total sites: 7, RV sites: 7, No water, No toilets, Tent & RV camping: $20, Reservations not accepted, Elevation: 6411ft/ 1954m, Telephone: 435-259-2100. Nearest town: Moab. GPS: 38.598765, -109.289473

150 • D4 | Ledge A

Total sites: 33, RV sites: 26, No water, Vault/pit toilet, Tent & RV camping: $20, Reservations not accepted, Stay limit: 14 days, Elevation: 4136ft/1261m, Telephone: 435-259-2100. Nearest town: Moab. GPS: 38.492832, -109.607175

151 • D4 | Ledge B

Total sites: 41, RV sites: 33, No water, Vault/pit toilet, Tent & RV camping: $20, Reservations not accepted, Stay limit: 14 days, Elevation: 4144ft/1263m, Telephone: 435-259-2100. Nearest town: Moab. GPS: 38.484609, -109.605737

152 • D4 | Ledge C

Dispersed sites, No water, Vault/pit toilet, Tents only: $20, Reservations not accepted, Stay limit: 14 days, Elevation: 4187ft/1276m, Telephone: 435-259-2100. Nearest town: Moab. GPS: 38.472531, -109.602053

153 • D4 | Ledge D

Total sites: 6, No water, Vault/pit toilet, Tents only: $20, Open all year, Reservations not accepted, Stay limit: 14 days, Elevation: 4209ft/1283m, Telephone: 435-259-2102. Nearest town: Moab. GPS: 38.468329, -109.600745

154 • D4 | Lockhart Rd South

Dispersed sites, No water, No toilets, Tent & RV camping: Free, Elevation: 4914ft/1498m. Nearest town: Moab. GPS: 38.182475, -109.668137

155 • D4 | Long Canyon Dispersed

Dispersed sites, No water, No toilets, Tent & RV camping: Free, Reservations not accepted, Elevation: 5870ft/1789m. Nearest town: Moab. GPS: 38.541811, -109.707506

156 • D4 | Lower Onion Creek

Total sites: 21, RV sites: 21, No water, Vault/pit toilet, Tent & RV camping: $20, Group site $60, Open all year,

Reservations not accepted, Stay limit: 14 days, Elevation: 4093ft/1248m, Telephone: 435-259-2100. Nearest town: Moab. GPS: 38.737172, -109.358436

157 • D4 | Mill Canyon

Dispersed sites, No water, No toilets, Tent & RV camping: Free, Reservations not accepted, Elevation: 4555ft/1388m, Telephone: 435-259-2100. Nearest town: Moab. GPS: 38.712414, -109.739554

158 • D4 | Mineral Point Road

Total sites: 7, RV sites: 2, No water, No toilets, Tent & RV camping: Free, Elevation: 5775ft/1760m. Nearest town: Moab. GPS: 38.585247, -109.826302

159 • D4 | Oak Grove

Total sites: 7, No water, Vault/pit toilet, Tents only: $20, Also walk-to sites, 4 walk-to sites, Open all year, Reservations not accepted, Stay limit: 14 days, Elevation: 4029ft/1228m, Telephone: 435-259-2100. Nearest town: Moab. GPS: 38.643624, -109.476348

160 • D4 | Picture Frame Arch

Total sites: 4, No water, No toilets, Tents only: Free, High-clearance vehicle recommended, Reservations not accepted, Elevation: 5544ft/1690m, Telephone: 435-259-2100. Nearest town: Moab. GPS: 38.435885, -109.502916

161 • D4 | Pucker Pass Dispersed

Dispersed sites, No water, No toilets, Tents only: Free, 4x4 required, Elevation: 6012ft/1832m. Nearest town: Moab. GPS: 38.540114, -109.715405

162 • D4 | Sand Flat Rec Area – Juniper

Total sites: 15, RV sites: 15, No water, Vault/pit toilet, Tents $15/RVs: $15-20, Reservations not accepted, Elevation: 5732ft/1747m. Nearest town: Moab. GPS: 38.579956, -109.429027

163 • D4 | Sand Flats – Area A

Total sites: 19, RV sites: 13, No water, Vault/pit toilet, Tents $15/RVs: $15-20, Open all year, Reservations not accepted, Stay limit: 14 days, Elevation: 4663ft/1421m, Telephone: 435-259-2100. Nearest town: Moab. GPS: 38.576479, -109.520135

164 • D4 | Sand Flats – Area B

Total sites: 16, No water, Vault/pit toilet, Tents only: $15, Open all year, Reservations not accepted, Stay limit: 14 days, Elevation: 4633ft/1412m, Telephone: 435-259-2100. Nearest town: Moab. GPS: 38.580921, -109.518597

165 • D4 | Sand Flats – Area C/D

Total sites: 26, RV sites: 0, No water, Vault/pit toilet, Tents only: $15, Open all year, Reservations not accepted, Stay limit: 14 days, Elevation: 4707ft/1435m, Telephone: 435-259-2100. Nearest town: Moab. GPS: 38.581751, -109.514182

166 • D4 | Sand Flats – Area E

Total sites: 9, RV sites: 7, No water, Vault/pit toilet, Tents: $15/RVs: $15-20, Group site: $50, Open all year, Reservations not accepted, Stay limit: 14 days, Elevation: 4754ft/1449m, Telephone: 435-259-2100. Nearest town: Moab. GPS: 38.580582, -109.499392

167 • D4 | Sand Flats – Area F/G/H

Total sites: 28, RV sites: 0, No water, Vault/pit toilet, Tents only: $15, Open all year, Reservations not accepted, Stay limit: 14 days, Elevation: 4769ft/1454m, Telephone: 435-259-2100. Nearest town: Moab. GPS: 38.582922, -109.485045

168 • D4 | Spring Canyon Road – Site 1

Dispersed sites, No water, No toilets, Tent & RV camping: Free, Elevation: 5111ft/1558m. Nearest town: Moab. GPS: 38.633541, -109.871174

169 • D4 | Spring Canyon Road – Site 2

Dispersed sites, No water, No toilets, Tent & RV camping: Free, Elevation: 5054ft/1540m. Nearest town: Moab. GPS: 38.634518, -109.897116

170 • D4 | Spring Canyon Road – Site 3

Dispersed sites, No water, No toilets, Tent & RV camping: Free, Elevation: 5297ft/1615m. Nearest town: Moab. GPS: 38.622306, -109.931642

171 • D4 | Spring Canyon Road – Site 4

Dispersed sites, No water, No toilets, Tent & RV camping: Free, Elevation: 5162ft/1573m. Nearest town: Moab. GPS: 38.630445, -109.953867

172 • D4 | Spring Canyon Road – Site 5

Dispersed sites, No water, No toilets, Tent & RV camping: Free, Elevation: 4830ft/1472m. Nearest town: Moab. GPS: 38.639143, -109.976254

173 • D4 | Spring Site

Total sites: 4, RV sites: 0, No water, Vault/pit toilet, Tents only: $5, Elevation: 4321ft/1317m. Nearest town: Moab. GPS: 38.518216, -109.594747

174 • D4 | Superbowl

Total sites: 16, RV sites: 16, No water, Vault/pit toilet, Tent & RV camping: $15, Group site: $65, Open all year, Reservations not accepted, Elevation: 4957ft/1511m, Telephone: 435-587-1500. Nearest town: Monticello. GPS: 38.148005, -109.621295

175 • D4 | Upper Big Bend

Total sites: 8, No water, Vault/pit toilet, Tents only: $20, Rough entrance road, Open all year, Reservations not accepted, Stay limit: 14 days, Elevation: 4042ft/1232m, Telephone: 435-259-2100. Nearest town: Moab. GPS: 38.649104, -109.488694

176 • D4 | Upper Onion Creek

Total sites: 14, RV sites: 14, No water, Vault/pit toilet, Tent & RV camping: $20, 2 group sites, Open all year, Reservations not accepted, Stay limit: 14 days, Elevation: 4222ft/1287m, Telephone: 435-259-2100. Nearest town: Moab. GPS: 38.721737, -109.343328

177 • D4 | White Wash Sand Dunes

Dispersed sites, No water, No toilets, Tent & RV camping: Free, Portable toilets required if not self-contained, Elevation: 4147ft/1264m, Telephone: 435-259-2100. Nearest town: Moab. GPS: 38.800522, -110.033257

178 • D4 | William's Bottom

Total sites: 17, RV sites: 17, No water, Vault/pit toilet, Tent & RV camping: $20, Only small RVs, Open all year, Reservations not accepted, Stay limit: 14 days, Elevation: 3995ft/1218m, Telephone: 435-259-2100. Nearest town: Moab. GPS: 38.538594, -109.603818

179 • D4 | Willow Springs Trail Dispersed 1

Dispersed sites, No water, No toilets, Tent & RV camping: Free, Open all year, Elevation: 4443ft/1354m. Nearest town: Moab. GPS: 38.697618, -109.692145

180 • D4 | Willow Springs Trail Dispersed 2

Dispersed sites, No water, No toilets, Tent & RV camping: Free, Open all year, Elevation: 4360ft/1329m. Nearest town: Moab. GPS: 38.696216, -109.673125

181 • D4 | Windwhistle

Total sites: 15, RV sites: 15, Central water, Vault/pit toilet, Tent & RV camping: $20, Reservable group site: $75, Only small RVs, Open all year, Reservations not accepted, Elevation: 6037ft/1840m, Telephone: 435-259-2102. Nearest town: Moab. GPS: 38.176227, -109.462162

182 • E1 | Apple Valley Dispersed 1

Dispersed sites, No water, No toilets, Tent & RV camping: Free, 4X4 or high clearance vehicles helpful, Reservations not accepted, Elevation: 4983ft/1519m. Nearest town: Apple Valley. GPS: 37.132225, -113.131616

183 • E1 | Apple Valley Dispersed 2

Dispersed sites, No water, No toilets, Tent & RV camping: Free, 4X4 or high clearance vehicles helpful, Reservations not accepted, Elevation: 4971ft/1515m. Nearest town: Apple Valley. GPS: 37.133377, -113.131562

184 • E1 | Apple Valley Dispersed 3

Dispersed sites, No water, No toilets, Tent & RV camping: Free, 4X4 or high clearance vehicles helpful, Reservations not accepted, Elevation: 4961ft/1512m. Nearest town: Apple Valley. GPS: 37.134322, -113.130351

185 • E1 | Apple Valley Dispersed 4

Dispersed sites, No water, No toilets, Tents only: Free, 4x4 required, Reservations not accepted, Elevation: 4907ft/1496m. Nearest town: Apple Valley. GPS: 37.139116, -113.128731

186 • E1 | Apple Valley Dispersed 5

Dispersed sites, No water, No toilets, Tent & RV camping: Free, 4X4 or high clearance vehicles helpful, Reservations not accepted, Elevation: 4731ft/1442m. Nearest town: Apple Valley. GPS: 37.138953, -113.110885

187 • E1 | Apple Valley Dispersed 6

Dispersed sites, No water, No toilets, Tent & RV camping: Free, 4X4 or high clearance vehicles helpful, Reservations not accepted, Elevation: 5031ft/1533m. Nearest town: Apple Valley. GPS: 37.138354, -113.143616

188 • E1 | Apple Valley Dispersed 7

Dispersed sites, No water, No toilets, Tent & RV camping: Free, 4X4 or high clearance vehicles helpful, Reservations not accepted, Elevation: 5034ft/1534m. Nearest town: Apple Valley. GPS: 37.142027, -113.146424

189 • E1 | Apple Valley Dispersed 8

Dispersed sites, No water, No toilets, Tent & RV camping: Free, 4X4 or high clearance vehicles helpful, Reservations not accepted, Elevation: 5087ft/1551m. Nearest town: Apple Valley. GPS: 37.141298, -113.150721

190 • E1 | Apple Valley Dispersed 9

Dispersed sites, No water, No toilets, Tent & RV camping: Free, 4X4 or high clearance vehicles helpful, Reservations not accepted, Elevation: 5040ft/1536m. Nearest town: Apple Valley. GPS: 37.152746, -113.158468

191 • E1 | Baker Dam

Total sites: 16, RV sites: 16, No water, Vault/pit toilet, Tent & RV camping: $6, Open all year, Reservations not accepted, Elevation: 4922ft/1500m, Telephone: 435-688-3200. Nearest town: St George. GPS: 37.377625, -113.643172

192 • E1 | Coal Pits Wash Dispersed

Dispersed sites, No water, No toilets, Tents only: Free, Elevation: 3677ft/1121m. Nearest town: Rockville. GPS: 37.170951, -113.081676

193 • E1 | Gaucamole TH

Dispersed sites, No water, No toilets, Tent & RV camping: Free, Steep narrow road - bad when wet, Elevation: 4467ft/1362m. Nearest town: Virgin. GPS: 37.227215, -113.114954

194 • E1 | Gooseberry Mesa Dispersed

Dispersed sites, No water, No toilets, Tent & RV camping: Free, Rough access road, Elevation: 5113ft/1558m, Telephone: 435-688-3200. Nearest town: Apple Valley. GPS: 37.140161, -113.156763

195 • E1 | Horseman Park Rd Dispersed

Dispersed sites, No water, No toilets, Tent & RV camping: Free, Reservations not accepted, Elevation: 4754ft/1449m. Nearest town: Dammeron Valley. GPS: 37.294358, -113.650176

196 • E1 | Horseman Park Rd Dispersed

Dispersed sites, No water, No toilets, Tent & RV camping: Free, Reservations not accepted, Elevation: 4792ft/1461m. Nearest town: Dammeron Valley. GPS: 37.295666, -113.647955

197 • E1 | Horseman Park Rd Dispersed

Dispersed sites, No water, No toilets, Tent & RV camping: Free, Reservations not accepted, Elevation: 4800ft/1463m. Nearest town: Dammeron Valley. GPS: 37.299309, -113.649016

198 • E1 | Horseman Park Rd Dispersed

Dispersed sites, No water, No toilets, Tent & RV camping: Free, Reservations not accepted, Elevation: 4818ft/1469m. Nearest town: Dammeron Valley. GPS: 37.300549, -113.647938

199 • E1 | Horseman Park Rd Dispersed

Dispersed sites, No water, No toilets, Tent & RV camping: Free, Reservations not accepted, Elevation: 4883ft/1488m. Nearest town: Dammeron Valley. GPS: 37.305408, -113.642457

200 • E1 | Hurricane Cliffs RA

Total sites: 12, RV sites: 3, No water, No toilets, Tent & RV camping: Free, Camp only in designated spots, 1 group site, Rough access road, Reservations not accepted, Elevation: 3647ft/1112m, Telephone: 435-688-3200. Nearest town: Hurricane. GPS: 37.187337, -113.223551

201 • E1 | Hurricane Cliffs RA

Total sites: 10, RV sites: 2, No water, No toilets, Tent & RV camping: Free, Camp only in designated spots, Reservations not accepted, Elevation: 3756ft/1145m, Telephone: 435-688-3200. Nearest town: Hurricane. GPS: 37.187725, -113.242263

202 • E1 | Hurricane Cliffs RA

Total sites: 6, RV sites: 1, No water, No toilets, Tent & RV camping: Free, Camp only in designated spots, Reservations not accepted, Elevation: 3787ft/1154m, Telephone: 435-688-3200. Nearest town: Hurricane. GPS: 37.182825, -113.245121

203 • E1 | Hurricane Cliffs RA

Total sites: 7, RV sites: 0, No water, No toilets, Tents only: Free, Camp only in designated spots, Reservations not accepted, Elevation: 3848ft/1173m, Telephone: 435-688-3200. Nearest town: Hurricane. GPS: 37.176539, -113.248409

204 • E1 | Hurricane Cliffs RA

Total sites: 12, RV sites: 2, No water, No toilets, Tent & RV camping: Free, Camp only in designated spots, Reservations not accepted, Elevation: 3882ft/1183m, Telephone: 435-688-3200. Nearest town: Hurricane. GPS: 37.165868, -113.253745

205 • E1 | Kolob Creekside

Dispersed sites, No water, No toilets, Tent & RV camping: Free, Elevation: 3610ft/1100m. Nearest town: Virgin. GPS: 37.220358, -113.161699

206 • E1 | La Verkin Overlook Rd

Dispersed sites, No water, No toilets, Tent & RV camping: Free, Open all year, Reservations not accepted, Elevation: 3717ft/1133m. Nearest town: La Verkin. GPS: 37.215053, -113.249844

207 • E1 | Long Valley Recreation Area

Dispersed sites, No water, No toilets, Tent & RV camping: Free, High clearance vehicle recommended - RV-accessible when dry, Reservations not accepted, Elevation: 2707ft/825m. Nearest town: St. George. GPS: 37.111014, -113.439026

208 • E1 | Manganese Wash Dispersed

Dispersed sites, No water, No toilets, Tent & RV camping: Free, High clearance vehicle required for river sites, Reservations not accepted, Elevation: 3495ft/1065m. GPS: 37.233899, -113.778946

209 • E1 | Red Cliffs

Total sites: 11, RV sites: 11, No water, Vault/pit toilet, Tent & RV camping: $15, 12' height restriction, Open all year, Reservations not accepted, Stay limit: 14 days, Elevation: 3281ft/1000m, Telephone: 435-688-3200. Nearest town: Leeds. GPS: 37.224789, -113.405613

210 • E1 | Road 033 Dispersed

Dispersed sites, No water, No toilets, Tent & RV camping: Free, Large area, Reservations not accepted, Elevation: 4816ft/1468m. Nearest town: Diamond Valley. GPS: 37.273811, -113.610736

211 • E1 | Sand Cove Primitive

Dispersed sites, No water, No toilets, Tent & RV camping: Free, Must provide portable toilet, Reservations not accepted, Stay limit: 7 days, Elevation: 3152ft/961m. Nearest town: Hurricane. GPS: 37.209671, -113.335844

212 • E1 | Smithsonian Butte Dispersed

Dispersed sites, No water, No toilets, Tent & RV camping: Free, 4x4 required, Must camp > .5 mile from main road, Elevation: 3764ft/1147m. Nearest town: Rockville. GPS: 37.150993, -113.058648

213 • E1 | Toquerville Falls

Dispersed sites, No water, No toilets, Tent & RV camping: Free, Elevation: 3764ft/1147m. Nearest town: Toquerville. GPS: 37.299361, -113.246888

214 • E1 | Virgin Dam Dispersed

Total sites: 1, RV sites: 1, No water, No toilets, Tent & RV camping: Free, Beware of private property boundaries, Reservations not accepted, Elevation: 3584ft/1092m. Nearest town: La Verkin. GPS: 37.204937, -113.231983

215 • E1 | Virgin Dam Dispersed

Total sites: 1, RV sites: 1, No water, No toilets, Tent & RV camping: Free, Beware of private property boundaries, Camp only in designated spots, Reservations not accepted, Elevation: 3587ft/1093m. Nearest town: La Verkin. GPS: 37.202553, -113.231866

216 • E1 | Virgin Dam Dispersed

Total sites: 1, RV sites: 0, No water, No toilets, Tents only: Free, Beware of private property boundaries, Reservations not accepted, Elevation: 3613ft/1101m. Nearest town: La Verkin. GPS: 37.206212, -113.237516

217 • E1 | Virgin Dam Dispersed

Total sites: 5, RV sites: 4, No water, No toilets, Tent & RV camping: Free, Beware of private property boundaries, Reservations not accepted, Elevation: 3620ft/1103m. Nearest town: La Verkin. GPS: 37.206323, -113.240447

218 • E1 | Zion View

Dispersed sites, No water, No toilets, Tent & RV camping: Free, Elevation: 5594ft/1705m. Nearest town: Virgin. GPS: 37.266967, -113.176154

219 • E2 | Buckskin Gulch Trailhead

Dispersed sites, No water, No toilets, Tent & RV camping: Free, Nearby BLM ranger station has maps and information on other camping areas, Elevation: 4836ft/1474m, Telephone: 435-688-3200. Nearest town: Page, AZ. GPS: 37.067008, -112.000579

220 • E2 | Cockscomb Dispersed

Dispersed sites, No water, No toilets, Tent & RV camping: Free, Reservations not accepted, Elevation: 4504ft/1373m. Nearest town: Kanab. GPS: 37.126449, -111.954795

221 • E2 | Coral Pink Sand Dunes – Meadows

Dispersed sites, No water, No toilets, Tent & RV camping: Free, Reservations not accepted, Elevation: 6151ft/1875m, Telephone: 435-644-1200. Nearest town: Kanab. GPS: 37.067627, -112.703822

222 • E2 | Coral Pink Sand Dunes – Ponderosa Grove

Total sites: 34, RV sites: 32, No water, Vault/pit toilet, Tent & RV camping: $5, Also walk-to sites, Reservations not accepted, Elevation: 6306ft/1922m, Telephone: 435-644-1200. Nearest town: Kanab. GPS: 37.088816, -112.672346

223 • E2 | Coral Pink Sand Dunes – Sand Spring

Dispersed sites, No water, No toilets, Tent & RV camping: Free, Reservations not accepted, Elevation: 6185ft/1885m, Telephone: 435-644-1200. Nearest town: Kanab. GPS: 37.077798, -112.661815

224 • E2 | Coral Pink Sand Dunes Dispersed

Dispersed sites, No water, No toilets, Tent & RV camping: Free, Reservations not accepted, Elevation: 5870ft/1789m, Telephone: 435-644-1200. Nearest town: Kanab. GPS: 37.033381, -112.747553

225 • E2 | Cottonwood Canyon Dispersed 1

Dispersed sites, No water, No toilets, Tent & RV camping: Free, 2nd site .25 mi west at end of road, Reservations not accepted, Elevation: 4784ft/1458m. Nearest town: Kanab. GPS: 37.117754, -111.853156

226 • E2 | Cottonwood Canyon Dispersed 2

Dispersed sites, No water, No toilets, Tent & RV camping: Free, 2 sites, Reservations not accepted, Elevation: 4867ft/1483m. Nearest town: Kanab. GPS: 37.119354, -111.849618

227 • E2 | Cottonwood Canyon Dispersed 3

Dispersed sites, No water, No toilets, Tent & RV camping: Free, Elevation: 4721ft/1439m. Nearest town: Paria. GPS: 37.240713, -111.920923

228 • E2 | Cottonwood Canyon Hoodoo TH Dispersed

Dispersed sites, No water, No toilets, Tent & RV camping: Free, High clearance vehicle recommended, Reservations not accepted, Elevation: 4854ft/1479m. Nearest town: Paria. GPS: 37.271492, -111.904477

229 • E2 | Crocodile Staging Area

Dispersed sites, No water, Vault/pit toilet, No tents/RVs: Free, Reservations not accepted, Stay limit: 14 days, Elevation: 5448ft/1661m, Telephone: 435-644-1300. Nearest town: Kanab. GPS: 37.143544, -112.393663

230 • E2 | Grand Staircase Escalante NM – Henrieville Creek

Dispersed sites, No water, No toilets, Tent & RV camping: Free, Free permit required, Elevation: 6665ft/2031m, Telephone: 435-644-1200. Nearest town: Henrieville. GPS: 37.617086, -111.896804

231 • E2 | Grand Staircase Escalante NM – Kitchen Corral Wash

Dispersed sites, No water, No toilets, Tent & RV camping: Free, Free permit required, Elevation: 5371ft/1637m, Telephone: 435-644-1200. Nearest town: Kanab. GPS: 37.140117, -112.091662

232 • E2 | Grand Staircase Escalante NM – Pump Canyon Springs

Dispersed sites, No water, No toilets, Tent & RV camping: Free, Free permit required, Elevation: 5241ft/1597m, Telephone: 435-644-1200. Nearest town: Kanab. GPS: 37.343314, -111.870779

233 • E2 | Grand Staircase Escalante NM – Rock Springs Bench

Dispersed sites, No water, No toilets, Tent & RV camping: Free, Free permit required, Elevation: 5809ft/1771m, Telephone: 435-644-1200. Nearest town: Henrieville. GPS: 37.494131, -111.981379

234 • E2 | Grand Staircase Escalante NM – Skutumpah Terrace

Dispersed sites, No water, No toilets, Tent & RV camping: Free, Free permit required, Elevation: 6018ft/1834m, Telephone: 435-644-1200. Nearest town: Kanab. GPS: 37.268283, -112.374518

235 • E2 | Grand Staircase Escalante NM – White House

Total sites: 12, RV sites: 7, No water, Vault/pit toilet, Tent & RV camping: $5, Also walk-to sites, Open all year, Reservations not accepted, Stay limit: 14 days, Elevation: 4426ft/1349m, Telephone: 435-644-1200. Nearest town: Page (AZ). GPS: 37.079755, -111.889953

236 • E2 | Mount Carmel

Dispersed sites, No water, No toilets, Tent & RV camping: Free, Elevation: 5500ft/1676m. Nearest town: Kanab. GPS: 37.207169, -112.675418

237 • E2 | Mount Carmel Jct ATV

Dispersed sites, No water, No toilets, Tent & RV camping: Free, Elevation: 5177ft/1578m. Nearest town: Mt Carmel. GPS: 37.215127, -112.684982

238 • E2 | Paria Contact Station

Dispersed sites, No water, No toilets, No tents/RVs: Free, Water at Contact Station, Reservations not accepted, Elevation: 4387ft/1337m, Telephone: 435-644-1200. Nearest town: Kanab. GPS: 37.106029, -111.903276

239 • E2 | Paria Contact Station

Dispersed sites, No water, No toilets, No tents/RVs: Free, Water at Contact Station, Reservations not accepted, Elevation: 4488ft/1368m, Telephone: 435-644-1200. Nearest town: Kanab. GPS: 37.101332, -111.902334

240 • E2 | Peek-A-Boo ATV Area

Dispersed sites, No water, No toilets, Tent & RV camping: Free, Stay limit: 14 days, Elevation: 5702ft/1738m, Telephone: 435-644-1300. Nearest town: Kanab. GPS: 37.154736, -112.573671

241 • E2 | Pine Spring Kiosk

Dispersed sites, No water, No toilets, Tent & RV camping: Free, Reservations not accepted, Elevation: 5793ft/1766m, Telephone: 435-644-1200. Nearest town: Hilldale. GPS: 37.048775, -112.831556

242 • E2 | Stateline

Total sites: 4, RV sites: 3, No water, Vault/pit toilet, Tent & RV camping: Free, Open all year, Elevation: 4977ft/1517m, Telephone: 435-688-3200. Nearest town: Kanab. GPS: 37.001113, -112.035385

243 • E2 | The Arch site 1

Dispersed sites, No water, No toilets, Tent & RV camping: Free, Reservations not accepted, Elevation: 5657ft/1724m. Nearest town: Kanab. GPS: 37.142956, -112.584759

244 • E2 | The Arch site 2

Dispersed sites, No water, No toilets, Tent & RV camping: Free, Reservations not accepted, Elevation: 5584ft/1702m. Nearest town: Kanab. GPS: 37.146552, -112.582172

245 • E2 | The Arch site 3

Dispersed sites, No water, No toilets, Tent & RV camping: Free, Reservations not accepted, Elevation: 5611ft/1710m. Nearest town: Kanab. GPS: 37.147408, -112.585359

246 • E2 | Twin Hollows Canyon Dispersed

Dispersed sites, No water, No toilets, Tent & RV camping: Free, Elevation: 5139ft/1566m. Nearest town: Mt Carmel Jct. GPS: 37.207192, -112.689751

247 • E2 | Yellowjacket Canyon Dispersed

Dispersed sites, No water, No toilets, Tent & RV camping: Free, Elevation: 5667ft/1727m. Nearest town: Kanab. GPS: 37.144836, -112.672894

248 • E2 | Yellowjacket Spring Dispersed

Dispersed sites, No water, No toilets, Tent & RV camping: Free, Elevation: 6145ft/1873m. Nearest town: Kanab. GPS: 37.089272, -112.696388

249 • E3 | Clay Hills

Dispersed sites, No water, Tent & RV camping: Free, Elevation: 3721ft/1134m. Nearest town: Blanding. GPS: 37.294118, -110.397711

250 • E3 | Grand Staircase Escalante NM – Dance Hall Rock

Dispersed sites, No water, No toilets, Tent & RV camping: Free, Free permit required, Elevation: 4618ft/1408m, Telephone: 435-644-1200. Nearest town: Escalante. GPS: 37.356413, -111.101489

251 • E3 | Grand Staircase Escalante NM – Forty Mile Spring

Dispersed sites, No water, Vault/pit toilet, Tent & RV camping: Free, Free permit required, Elevation: 4793ft/1461m, Telephone: 435-644-1200. Nearest town: Escalante. GPS: 37.392523, -111.048634

252 • E3 | Grand Staircase Escalante NM – Harris Wash

Dispersed sites, No water, No toilets, Tent & RV camping: Free, Free permit required, Elevation: 5436ft/1657m, Telephone: 435-644-1200. Nearest town: Henrieville. GPS: 37.605248, -111.422393

253 • E3 | Grand Staircase Escalante NM – Sooner Rocks

Dispersed sites, No water, No toilets, Tent & RV camping: Free, Free permit required, Elevation: 4356ft/1328m, Telephone: 435-644-1200. Nearest town: Escalante. GPS: 37.32793, -111.058817

254 • E3 | Halls Creek

Dispersed sites, No water, No toilets, Tents only: Free, Very rough gravel road to overlook, but plenty of camping available on the graded roads nearby, Elevation: 5276ft/1608m. GPS: 37.717794, -110.930149

255 • E3 | Jacob's Chair

Dispersed sites, No water, No toilets, No tents/RVs: Free, Elevation: 4810ft/1466m. Nearest town: Fry Canyon. GPS: 37.706932, -110.239412

256 • E4 | Arch Canyon/Comb Wash

Dispersed sites, No water, Vault/pit toilet, Tent & RV camping: Free, Open all year, Reservations not accepted, Elevation: 4845ft/1477m, Telephone: 435-587-1500. Nearest town: Blanding. GPS: 37.507801, -109.655044

257 • E4 | Bailey S Lower Rd

Dispersed sites, No water, No toilets, Tent & RV camping: Free, Elevation: 6099ft/1859m. Nearest town: Blanding. GPS: 37.522409, -109.748447

258 • E4 | Grand Gulch

Dispersed sites, No water, No toilets, Tents only: Free, 4x4 required, Elevation: 6811ft/2076m, Telephone: 435-688-3200. Nearest town: Blanding. GPS: 37.582891, -109.893581

259 • E4 | Jct 95-261

Dispersed sites, No water, No toilets, Tent & RV camping: Free, 4x4 recommended, Elevation: 6791ft/2070m. Nearest town: Blanding. GPS: 37.570625, -109.882595

260 • E4 | Mexican Hat Dispersed

Dispersed sites, No water, No toilets, Tent & RV camping: Free, Numerous sites in area, Reservations not accepted, Elevation: 4234ft/1291m. Nearest town: Mexican Hat. GPS: 37.171099, -109.849266

261 • E4 | Muley Point

Dispersed sites, No water, No toilets, Tent & RV camping: Free, 5-mile dirt road, Reservations not accepted, Elevation: 6194ft/1888m. Nearest town: Mexican Hat. GPS: 37.235377, -109.992191

262 • E4 | Recapture Reservoir East Side

Dispersed sites, No water, No toilets, Tent & RV camping: Free, Elevation: 6062ft/1848m. Nearest town: Blanding. GPS: 37.667694, -109.437298

263 • E4 | Recapture Reservoir West Side

Dispersed sites, No water, No toilets, Tent & RV camping: Free, Elevation: 6076ft/1852m. Nearest town: Blanding. GPS: 37.667068, -109.443783

264 • E4 | San Juan River – Sand Island

Total sites: 24, RV sites: 24, Central water, Vault/pit toilet, No showers, No RV dump, Tent & RV camping: $15, Group fee: $65-$85, Open all year, Reservations not accepted, Elevation: 4287ft/1307m, Telephone: 435-259-2102. Nearest town: Bluff. GPS: 37.261056, -109.617842

265 • E4 | San Juan River – Swinging Bridge

Dispersed sites, No water, No toilets, Tents only: Free, Also boat-in sites, Elevation: 4339ft/1323m. Nearest town: Bluff. GPS: 37.279537, -109.492814

266 • E4 | Valley of the Gods

Dispersed sites, No water, No toilets, Tent & RV camping: Free, No campfires, Reservations not accepted, Elevation: 4997ft/1523m, Telephone: 435-587-1500. Nearest town: Bluff. GPS: 37.316424, -109.850376

Washington

IDAHO

BRITISH COLUMBIA

WASHINGTON

OREGON

BRITISH COLUMBIA

Pacific Ocean

Colville

Spokane

Pullman

15

5 7
5
6

13

14

1 2
3

Okanogan

4

Wenatchee

9

12 10
8 11

Yakima

Kennewick

Bellingham

Seattle

Olympia

Vancouver

2

195

395

90

26

12

12

97

97

2

395

90

26

82

82

97

90

2

90

12

5

5

5

Washington

Oregon/Washington State Office
1220 SW 3rd Ave
Portland OR 97204

Phone: 503-808-6001

Name	ID	Map	RVs	Tents	Free
Big Pines	8	C3	✓	✓	
Chopaka Lake	1	A4	✓	✓	✓
Coffeepot Lake	5	B4	✓	✓	✓
Douglas Creek	4	B3	✓	✓	✓
Escure Ranch	15	C5	✓	✓	✓
Juniper Dunes OHV Area	13	C4	✓	✓	✓
Liberty Rec Area	9	C3	✓	✓	✓
Lmuma Creek	10	C3	✓	✓	
Loomis Loop	2	A4	✓	✓	✓
Moses Lake	14	C4	✓	✓	✓
Pacific Lake	6	B4	✓	✓	✓
Roza	11	C3	✓	✓	
Twin Lakes	7	B4	✓	✓	✓
Umtanum	12	C3	✓	✓	
Washburn Lake	3	A4	✓	✓	

1 • A4 | Chopaka Lake

Total sites: 8, RV sites: 8, No water, Vault/pit toilet, Tent & RV camping: Free, Road may be inaccessible in winter, Open all year, Reservations not accepted, Elevation: 2920ft/890m, Telephone: 509-536-1200. Nearest town: Tonasket. GPS: 48.916938, -119.702052

2 • A4 | Loomis Loop

Dispersed sites, No water, No toilets, Tent & RV camping: Free, Also boat-in sites, Elevation: 1131ft/345m. Nearest town: Oroville. GPS: 48.986518, -119.569832

3 • A4 | Washburn Lake

Total sites: 3, RV sites: 3, No water, No toilets, Tent & RV camping: Fee unk, Elevation: 3149ft/960m, Telephone: 509-536-1200. Nearest town: Loomis. GPS: 48.844868, -119.594738

4 • B3 | Douglas Creek

Dispersed sites, No water, No toilets, Tent & RV camping: Free, Open Mar-Nov, Reservations not accepted, Stay limit:

14 days, Elevation: 1488ft/454m, Telephone: 509-536-1200. Nearest town: Waterville. GPS: 47.484562, -119.898208

5 • B4 | Coffeepot Lake

Dispersed sites, No water, Vault/pit toilet, Tent & RV camping: Free, Open all year, Reservations not accepted, Elevation: 1844ft/562m, Telephone: 509-536-1200. Nearest town: Odessa. GPS: 47.500043, -118.556805

6 • B4 | Pacific Lake

Dispersed sites, Vault/pit toilet, Tent & RV camping: Free, Reservations not accepted, Elevation: 1604ft/489m, Telephone: 509-536-1200. Nearest town: Odessa. GPS: 47.415097, -118.732898

7 • B4 | Twin Lakes

Total sites: 5, RV sites: 5, No water, Vault/pit toilet, Tent & RV camping: Free, Open all year, Reservations not accepted, Stay limit: 14 days, Elevation: 1896ft/578m, Telephone: 509-536-1200. Nearest town: Harrington. GPS: 47.529959, -118.506223

8 • C3 | Big Pines

Total sites: 41, RV sites: 38, No water, Vault/pit toilet, Tent & RV camping: $15, Also walk-to sites, 3 walk-to sites, Open May-Sep, Reservations accepted, Stay limit: 14 days, Elevation: 1250ft/381m, Telephone: 509-536-1200. Nearest town: Ellensburg. GPS: 46.7943, -120.45882

9 • C3 | Liberty Rec Area

Total sites: 15, RV sites: 15, No water, Vault/pit toilet, Tent & RV camping: Free, Winter access may be limited, Open all year, Reservations not accepted, Stay limit: 14 days, Elevation: 2730ft/832m, Telephone: 509-665-2100. Nearest town: Teanaway. GPS: 47.253323, -120.670489

10 • C3 | Lmuma Creek

Total sites: 7, RV sites: 7, No water, Vault/pit toilet, Tent & RV camping: $15, Free in winter, Open all year, Reservations accepted, Stay limit: 14 days, Elevation: 1355ft/413m, Telephone: 509-536-1200. Nearest town: Ellensburg. GPS: 46.81384, -120.4493

11 • C3 | Roza

Total sites: 5, RV sites: 5, No water, Vault/pit toilet, Tent & RV camping: $15, Open May-Sep, Reservations accepted, Stay limit: 14 days, Elevation: 1230ft/375m, Telephone: 509-536-1200. Nearest town: Ellensburg. GPS: 46.76438, -120.45676

12 • C3 | Umtanum

Total sites: 8, RV sites: 8, No water, Vault/pit toilet, Tent & RV camping: $15, Open May-Sep, Reservations accepted, Elevation: 1434ft/437m, Telephone: 509-536-1200. Nearest town: Ellensburg. GPS: 46.85608, -120.48195

13 • C4 | Juniper Dunes OHV Area

Dispersed sites, No water, No toilets, Tent & RV camping: Free, High clearance 4x4 Only, Open fires prohibited, Open all year, Elevation: 782ft/238m, Telephone: 509-536-1200. Nearest town: Kennewick. GPS: 46.357892, -118.908722

14 • C4 | Moses Lake

Dispersed sites, No water, No toilets, Tent & RV camping: Free, Open all year, Elevation: 1043ft/318m. Nearest town: Moses Lake. GPS: 47.062779, -119.320773

15 • C5 | Escure Ranch

Total sites: 15, RV sites: 15, Vault/pit toilet, Tent & RV camping: Free, Reservations not accepted, Elevation: 1459ft/445m. Nearest town: Ritzville. GPS: 47.015048, -117.943425

Wyoming

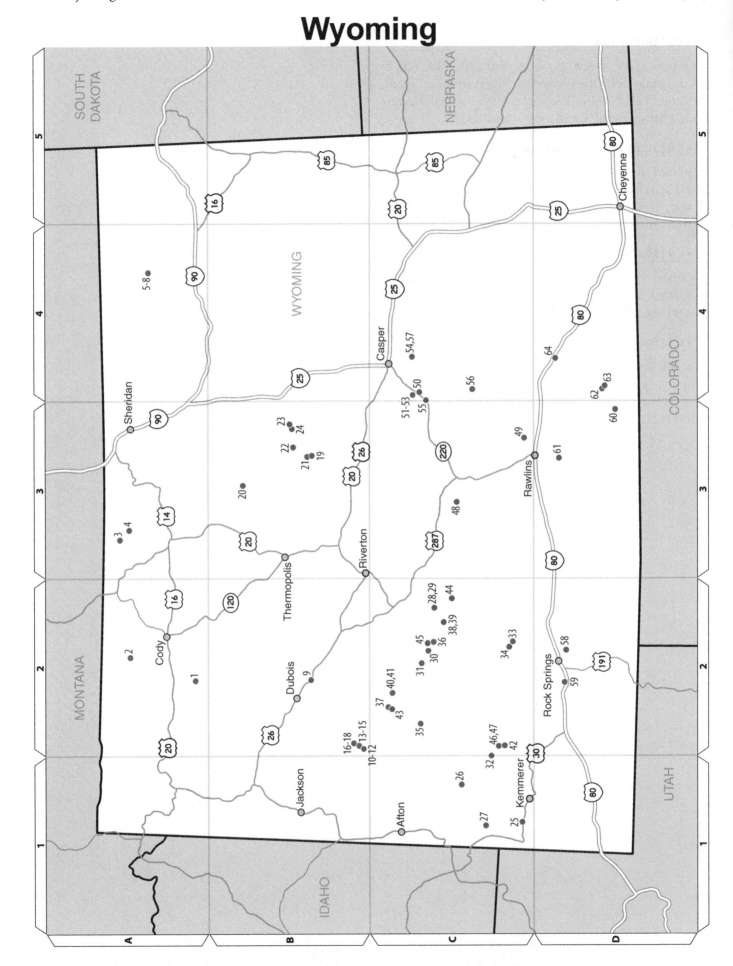

Wyoming

Wyoming State Office
5353 Yellowstone Rd
Cheyenne WY 82009

Phone: 307-775-6256

Name	ID	Map	RVs	Tents	Free
Atlantic City	28	C2	✓	✓	
Bennett Peak	62	D4	✓	✓	
Big Atlantic Gulch	29	C2	✓	✓	
Blucher Creek	30	C2	✓	✓	✓
Bobcat-Houlihan	1	A2	✓	✓	✓
Bolton Creek Dispersed	50	C4	✓	✓	✓
Buffalo Creek	19	B3	✓	✓	✓
Buffaloberry	51	C4	✓	✓	
Castle Gardens Scenic Area	20	B3		✓	✓
Chalk Bluffs	52	C4	✓	✓	✓
Corral Creek	63	D4	✓	✓	✓
Cottonwood	48	C3	✓	✓	
Cottonwood Creek TH	3	A3	✓	✓	✓
Dubois	9	B2	✓	✓	✓
Dugway	49	C3	✓	✓	✓
Dutch Joe Dispersed	31	C2	✓	✓	✓
Encampment River	60	D3	✓	✓	
Five Springs Falls	4	A3	✓	✓	
Fontenelle Creek	32	C2	✓	✓	
Fossil Butte Dispersed	25	C1	✓	✓	✓
Golden Currant	53	C4		✓	✓
Grave Springs	21	B3	✓	✓	✓
Hogan and Luce CG	2	A2	✓	✓	✓
Killpecker Sand Dunes – North Table Rock	33	C2	✓	✓	✓
Killpecker Sand Dunes Dispersed	34	C2	✓	✓	✓
La Barge Creek	26	C1	✓	✓	✓
Lodgepole	54	C4	✓	✓	
Middle Baxter Rd Dispersed	58	D2	✓	✓	✓
Middle Fork of the Powder River	22	B3	✓	✓	✓
Middle Fork Powder River Dispersed	23	B3	✓	✓	✓
New Fork River – W-351 Bridge	35	C2	✓	✓	✓
No Name	36	C2	✓	✓	✓
North Boulder Lake	37	C2	✓	✓	✓

Name	ID	Map	RVs	Tents	Free
Outlaw Cave	24	B3		✓	✓
Pete's Draw	55	C4	✓	✓	
Pine Creek	27	C1		✓	✓
Pine Creek Camping Area	38	C2	✓	✓	✓
Pine Creek Dispersed	39	C2	✓	✓	✓
Prior Flat	56	C4	✓	✓	✓
Rim	57	C4	✓	✓	
Scab Creek	40	C2	✓		✓
Scab Creek Large Vehicle CG	41	C2	✓		✓
Slate Creek	42	C2	✓	✓	✓
Stokes Crossing	43	C2	✓	✓	✓
Sweetwater Bridge	44	C2	✓	✓	✓
Sweetwater River	45	C2	✓	✓	✓
Tail Race	46	C2		✓	✓
Teton Reservoir	61	D3	✓	✓	✓
Wagonhound	64	D4	✓	✓	✓
Warren Bridge	10	B2	✓	✓	
Warren Bridge/Green River Access #1	11	B2	✓	✓	✓
Warren Bridge/Green River Access #2	12	B2	✓	✓	✓
Warren Bridge/Green River Access #3	13	B2	✓	✓	✓
Warren Bridge/Green River Access #4	14	B2	✓	✓	✓
Warren Bridge/Green River Access #5	15	B2	✓	✓	✓
Warren Bridge/Green River Access #6	16	B2	✓	✓	✓
Warren Bridge/Green River Access #7	17	B2	✓	✓	✓
Warren Bridge/Green River Access #8	18	B2		✓	✓
Weeping Rock	47	C2	✓	✓	✓
Weston Hills Rec Area Site 1	5	A4	✓	✓	✓
Weston Hills Rec Area Site 2	6	A4	✓	✓	✓
Weston Hills Rec Area Site 3	7	A4	✓	✓	✓
Weston Hills Rec Area Site 4	8	A4		✓	✓
White Mountain Road	59	D2	✓	✓	✓

1 • A2 | Bobcat-Houlihan

Dispersed sites, No water, No toilets, Tent & RV camping: Free, Hitching rails, Stay limit: 14 days, Elevation: 6024ft/ 1836m, Telephone: 307-578-5900. Nearest town: Cody. GPS: 44.29262, -109.485147

2 • A2 | Hogan and Luce CG

Total sites: 5, RV sites: 5, Vault/pit toilet, Tent & RV camping: Free, Open all year, Reservations not accepted, Elevation:

4826ft/1471m, Telephone: 307-578-5900. Nearest town: Cody. GPS: 44.787463, -109.257649

3 • A3 | Cottonwood Creek TH

Total sites: 5, RV sites: 5, Vault/pit toilet, Tent & RV camping: Free, 4 corrals, Reservations not accepted, Elevation: 4836ft/1474m, Telephone: 307-578-5900. Nearest town: Lovell. GPS: 44.869417, -108.071986

4 • A3 | Five Springs Falls

Total sites: 19, RV sites: 10, Central water, Vault/pit toilet, No showers, No RV dump, Tent & RV camping: $7, Open all year, Reservations not accepted, Stay limit: 14 days, Elevation: 6647ft/2026m, Telephone: 307-578-5900. Nearest town: Lovell. GPS: 44.804364, -107.969709

5 • A4 | Weston Hills Rec Area Site 1

Dispersed sites, No water, No toilets, Tent & RV camping: Free, Reservations not accepted, Elevation: 3900ft/1189m, Telephone: 307-684-1100. Nearest town: Gillette. GPS: 44.635982, -105.355455

6 • A4 | Weston Hills Rec Area Site 2

Dispersed sites, No water, No toilets, Tent & RV camping: Free, Reservations not accepted, Elevation: 3917ft/1194m, Telephone: 307-684-1100. Nearest town: Gillette. GPS: 44.636713, -105.360578

7 • A4 | Weston Hills Rec Area Site 3

Dispersed sites, No water, No toilets, Tent & RV camping: Free, Reservations not accepted, Elevation: 3942ft/1202m, Telephone: 307-684-1100. Nearest town: Gillette. GPS: 44.635527, -105.365081

8 • A4 | Weston Hills Rec Area Site 4

Dispersed sites, No water, No toilets, Tents only: Free, Reservations not accepted, Elevation: 3944ft/1202m, Telephone: 307-684-1100. Nearest town: Gillette. GPS: 44.635633, -105.366592

9 • B2 | Dubois

Total sites: 6, RV sites: 6, No water, No toilets, Tent & RV camping: Free, Elevation: 6371ft/1942m. Nearest town: Dubois. GPS: 43.432689, -109.445977

10 • B2 | Warren Bridge

Total sites: 17, RV sites: 17, Water at site, Vault/pit toilet, No showers, RV dump, Tent & RV camping: $10, Dump fee: $5, Open May-Sep, Reservations not accepted, Elevation: 7480ft/2280m, Telephone: 307-367-5300. Nearest town: Pinedale. GPS: 43.01709, -110.120117

11 • B2 | Warren Bridge/Green River Access #1

Total sites: 5, RV sites: 5, No water, No toilets, Tent & RV camping: Free, 12 sites along 9 miles of river, Elevation: 7498ft/2285m, Telephone: 307-367-5300. Nearest town: Pinedale. GPS: 43.024467, -110.103173

12 • B2 | Warren Bridge/Green River Access #2

Dispersed sites, No water, No toilets, Tent & RV camping: Free, Elevation: 7514ft/2290m, Telephone: 307-367-5300. Nearest town: Pinedale. GPS: 43.033077, -110.101697

13 • B2 | Warren Bridge/Green River Access #3

Total sites: 3, RV sites: 3, No water, No toilets, Tent & RV camping: Free, Elevation: 7559ft/2304m, Telephone: 307-367-5300. Nearest town: Pinedale. GPS: 43.060059, -110.085445

14 • B2 | Warren Bridge/Green River Access #4

Total sites: 4, RV sites: 4, No water, Vault/pit toilet, Tent & RV camping: Free, Elevation: 7562ft/2305m, Telephone: 307-367-5300. Nearest town: Pinedale. GPS: 43.065721, -110.081076

15 • B2 | Warren Bridge/Green River Access #5

Total sites: 2, RV sites: 2, No water, No toilets, Tent & RV camping: Free, Elevation: 7575ft/2309m, Telephone: 307-367-5300. Nearest town: Pinedale. GPS: 43.072302, -110.074066

16 • B2 | Warren Bridge/Green River Access #6

Total sites: 3, RV sites: 3, No water, Vault/pit toilet, Tent & RV camping: Free, Elevation: 7587ft/2313m, Telephone: 307-367-5300. Nearest town: Pinedale. GPS: 43.080704, -110.066597

17 • B2 | Warren Bridge/Green River Access #7

Total sites: 7, RV sites: 7, No water, No toilets, Tent & RV camping: Free, Elevation: 7592ft/2314m, Telephone: 307-367-5300. Nearest town: Pinedale. GPS: 43.089371, -110.066434

18 • B2 | Warren Bridge/Green River Access #8

Dispersed sites, No water, No toilets, Tent & RV camping: Free, Elevation: 7608ft/2319m, Telephone: 307-367-5300. Nearest town: Pinedale. GPS: 43.098339, -110.063323

19 • B3 | Buffalo Creek

Total sites: 4, RV sites: 4, No water, Vault/pit toilet, Tent & RV camping: Free, Open May-Sep, Reservations not accepted, Stay limit: 14 days, Elevation: 8159ft/2487m, Telephone:

307-587-9227. Nearest town: Arminto. GPS: 43.437912, -107.223752

20 • B3 | Castle Gardens Scenic Area

Total sites: 4, RV sites: 0, No water, Vault/pit toilet, Tents only: Free, Open all year, Reservations not accepted, Elevation: 5026ft/1532m, Telephone: 307-347-5100. Nearest town: Ten Sleep. GPS: 43.956922, -107.517179

21 • B3 | Grave Springs

Total sites: 12, RV sites: 10, No water, Vault/pit toilet, Tent & RV camping: Free, Limited winter access, Open all year, Reservations not accepted, Stay limit: 14 days, Elevation: 8268ft/2520m, Telephone: 307-261-7600. Nearest town: Arminto. GPS: 43.464031, -107.228659

22 • B3 | Middle Fork of the Powder River

Total sites: 5, RV sites: 5, No water, Vault/pit toilet, Tent & RV camping: Free, Reservations not accepted, Elevation: 7323ft/2232m, Telephone: 307-684-1100. Nearest town: Powder River. GPS: 43.577034, -107.142292

23 • B3 | Middle Fork Powder River Dispersed

Dispersed sites, No water, Vault/pit toilet, Tent & RV camping: Free, Reservations not accepted, Elevation: 5505ft/1678m. Nearest town: Kaycee. GPS: 43.597122, -106.911523

24 • B3 | Outlaw Cave

Total sites: 12, RV sites: 0, No water, Vault/pit toilet, Tents only: Free, 4x4 recommended, Land-owner permission required for access, Open Apr-Nov, Reservations not accepted, Stay limit: 14 days, Elevation: 6070ft/1850m, Telephone: 307-347-5100. Nearest town: Barnum. GPS: 43.589846, -106.947896

25 • C1 | Fossil Butte Dispersed

Dispersed sites, No water, No toilets, Tent & RV camping: Free, Reservations not accepted, Elevation: 6760ft/2060m. Nearest town: Kemmerer. GPS: 41.828991, -110.781379

26 • C1 | La Barge Creek

Dispersed sites, No water, Tent & RV camping: Free, Elevation: 7299ft/2225m, Telephone: 307-777-4600. Nearest town: La Barge. GPS: 42.293963, -110.440055

27 • C1 | Pine Creek

Total sites: 7, No water, Vault/pit toilet, Tents only: Free, Near ski area, Reservations not accepted, Stay limit: 14 days, Elevation: 6868ft/2093m, Telephone: 307-828-4500. Nearest town: Cokeville. GPS: 42.104735, -110.828238

28 • C2 | Atlantic City

Total sites: 18, RV sites: 18, Central water, Vault/pit toilet, No showers, No RV dump, Tent & RV camping: $6, Open Jun-Oct, Reservations not accepted, Stay limit: 14 days, Elevation: 8130ft/2478m, Telephone: 307-332-8400. Nearest town: Lander. GPS: 42.515869, -108.723633

29 • C2 | Big Atlantic Gulch

Total sites: 10, RV sites: 10, Central water, Vault/pit toilet, Tent & RV camping: $6, Water dependent on weather, Open Jun-Oct, Reservations not accepted, Stay limit: 14 days, Elevation: 8100ft/2469m, Telephone: 307-332-8400. Nearest town: Atlantic City. GPS: 42.520508, -108.7146

30 • C2 | Blucher Creek

Dispersed sites, No water, Vault/pit toilet, Tent & RV camping: Free, Stay limit: 14 days, Elevation: 8577ft/2614m, Telephone: 307-352-0256. Nearest town: Boulder. GPS: 42.561771, -109.141683

31 • C2 | Dutch Joe Dispersed

Dispersed sites, No water, No toilets, Tent & RV camping: Free, Reservations not accepted, Stay limit: 14 days, Elevation: 8442ft/2573m, Telephone: 307-352-0256. Nearest town: Pinedale. GPS: 42.606732, -109.260238

32 • C2 | Fontenelle Creek

Total sites: 55, RV sites: 55, Central water, Vault/pit toilet, No showers, RV dump, Tent & RV camping: $7, $3 dump fee, Open May-Oct, Reservations not accepted, Stay limit: 14 days, Elevation: 6522ft/1988m, Telephone: 307-828-4500. Nearest town: LaBarge. GPS: 42.073129, -110.152671

33 • C2 | Killpecker Sand Dunes – North Table Rock

Dispersed sites, No water, No toilets, Tent & RV camping: Free, Reservations not accepted, Stay limit: 14 days, Elevation: 7140ft/2176m, Telephone: 307-352-0256. Nearest town: Rock Springs. GPS: 41.940933, -109.036778

34 • C2 | Killpecker Sand Dunes Dispersed

Dispersed sites, No water, Vault/pit toilet, Tent & RV camping: Free, Stay limit: 14 days, Elevation: 7168ft/2185m, Telephone: 307-352-0256. Nearest town: Rock Springs. GPS: 41.961338, -109.081383

35 • C2 | New Fork River – W-351 Bridge

Total sites: 2, RV sites: 2, No water, Vault/pit toilet, Tent & RV camping: Free, Reservations not accepted, Elevation: 6847ft/2087m, Telephone: 307-367-5300. Nearest town: Pinedale. GPS: 42.606199, -109.855856

36 • C2 | No Name

Total sites: 10, RV sites: 7, No water, Vault/pit toilet, Tent & RV camping: Free, Reservations not accepted, Elevation: 7888ft/2404m. Nearest town: Atlantic City. GPS: 42.519618, -109.048365

37 • C2 | North Boulder Lake

Total sites: 5, RV sites: 5, No water, Vault/pit toilet, Tent & RV camping: Free, Open Jun-Sep, Reservations not accepted, Elevation: 7323ft/2232m, Telephone: 307-367-5300. Nearest town: Pinedale. GPS: 42.841404, -109.702373

38 • C2 | Pine Creek Camping Area

Dispersed sites, No water, No toilets, Tent & RV camping: Free, Reservations not accepted, Stay limit: 14 days, Elevation: 7944ft/2421m, Telephone: 307-352-0256. Nearest town: Atlantic City. GPS: 42.452014, -108.862612

39 • C2 | Pine Creek Dispersed

Dispersed sites, No water, No toilets, Tent & RV camping: Free, Nothing larger than truck camper, Reservations not accepted, Elevation: 7922ft/2415m, Telephone: 307-352-0256. Nearest town: Farson. GPS: 42.450261, -108.857221

40 • C2 | Scab Creek

Total sites: 9, RV sites: 9, No water, Vault/pit toilet, Tent & RV camping: Free, No large RVs, Open May-Nov, Reservations not accepted, Stay limit: 14 days, Elevation: 8255ft/2516m, Telephone: 307-367-5300. Nearest town: Pinedale. GPS: 42.820904, -109.553253

41 • C2 | Scab Creek Large Vehicle CG

Total sites: 7, RV sites: 7, No water, No toilets, No tents/RVs: Free, Toilet/water at nearby stock staging area, Reservations not accepted, Stay limit: 14 days, Elevation: 8209ft/2502m, Telephone: 307-367-5300. Nearest town: Pinedale. GPS: 42.818141, -109.562994

42 • C2 | Slate CreeK

Total sites: 8, RV sites: 8, No water, Vault/pit toilet, Tent & RV camping: Free, Reservations not accepted, Stay limit: 14 days, Elevation: 6381ft/1945m, Telephone: 307-828-4500. Nearest town: Fontenelle. GPS: 41.983962, -110.044609

43 • C2 | Stokes Crossing

Total sites: 2, RV sites: 2, No water, Vault/pit toilet, Tent & RV camping: Free, Reservations not accepted, Stay limit: 14 days, Elevation: 7201ft/2195m, Telephone: 307-367-5300. Nearest town: Pinedale. GPS: 42.819321, -109.715796

44 • C2 | Sweetwater Bridge

Total sites: 8, RV sites: 8, No water, Vault/pit toilet, No showers, No RV dump, Tent & RV camping: Free, Winter access may be limited, Open all year, Reservations not accepted, Stay limit: 14 days, Elevation: 7246ft/2209m, Telephone: 307-352-0256. Nearest town: Atlantic City. GPS: 42.392749, -108.624442

45 • C2 | Sweetwater River

Total sites: 10, RV sites: 10, No water, Vault/pit toilet, Tent & RV camping: Free, Reservations not accepted, Elevation: 8287ft/2526m, Telephone: 307-352-0256. Nearest town: Rock Springs. GPS: 42.562074, -109.062969

46 • C2 | Tail Race

Total sites: 9, RV sites: 9, No water, Vault/pit toilet, Tent & RV camping: Free, Reservations not accepted, Elevation: 6417ft/1956m, Telephone: 307-828-4500. Nearest town: Fontenelle. GPS: 42.024968, -110.061183

47 • C2 | Weeping Rock

Total sites: 10, RV sites: 10, No water, Vault/pit toilet, Tent & RV camping: Free, Open all year, Reservations not accepted, Elevation: 6447ft/1965m, Telephone: 307-828-4500. Nearest town: Fontenelle. GPS: 42.020655, -110.047654

48 • C3 | Cottonwood

Total sites: 18, RV sites: 18, Central water, Vault/pit toilet, No showers, No RV dump, Tent & RV camping: $6, Open Jun-Oct, Reservations not accepted, Stay limit: 14 days, Elevation: 7789ft/2374m, Telephone: 307-332-8400. Nearest town: Afton. GPS: 42.360167, -107.684339

49 • C3 | Dugway

Total sites: 5, RV sites: 5, No water, Vault/pit toilet, Tent & RV camping: Free, Open all year, Reservations not accepted, Stay limit: 14 days, Elevation: 6440ft/1963m, Telephone: 307-328-4200. Nearest town: Sinclair. GPS: 41.860593, -107.054107

50 • C4 | Bolton Creek Dispersed

Dispersed sites, No water, No toilets, Tent & RV camping: Free, Reservations not accepted, Elevation: 5294ft/1614m, Telephone: 307-261-7600. Nearest town: Alcova. GPS: 42.631105, -106.605351

51 • C4 | Buffaloberry

Total sites: 4, RV sites: 4, No water, Vault/pit toilet, No showers, No RV dump, Tent & RV camping: $10, Open all year, Reservations not accepted, Stay limit: 14 days,

Elevation: 5261ft/1604m, Telephone: 307-261-7600. Nearest town: Alcova. GPS: 42.683014, -106.622923

52 • C4 | Chalk Bluffs

Total sites: 11, RV sites: 11, No water, Vault/pit toilet, Tent & RV camping: Free, Reservations not accepted, Stay limit: 14 days, Elevation: 5268ft/1606m, Telephone: 307-261-7600. Nearest town: Alcova. GPS: 42.675737, -106.623692

53 • C4 | Golden Currant

Total sites: 4, RV sites: 0, No water, Vault/pit toilet, Tents only: Free, Elevation: 5266ft/1605m. Nearest town: Alcova. GPS: 42.664741, -106.632193

54 • C4 | Lodgepole

Total sites: 15, RV sites: 15, Central water, Vault/pit toilet, Tent & RV camping: $7, Reservations not accepted, Stay limit: 14 days, Elevation: 8264ft/2519m, Telephone: 307-261-7600. Nearest town: Casper. GPS: 42.677423, -106.263384

55 • C4 | Pete's Draw

Total sites: 6, RV sites: 6, No water, Vault/pit toilet, Tent & RV camping: $10, Reservations not accepted, Elevation: 5397ft/1645m, Telephone: 307-261-7600. Nearest town: Casper. GPS: 42.580511, -106.686761

56 • C4 | Prior Flat

Total sites: 15, RV sites: 15, No water, Vault/pit toilet, Tent & RV camping: Free, Open Jun-Nov, Reservations not accepted, Stay limit: 14 days, Elevation: 7733ft/2357m, Telephone: 307-328-4200. Nearest town: Medicine Bow. GPS: 42.241569, -106.584398

57 • C4 | Rim

Total sites: 8, RV sites: 8, No water, Vault/pit toilet, Tent & RV camping: $7, Potable water at Lodgepole, Open Jun-Nov, Reservations not accepted, Stay limit: 14 days, Elevation: 8281ft/2524m, Telephone: 307-261-7600. Nearest town: Casper. GPS: 42.681229, -106.256587

58 • D2 | Middle Baxter Rd Dispersed

Dispersed sites, No water, No toilets, Tent & RV camping: Free, Reservations not accepted, Elevation: 6639ft/2024m. Nearest town: Rock Springs. GPS: 41.540188, -109.108509

59 • D2 | White Mountain Road

Dispersed sites, No water, No toilets, Tent & RV camping: Free, Reservations not accepted, Elevation: 7165ft/2184m. Nearest town: Green River. GPS: 41.548516, -109.421571

60 • D3 | Encampment River

Total sites: 8, RV sites: 8, No water, Vault/pit toilet, Tent & RV camping: $10, Open Jun-Nov, Reservations not accepted, Elevation: 7310ft/2228m, Telephone: 307-328-4200. Nearest town: Encampment. GPS: 41.182611, -106.794052

61 • D3 | Teton Reservoir

Total sites: 5, RV sites: 5, No water, Vault/pit toilet, Tent & RV camping: Free, Open all year, Reservations not accepted, Stay limit: 14 days, Elevation: 7021ft/2140m, Telephone: 307-828-4500. Nearest town: Rawlins. GPS: 41.603208, -107.255528

62 • D4 | Bennett Peak

Total sites: 11, RV sites: 11, Central water, Vault/pit toilet, No showers, No RV dump, Tent & RV camping: $10, Open Jun-Nov, Reservations not accepted, Stay limit: 14 days, Elevation: 7211ft/2198m, Telephone: 307-328-4200. Nearest town: Riverside. GPS: 41.270369, -106.589302

63 • D4 | Corral Creek

Total sites: 6, RV sites: 6, No water, Vault/pit toilet, Tent & RV camping: Free, Not for large RVs, Open Jun-Nov, Reservations not accepted, Elevation: 7224ft/2202m, Telephone: 307-328-4200. Nearest town: Riverside. GPS: 41.261296, -106.572779

64 • D4 | Wagonhound

Dispersed sites, No water, No toilets, Tent & RV camping: Free, Elevation: 7595ft/2315m. Nearest town: Arlington. GPS: 41.623326, -106.291714

Other Public Campground Guides

Visit our website at www.roundaboutpublications.com to learn more about the titles below and other books about camping and traveling in America.

Free RV Camping Guides

Two books provide details about officially designated camping areas in the United States. The Free RV Camping American West edition describes 1,902 formal campgrounds and dispersed camping areas in 11 states across America's West. The Free RV Camping American Heartland edition describes 1,784 camping areas across 12 states in America's heartland. Both guides include camping areas managed by federal, state, local, and other public agencies.

National Forest Camping

The U.S. Forest Service manages nearly 193 million acres of public land in 154 national forests and 20 national grasslands. These areas provide a wide variety of opportunities for outdoor recreation. From remote mountaintops to secluded canyons, alongside streams, rivers, and lakes, Forest Service areas offer some of the best camping experiences in the United States. In this directory, you'll discover 3,704 camping areas in 41 states.

RV Camping in Corps of Engineers Parks

This is the best guide to all RV-friendly camping areas operated by the Corps of Engineers. It's perfect for RV travelers because all of the hike-in, boat-in, and tent only camping areas are not included, making it very easy to locate campgrounds that can accommodate RVs. Includes details about 644 campgrounds at 210 lakes in 34 states. Corps of Engineers parks are considered by many RVers to be the best public campgrounds in the USA.

RV Camping in National Parks

This book describes all of the RV-friendly campgrounds in national parks, recreation areas, monuments, and other areas managed by the National Park Service. Included are 254 campgrounds in 90 national park areas in 31 states.

RV Camping in State Parks

RV Camping in State Parks describes camping areas in 1,644 parks in 49 states. The book provides contact information, phone numbers, directions, and GPS coordinates for each state park. It also includes activities available like boating, fishing, swimming, and hiking. Camping details include the season, number of sites, cost per night, type of hookups available, and facilities such as restrooms, showers, dump station, etc.

The Ultimate Public Campground Project

This is a 17-volume series of guidebooks that describe over 38,000 public camping areas across the United States. Included are camping areas managed by federal, state, local, and other public agencies.

Made in the USA
Las Vegas, NV
22 September 2023

77930288R00070